Writing the Republic

Writing the Republic

LIBERALISM AND MORALITY
IN AMERICAN POLITICAL FICTION

Anthony Hutchison

Columbia University Press   *New York*

Columbia University Press
Publishers Since 1893
New York   Chichester, West Sussex
Copyright © 2007 Columbia University Press
Library of Congress Cataloging-in-Publication Data
Hutchison, Anthony, 1969–
Writing the republic : liberalism and morality in American political fiction /
Anthony Hutchison.
p. cm.
Includes bibliographical references and index.
ISBN-13: 978–0–231–14138–3 (cloth : acid-free paper)
ISBN-13: 978–0–231–51190–2 (e-book)
1. Political fiction, American—History and criticism. 2. Liberalism in literature.
3. Ethics in literature. 4. Politics in literature. 5. United States—In literature.
6. American fiction—19th century—History and criticism. 7. American fiction—
20th century—History and criticism. I. Title.
PS374.P6H87 2007
810.9'358—dc22
∞
Columbia University Press books are printed on permanent and durable acid-free
paper.
This book is printed on paper with recycled content.
Printed in the United States of America
c 10 9 8 7 6 5 4 3 2 1

for Sarah Barrett
(1940–1996)

and Damian Yates
(1969–2006)

CONTENTS

ACKNOWLEDGMENTS

This book couldn't have been written without the influence and input of several members—past and present—of the School of American and Canadian Studies at the University of Nottingham. To begin at the very beginning, I will always be grateful for having taken Douglas Tallack's courses in U.S. intellectual history, which played a formative role in this project, igniting my interest in the relationship between ideas and American culture at an early stage. Sharon Monteith has offered helpful comments and suggestions on earlier versions of this work. Dave Murray should also be thanked profusely for his careful supervision of this project in its doctoral incarnation as well as for introducing me to the endless ambiguities of Herman Melville. Paul Giles, now of the Rothermere American Institute at Oxford, offered some useful tips at the very end of the process.

My greatest academic debt, however, is to Richard King, a genuine polymath, who has overseen this work's progress (and arrested its regress) from the start. The continuing relevance of Hannah Arendt's thought is just one of the many influences of his that this book bears. As a result of our many conversations over the years, I also now know how to successfully stage a one-man protest at the Grand Ole Opry and what a Tennessean might mean when he claims "that dog won't hunt"—just about the only knowledge I've gathered from Richard that I've not managed to incorporate here.

Beyond Nottingham, I would like to thank Professor Ian Bell of the University of Keele for his comments and advice within the context of a *viva voce* that was much more straightforward than it had a right to be. The readers approached by Columbia University Press also produced extremely thorough and erudite commentaries that identified more than a few vulnerable spots. This work, I feel sure, is significantly sharper for their efforts. I also greatly appreciate the professionalism and conscientiousness of CUP editors Jennifer Crewe and Rob Fellman on my behalf.

I'd also like to thank my father and my brother Andy for always being there for me. If she were still alive, I know my mother would have been proud too—or, more likely, too proud. My children, Madeleine and Harry, quite naturally, have done nothing whatsoever to help bring this book to completion any quicker but have been a whole lot of fun. It is to my wife, Joanne, though, finally, that I owe by far the most in all manner of ways. Without her constant encouragement, support, and preternatural capacity just to put up with me I couldn't have come close.

Short sections of chapters 3 and 4 have previously been published in *Comparative American Studies* and *Rethinking History*, respectively. A truncated version of chapter 2 has also appeared in the *Journal of American Studies*.

LIBERALISM AND THE PROBLEM OF
TRADITION IN AMERICAN LITERATURE

I should say more than I mean if I asserted that a nation's literature is
always subordinated to its social state and political constitution. I know
that, apart from these, there are other causes that give literature certain
characteristics, but those do seem the most important to me.

There are always numerous connections between the social and the political condition of a people and the inspiration of its writers. He who knows
the one is never completely ignorant of the other.

—ALEXIS DE TOCQUEVILLE, *Democracy in America*

T ocqueville's early recognition of an intimacy between literary and
sociopolitical traditions emerges alongside his view that in a
democracy "each generation is a new people." This leads him to
suggest that the literature produced by democracies such as the United
States may well be characterized by a certain immaturity, manifest in "facile
forms of beauty, self-explanatory and immediately enjoyable." Unhampered
by the weight of a literary tradition and its accompanying "anxiety of influence," writers in a democracy need merely respond to readers who
"above all ... like things unexpected and new." The style cultivated among
such authors will thus "often be strange, incorrect, overburdened, and
loose, and almost always strong and bold."[1]

This particular sense of American "exceptionalism" was pursued further by twentieth-century cultural critics of the United States beginning
with D. H. Lawrence who, in *Studies in Classic American Literature* (1923),
identified and championed a distinctive "new voice" in a nascent literary
heritage hitherto dismissed as a mere accumulation of "children's tales."[2]
Yet the fiction produced by Cooper, Melville, Twain, and others, as Lawrence attests, is far more complex than this characterization permits. Such

ostensibly "childish" themes of generational rebirth, renewal, reinvention, and, most potently and problematically, American "innocence" are explored in these narratives as a form of democratic and cultural "rebellion against the old parenthood of Europe."[3] The great cultural progenitor of this in the aesthetic and philosophical realm is, of course, Ralph Waldo Emerson—a figure who will be explored in chapter 2.

This "antitradition" tradition, so to speak, was most powerfully delineated in the works of a group of literary and cultural critics published in the years following World War II. Indeed, seminal studies such as Henry Nash Smith's *Virgin Land* (1950), R. W. B. Lewis's *The American Adam* (1955), and Leo Marx's *The Machine in the Garden* (1964) played an instrumental role in the institutionalization of American Studies that attended and reinforced the United States's rise to political, economic, and cultural eminence during this period. The mythopoeic quality of this criticism served to illuminate the influence of Emersonian individualism with reference to a wide range of tropes; these included, most prominently, the frontier or "West" (Smith), the "Adamic" figure (Lewis), and the pastoral (Marx). One important shared characteristic of this critical milieu was a concern with the presence of "innocence"—lost and/or regained—as a recurring theme in the American literary tradition.

Foremost among the consequences of this particular thematic, it was alleged, was a reluctance to engage with *society* in the fashion familiar from the tradition of the nineteenth- century European novel. Rebelling against this understanding of the novel, American fiction instead associated society with corruption, compromise, and loss of innocence. American authors chose to "purify" the form by showcasing characters whose central subjectivity-defining relationship was with nature as opposed to "culture" in the more rarefied sense (or nineteenth-century bourgeois conceptions of "society"). "Adamic" figures from Natty Bumppo to Huck Finn are thus portrayed as in retreat from society in some profound way and, as a consequence, still defined and energized by a pristine and frequently pastoral vision of American innocence.

This downgrading of social relations, it has been argued, explains a certain lacuna of the political in American fiction. American commentators on the political novel as a genre have outlined this problem with implicit acknowledgements of the obstacles presented by the U.S. literary tradition. "If a 19th century American novelist chose a political theme," Irving Howe noted in *Politics and the Novel* (1957), "he generally did so in order to expose the evils of corruption in government (America's substi-tute, as someone has said, for ideology) or to bemoan the vulgarities of public life that were driving sensitive men into retreat."[4] Robert Boyers, in a preface to his study of the genre a few decades later, *Atrocity and Amnesia* (1985), extends the charge of such "exceptionalism" as a hindrance to political fiction to a new postwar generation of American novelists: "To discuss the relevant [postwar American] novels ... would require an ex-tended focus on the peculiar 'Americanness' of these works and direct us to matters largely unrelated to the themes of this book."

This idea of a disjunction between politics and literature, or what Boy-ers more precisely describes in terms of the cultural slippage in the United States between "political intelligence" and "advanced literary thinking," was ostensibly addressed by a group of "New Americanist" critics in the 1980s and 1990s. Historicist in focus, scholars such as Donald Pease, Myra Jehlen, and Sacvan Bercovitch not only advanced a wide-ranging critique of the literary "mythologies" produced by critics such as Lewis and Smith but also launched a broader assault on the intellectual culture of the cold war. The central organizing concept in their critical arsenal was that of "ideology," that is, in this instance, the prevailing systems of ideas out of which American myth can only ever be generated.

Their position hinged on a rejection of the myth critics' notion of America as "exceptional," as essentially a nation untainted by political ide-ologies. This was also the conclusion drawn by influential "consensus his-torians" of the 1950s, such as Louis Hartz and Daniel Boorstin, whose promotion of liberalism as the key to understanding such American ex-ceptionalism provides one important context for the discussion to follow in chapter 1. This idea, it was argued, was merely a symptom of rhetorical excess on the part of a liberal culture, society, and polity threatened by the increasingly global reach of Soviet communist ideology. The popular mid-century "end of ideology" thesis, therefore, articulated by social commen-tator Daniel Bell (and legitimated in the work of the consensus school), served only to further obscure liberalism's own status as the predominant *ideology* in the United States. In other words, it was a liberal "end-of-ideology" ideology. As we shall also see in the following chapter, a later "postconsen-sus" school of American intellectual historians publishing in the late 1960s and 1970s did much of the groundwork for the New Americanists of the 1980s in their exposure of liberalism as ideology or one competing group of ideas among others at various historical points.

Perhaps the pivotal text in the shift from "myth" to "New Americanist" understandings of the American literary tradition was the Bercovitch and Jehlen–edited collection *Ideology and Classic American Literature* (1986). Here, several of the older generation of critics such as Henry Nash Smith and Leo Marx, in a section entitled "Reassessments," addressed those who had come to associate their earlier works with the "pervasive ideological distortion" that largely determined the intellectual climate of the cold war.[5] This, it was contended, originated from a similar ideological strategy that prompted a contemporaneous "consensus" historiography to view the concept of "ideology" itself as quintessentially un-American.

Elsewhere in the volume, Donald Pease builds on such criticism to critique forty years of "cold war" readings of *Moby Dick*, beginning with that put forward by F. O. Matthiesson in *American Renaissance* (1941). Matthiesson's reading, Pease argues, largely set the tone for the postwar reception of Melville's novel that ultimately led to its canonical status. It did so, nonetheless, by reductively equating Ahab with a reckless totalitarian will and Ishmael with "the principle of America's freedom who hands us over to our heritage."[6] This, however, Pease argues, represents an ideological distortion of a complex text, a text that also crucially "reveal[s] the way Ishmael's obsession depends on Ahab's compulsion"—an obsession, for Pease, analogous to the formidable "totalizing logic" of cold war liberalism. U.S. liberalism, in yet another cultural context, proves to be the ideology that dare not speak its name. Melville here, then, in Pease's post–cold war reading, is taking aim not only at "totalitarian" ideology but also at the type of ideological maneuvering evident in postwar liberalism. In doing so, Pease concludes, he is "asking us if we can survive the free world Ishmael has handed down to us."[7]

This and other interventions by the New Americanist critics would appear to have belatedly introduced a political dimension to our understanding of the American literary tradition. However, as John Whalen-Bridge has made clear in a timely response to what has become, by now, a New Americanist orthodoxy, this critical-theoretical development has curiously failed to upgrade the status of the political novel. "The 'political novel' per se," he writes in *Political Fiction and the American Self* (1998), "is not a factor in contemporary criticism though politics is supposedly more important than ever before. We no longer discuss the political novel though there is a great deal of discussion about politics 'in' and the politics 'of.'"[8] What we have instead is a notion of the literary text as contaminated by ideology, with literary theory or political criticism as the only feasible decontaminant.

This too, of course, is characteristic of the New Historicist school of criticism that has dominated the study of English literature in the United States since the publication of Stephen Greenblatt's *Renaissance Self-Fashioning: From More to Shakespeare* (1980). In the context of American studies, Walter Benn Michaels' *The Gold Standard and the Logic of Naturalism* (1982) shared with Greenblatt and the New Historicism a concern with the reinterpretation of texts in the light of Michel Foucault's post-Marxist reframings of power and subjectivity. Likewise, a decade later, the collection edited by Philip Fisher, *The New American Studies: Essays from Representations* (1991), indicated how New Historicist currents were now making their presence felt in this new sphere. However, Foucault's influence aside, it remains difficult to see how New Historicism differs radically from various earlier forms of materialist criticism, Marxist or otherwise. The concept that seems to recur most frequently within New Americanist (and most other New Historicist) scholarship continues to be "ideology," albeit ideology in the more sophisticated antireductionist terms first delineated by Western Marxists in the 1960s.

For this reason, no doubt, Fredric Jameson's *The Political Unconscious* (1981) must be regarded as at least of equally significant importance to the New Americanists. An ambitious dialectical reflection on the problem of interpretation, which brought an array of psychoanalytic and Marxist social and cultural criticism to the table, Jameson's work presented a hermeneutic premised on the return of "repressed" social and political struggles buried beneath the surface of literary history. In a similar fashion, Donald Pease, in his introduction to an edition of *boundary* 2 devoted to the New Americanist phenomenon, talks of retrieving "questions of class, race and gender from the political unconscious of American studies."[9] Drawing on the psychoanalytic vocabulary familiar from Jameson's work, he later adds that the "political unconscious of the primal scene of New Historicist readings embodies *both* the *repressed* relationships between the literary and the political and the *disenfranchised groups unrepresentable in this relationship.*"[10]

It is perhaps unsurprising then that a work such as Jameson's—which begins by committing itself without undue self-consciousness to the slogan "always historicize!"—should later find a receptive audience among literary scholars under the sway of a "new" historicism. Most crucially, though Jameson goes beyond this in *The Political Unconscious* by announcing that all interpretation and thus all "historicization"—if it is to free itself from the "reification and privatisation of contemporary life"—must begin with "the recognition that there is nothing that is not social and historical—indeed that everything is 'in the last analysis' political."[11] If we follow Jameson's observation, of course, it no longer makes any sense to speak of a "political novel," as every novel—indeed every act of interpretation—qualifies "in the last analysis" as political.

Whalen-Bridge takes issue with Jameson's thesis and its influence, believing it to have helped to reduce literary criticism and theory to "a mode of discourse that offers psychic self-defense in a world of ideological oppression."[12] The therapeutic tendencies of this discourse might even be related to the preoccupation with purity Whalen-Bridge skillfully uncovers in both earlier "Adamic" mythology critics *and* their New Americanist antagonists. It is in this respect, he argues persuasively, that the 1990s might be said to have witnessed the emergence of some "new American Adams." Here, incidentally, we find an academic disciplinary instantiation—that of American Studies—of a generational conflict over the meaning of the liberal tradition that will feature heavily in other contexts over the remaining chapters. Whalen-Bridge supports his view by noting how Pease, in that same *boundary 2* piece, feels an urgent need to reestablish a form of "virgin land" in order to differentiate—that is, overdifferentiate—New Americanist criticism from the "Old Americanist" counterrevolutionary criticism of Frederick Crews:

> Crews criticizes the younger generation of critics for not respecting the disciplinary boundaries that have given the study of American literature its meaning. According to Pease, Crews has not merely criticized the New Americanists, he has rejected them as followers in the path of American Studies. Pease embraces the claim that American Studies is a bastard discipline (and he exaggerates Crews's "rejection" to do this) because the illegitimacy of the newer discipline is, paradoxically, the ground of its legitimacy—as counter-hegemonic formation.
>
> New Americanism—Call it Ishmael! To transcend the mob, to light out for the territory, or to maintain some connection to innocence—these are the marks of the American Adam—as described by Lewis.[13]

This self-dramatizing act of institutional and generational rebellion—what Whalen-Bridge describes in terms of a "self purification [that] provides a way to see oneself in opposition to the national sins (slavery, imperialism) [and] a depoliticised academy"[14]—may or may not make for political criticism. It has, however, by dominating the study of American literature, done little to raise the profile of the political novel or address the question of what it might mean to treat writers of fiction as serious political thinkers. Like Whalen-Bridge, my own view is that the New Americanist criticism is symptomatic of the critical tradition it seeks to displace. Again, like Whalen-Bridge and contra Jameson, my concern here is with *explicitly* political fiction. Rather than operating on the premise, as Jameson suggests, that all fiction is "in the last analysis" political, I wish to draw attention to the importance of the Althusserian qualification by asking what might be political *in the first instance*.[15] As opposed, then, to the perennial focus of contemporary critics on the politics of representation (in which every fictional text inevitably has a stake), my concern here might be said to be with those fictions that explicitly seek to *represent politics*. There is, of course, no hard and fast distinction that can consistently be drawn between the two—all novels represent politics "in the last instance" presumably—but the emphasis in this study will track the role of political ideas in shaping culture and identity, rather than vice versa. In the American context, the novel that explicitly seeks to represent politics is ineluctably challenged by the powerful presence of a political tradition that renders the relationship between art and political ideas less abstract or indirect than is commonly assumed. Here, we might do well to recall Richard Hofstadter's famous dictum that rather than simply "having" an ideology, America *is* an ideology.

Thus to write a novel "about" America, that is, to write a novel in which the idea of America functions as an intermittent refrain, is to write not only a political novel but a novel that engages with a varying set of historically inflected political ideas. This is not the same as, say, writing a novel about the breakup of a marriage that has an American setting. The former will always be political in the first instance; the latter may be in some secondary sense, but for it to be understood as a "political novel," its status as a novel "about" the breakup of a marriage would require downgrading. Such a discrimination between types is sustainable largely as a result of the division between public and private characteristic of both liberal and republican thinking in classical and modern Western societies.[16] Consequently, the only conceivable context in which a novel about the breakup of a marriage might be construed as a political novel in the sense understood here is one in which such a distinction has collapsed. This perhaps explains why the most "intimate" of political fictions tend to be those set against the backdrop of totalitarian societies in which the private sphere is all but abolished.[17]

It must be asserted that the types of distinctions drawn here are not meant to privilege novels that emphasize the public rather than the private and the political rather than the personal. Aesthetic judgment should never be hostage to such narrow generic considerations. A novel depicting marital breakdown is no less likely to succeed as a political novel is to fail. The issue, rather, in the American context, is the reluctance within studies of U.S. literature to develop a taxonomy that insists, among other things, on the political novel as a discrete entity. The effect has been the closure of a number of potentially rewarding avenues of critical inquiry. Several of these will become apparent in the pages that follow, but chief among them—and in some sense underpinning them all—is the idea that the novel has something important to contribute to political thinking. This is not simply in terms of the particular political issues it seeks to explore, but in the formal properties and tools it makes available to the writer interested in political thought and the overlapping discipline of intellectual history. This area is largely unexamined within literary studies itself.

This broader, more sophisticated understanding of the relationship between literature and politics has, however, in recent years been a feature of the work of a few renegade political philosophers. In their introduction to *Literature and the Political Imagination* (1996), a collection of essays in this grain, John Horton and Andrea Baumeister propose the study of fiction as an antidote to the demand for "closure"—perhaps equally a demand in response to the need for "psychic self-defense"—in their own intellectual discipline:

> It is in developing a richer, more nuanced and realistic understanding of political deliberation that imaginative literature may have an especially valuable role to play. Novels and plays, for example, seem much better at exhibiting the complexities of political experience and the open-textured and necessarily incomplete character of real political arguments . . . than the linear discourse of philosophy.

Horton and Baumeister go on, furthermore, to stress the capacity of literature to "shape and inform the very terms in which [particular political] issues are conceived."[18] This brings us somewhat closer to the design of the present study, which, by focusing on the tension between issues of liberalism and morality in the political thought of several American novelists, hopes to generate a more "nuanced" and "open-textured" understanding of the U.S. political tradition.

The type of cross-fertilization between literature and political theory endorsed above has also failed to materialize in the United States despite the interdisciplinary pressure placed on the study of American literature since the 1960s. Yet if this has led American literary critics to bracket awkward questions of the character or form taken by the political novel in a tradition supposedly determined by myth and an antipolitical predilection toward themes of innocence, nature, and the pastoral, then the same cannot be said of critics with a background in political philosophy. Scholars such as Maureen Whitebrook, Catherine Zuckert, and Ethan Canin have all sought to engage with American works of fiction in order to illuminate some of the broader as well as finer details of an overarching liberal political tradition. Indeed, Zuckert's study *Natural Right and the Political Imagination* (1990), which examines canonical writers such as Cooper, Twain, and Faulkner, effectively repudiates the notion that a Lockean liberal tradition rooted in "natural law" disqualifies meaningful artistic exploration of politics and society. The final claim posited in this work is instructive for my purposes here:

> Taken as a whole these fictional depictions of a man's withdrawal from civil society to live in the state of nature have served to reiterate the major elements of the social contract theory underlying the U.S. Constitution, in the face of European philosophical criticism. The novels have not taken the truth of the "self-evident" propositions of the Declaration for granted, however. On the contrary, by leading their readers to raise questions about the adequacy of the philosophic foundations of the American regime, these novelists have reminded us of the need repeatedly to reconsider the nature of the "truths" themselves as well as their practical meaning in ever-changing historical circumstances.[19]

The implicit point made here is that even those canonical authors championed by the "myth" critics confronted the American liberal tradition by problematizing as well as affirming its Lockean origins in a theory of "nature" and "self-evident truths." My argument is an extension of this undertaking in so far as I focus on a number of postwar American novels that I believe significantly extend this form of novelistic political-philosophical inquiry. The aim is not solely to continue an effort to bridge the gap between literature and political thought in a particular context, useful as this may be, but also to bring to bear an intellectual-historical approach capable of discerning why some novels might offer us a greater degree of political understanding than others. The liberal political tradition in the United States will thus be examined in various "historical circumstances" as it finds expression in postwar American political fiction.

In the central chapters, novels by Gore Vidal, Russell Banks, Lionel Trilling, and Philip Roth foreground the critique of liberalism put forward by republicanism, Transcendentalism, Marxism, and neoconservatism at their respective historical moments of ascent. The aim here, primarily, as previously stated, is to treat novelists seriously as political thinkers; much of the analysis is, accordingly, interdisciplinary in approach, drawing from artists, philosophers, and theorists such as Herman Melville, Fyodor Dostoevsky, Hannah Arendt, John Dewey, Leon Trotsky, and numerous contemporary commentators and historians as well as the novelists listed above. This approach, it must be said, is also an attempt to establish some wider points of intellectual reference than is perhaps customary in the study of American literature as currently practiced. William V. Spanos has recently offered a quite sweeping critique of New Americanist literary and cultural criticism on the basis of such alleged insularity. Much of this simply turns New Americanist accusations toward earlier critics back against them in the manner of Whalen-Bridge, though the charge here relates to both groups' "antitheoretical" impulses rather than political quietism. Spanos argues, finally, from a position that would repudiate the influence of homegrown pragmatist and empiricist perspectives within American studies in favor of tools derived from the supposedly more radical tradition of continental philosophy.

While I do not share this suspicion of immanent critique (or what is described as a tendency "to articulate opposition in the terms laid down by the American discourse it would resist") and remain skeptical with regard to certain assumptions behind any critical project designed to combat the "global colonization of thinking by American instrumentalism," many of Spanos's less grandiloquent criticisms hit the mark. What is characterized as the New Americanist studies' "tendency to overdetermine the New

Historicism" undoubtedly explains why it "remains vestigially and disablingly local in scope" and why its adherents "restrict their discursive references to others within the hermetic field imaginary of American studies, that is to other prominent Americanists."[20]

Sharing then at least some of Spanos's reservations as to the relative disciplinary and intellectual parochialism within American studies today, this work seeks to utilize as well as scrutinize the ideas of figures such as Arendt, Dostoevsky, and Trotsky as a way of offering fresh insight into issues and tensions within American liberalism. Other figures such as Dewey, Richard Rorty, and Lionel Trilling fall within those empirical-pragmatist theoretical precincts that both New Americanists and postmodernist critics such as Spanos disdain. Melville, however, whom, with Henry Adams, Spanos cites approvingly as an "ontological exile"[21] who offers a radical antidote to (New) Americanist orthodoxies, features prominently in several chapters. By embracing such a method, the intention is to take up Günther Lenz's challenge, voiced in the same collection as Spanos's piece, to

> widen the scope of our rereading of American cultural studies from the 1930s to the 1960s beyond the limits of academic American studies departments to include cultural, historical and social critics from other departments and from outside academia [in order to] rediscover and reclaim important and challenging strategies of radical cultural critique.[22]

The "republican" form of cultural critique that ultimately emerges from what follows is the product of the political acumen evident with the novels themselves when exposed to the light of ideas from this more eclectic array of intellectual sources. The result can be enlightening, complex, and sometimes shocking in the picture of the historical record and contested political tradition it presents. Genealogy, too, in both figurative and nonfigurative fashion, is an important theme in this writing of the republic. This, no doubt, relates to the forms of association Russ Castronovo highlights when he notes the tension between republicanism and the "authority of origins":

> Republicanism entails remembrance of the past but it does not intend to solemnize the past with the myth of inviolate origins. Rather, republicanism

as a genealogical practice acknowledges the blood and violence: like Machiavelli it acknowledges that Rome was founded upon fratricide; like Nietzsche, it marks the beginning of civilization in sacrifice, mutilation and torture; like Foucault, it embraces a historiography that assumes that the authority of origins deserves to be dissipated and toppled.[23]

Although not all of the primary literary works under consideration can be said to be "historical" in the strict generic sense (several straddle two or more epochs in their narrative design), they nonetheless take very specific historical periods and episodes for their central subject matter. More importantly, for my purposes, they do so in order to interrogate, critique, and contextualize several pivotal moments in the intellectual history of American liberalism. To speak of "liberalism" or a "liberal tradition" in this way, of course, no doubt invites qualms about conceptual clarity and definitional boundaries. In the chapters that follow, my intention is primarily to *show* what was meant by liberalism and how it confronted and reconstituted itself in the face of competing ideological pressures. The novel itself will constitute the primary source for what is essentially a history of political ideas in America; political novelists will also be shown as identifiable as such in their often sophisticated negotiations of themes and ideas more commonly discussed in political philosophy and intellectual history. The study, however, is divided into nineteenth- and twentieth-century contexts for liberalism, as a fairly clear distinction, it seems to me, can be drawn between the two.

Part 1 is concerned with the nineteenth-century context of "classical liberalism," which has its philosophical roots in the work of Adam Smith and, most importantly, John Locke. Its precepts include a commitment to representative government, hostility to aristocratic privilege, some conception of government as a contract between those who govern and those who are governed, a belief in individualism premised on those "natural rights" guaranteed by an immoveable law of "nature," and, perhaps most centrally, a faith in the workings of a modern capitalist economy (itself governed by the laws of nature that operate the market's "price mechanism"—a process Adam Smith referred to as akin to an "invisible hand"). Nowhere did these ideas hold greater sway than in the United States, whose "natural state" Locke himself identified as providing the archetypal site of such natural law. Notwithstanding this influence, the chapters in part 1 seek to show how novels such as Gore Vidal's *Burr* and Russell Banks's *Cloudsplitter* not only represent certain historical manifestations of "classical" liberal politics but also the ideological pressure brought to bear on this politics by the sometimes distinct, sometimes overlapping politics of republicanism and Transcendentalism, respectively.

The studies in part 2 equally accept many of the above "classical" understandings of liberalism, but they do so while also seeking to absorb the significant American inflections given to the term as a result of more recent historical developments beginning with the New Deal era of the 1930s. It was during this period, as Dorothy Ross has observed, that "liberalism first became a focus of serious intellectual debate in the United States."[24] Whereas the "classical" understanding of the term is now largely restricted to specialist political theorists, economists, and intellectual historians in the academy, by the late twentieth-century, liberalism in the United States had acquired a largely negative political—not to mention cultural—resonance. The chapters in part 2—on Lionel Trilling's *The Middle of the Journey* and Philip Roth's recent fictional portrayals of particular "representative" postwar American lives—seek to monitor and explain this bifurcation in the more recent conceptual career of American liberalism. In doing so, they utilize the abundance of insight evident in Trilling's and Roth's accounts of liberalism's encounter with both neoconservatism and various incarnations of the American Left since the 1930s.

The study concludes with some reflections on the meaning of the American political novel in the light of the preceding analyses. These will include a more sustained engagement with some of the developments and arguments noted here connected with U.S. political fiction's somewhat "semidetached" relationship with a more general literary tradition. In particular, Whalen Bridge's reading of *Moby Dick* as a "submerged political novel" will come under scrutiny as a preliminary step in the articulation of a theory of American political fiction. This subgenre, it will be contended, emerges from a complex but nonetheless distinguishable cross-fertilization between American political and literary cultures. More specifically, this theory can only be grasped once we render intelligible the manifold ways in which a culture of republicanism serves to generate a particular narrative form. An understanding of this recognizable narrative structure for political fiction in the United States, I close by arguing, is crucial if we are to excavate and comprehend a countertradition of political and cultural critique that takes the health of the American republic in time as its overriding concern.

Writing the Republic

PART I

THE NINETEENTH-CENTURY CONTEXT

ELUSIVE REPUBLICANISM

Thomas Jefferson and the Foundations of American Politics in Gore Vidal's *Burr*

Sons have generally followed in the footsteps of their fathers ...

—MARTIN VAN BUREN,
Inquiry Into the Origins and Course of Political Parties in the United States

---

I set down as calumny every tale calculated to disturb our harmony.

—AARON BURR,
in a letter to Thomas Jefferson, February 12, 1801

The Republican Synthesis

In the immediate post–World War II period, the political tradition of the United States was explained in terms of the triumph of liberalism and, in particular, the liberal political philosophy of John Locke. America's self-image, it was claimed, was rooted more or less exclusively in Lockean "natural rights." Such rights were part of a contract freely entered into by citizens, the consent of the governed premised on institutionalized recognition of the private individual's entitlement to life, liberty, and property. For its proponents, the liberal, pragmatic disdain for ideology that grew out of such a "privatized" notion of rights constituted the "genius" of American politics; less sanguine critics, meanwhile, had to be content with pointing out how this atavistic individualism at least explained the diminished appeal of socialist doctrines in the United States.[1]

This consensus, however, began to crack in the late 1960s with the appearance of two seminal works. Bernard Bailyn's *The Ideological Origins of the American Revolution* (1967) and his former pupil Gordon Wood's *The Creation of the American Republic* (1969) were the first important expressions of what ultimately came to be regarded as "a declaration of independence from older scholarship in American political history."[2] Instead of emphasizing the extent to which the fight for independence and founding of an American republic was a *beginning* that ushered in new organizing principles for government, Bailyn and Wood each stressed the ways in which events were interpreted via a body of thought originating in the English parliamentary crises of the seventeenth and early eighteenth centuries. Although Bailyn's study was concerned only with the effects of this hitherto submerged ideology on the American revolution, Wood pursued the link through to the constitutional convention of 1787. It was during this critical period between 1776 and 1787, Wood claimed, that republican ideology began to dissipate as the constitution makers confronted their own crises of authority in the turbulent political climate of the 1780s. Thus, he concluded, the signing of the Constitution signaled the eclipse of classical republicanism as a major component of American political thought, the volatile historical moment forcing the delegates to embrace a more jaundiced view of human nature and consequently to place greater emphasis on those "negative" liberties associated with property rights. This shift finally brought about what Wood describes as "the end of classical politics" in the United States. In historiographical terms, it prompted what, a few years after Wood's work appeared, would be labeled the "republican synthesis."[3]

By the end of the 1970s, however, the influence of classical politics in the United States was actually being extended by scholars into the early nineteenth century. Focusing on the early national period, Lance Banning and Drew R. McCoy detected the persistence of republican ideology among both Federalists and Republicans during the first party quarrel and beyond. The main way in which this ideology found expression in the early decades of the new republic, they asserted, was in the hypersensitivity of Americans to those "corrupted" aspects of government they had previously associated with the British parliament prior to the War of Independence.[4] The Glorious Revolution of 1688 in England had established the principle of a polity headed by a Protestant monarch but premised on the notion of "mixed" government. Power was divided between social groups of the one (the Crown), the few (the Lords), and the many (the Commons). This abridgement of monarchical power, combined with what was anticipated as a conclusive affirmation of parliament's sovereignty, realigned the English political system with a premodern tradition of republican thought. The new mixed constitution, consisting of a tripartite social order with the King as first magistrate, was regarded by many as republican in spirit and was admired by Montesquieu in particular, whose *Considerations on the Causes of the Greatness of the Romans and Their Decline* (1734) and *The Spirit of the Laws* (1748) were highly regarded by many of the delegates who attended the Constitutional Convention in 1787.[5]

Such accounts of the *continuity* of republican thought in a widened Anglo-American context were bolstered further by the even broader historical sweep of J. G. A. Pocock's *The Machiavellian Moment: Florentine Political Thought and the Atlantic Republican Tradition* (1975). Pocock's work traced the meaning of a number of concepts as they appeared at various republican historical junctures. Most prominent among these was the notion of "virtue," which, first politicized in Aristotelian civic humanism, was further cultivated in the writings of Machiavelli during the Renaissance and revived once more by the English commonwealth men and James Harrington in the seventeenth century before finally reappearing in early Enlightenment Europe and revolutionary America. By giving the "republican synthesis" such a comprehensive historical grounding, Pocock illuminated more dramatically the problems inherent in the American republic's confrontation with modernity and its emerging capitalist economy. In this way, he was able to elaborate on an earlier assertion—resting on his "classical republican" reading of early American political thought—that the revolt of the colonies might be perceived "less as the first political act of revolutionary enlightenment than the last great act of the Renaissance."[6] Pocock's more determined attempt to relegate the influence of Lockean thought in the early modern period as well as his explicit dependence on a Kuhnian "paradigmatic" framework, furthermore, appeared to up the stakes of the debate. Some historians now began to talk of a "republican paradigm" rather than "synthesis."[7]

Central to the political and civic notion of virtue that Pocock places at the heart of his study is—in contrast to the Lockean emphasis on negative liberty and the autonomy of the private sphere—the elevation of the public sphere and the importance of preserving its capacity to generate the positive sense of liberty associated with participation in civic affairs. The health of the public sphere—which eighteenth-century republican thinkers measured in terms of "public happiness"[8]—is premised on the willingness of citizens to demonstrate "virtue" by subordinating private interests to a higher notion of the public good. Only a virtuous citizenry—whose virtue and autonomy are assured by their status as property holders and associated freedom from the economy—could be sufficiently "disinterested" in political matters to maintain the moral rectitude of the republic. Pocock claims that it is only with the appearance in early eighteenth-century England of an oligarchy dedicated to financial reforms designed to buttress a modern capitalist economy that a countervailing republican discourse of opposition began to engage with modernity.

This opposition disdained the economy's "corrupting" impingement on the body politic as longstanding principles of commerce became distorted by a parasitic "mercantilism." Such developments were attributed to the financial revolution that led to the new and unsavory phenomena of paper money, "stockjobbers" (investors in the stock exchange), and public debt. The opposition in England took the form of the "country" critics of the "court" Walpole administration who saw themselves as attempting to defend the ideals of civic virtue and "disinterested" public service in the face of a relentless "commercialization" of such values. The English oppositionists, as their American heirs would sixty years later, spanned the political spectrum of the day to include Tories such as Henry St. John, Viscount Bolingbroke, as well as the more radical "old Whigs" such as Trenchard and Gordon, the authors of *Cato's Letters*.[9] For Pocock, these critics were invoking the Machiavellian cry of *ridurre ai principii* (return to first principles), the response of those loyal to the founding values of the city-state republics whenever those values were perceived to be threatened by "corruption." This informs Pocock's central organizing concept, which understands this republican discourse as a response to the temporal pressures exacted on all polities founded on the ideal of civic virtue. Republics are thus to be defined by their *contingency*. "The Machiavellian moment," he writes,

> is a name for the moment in conceptualised time in which the republic was seen as confronting its own temporal finitude, as attempting to remain morally and politically stable in a stream of irrational events conceived as essentially destructive of all systems of secular stability. In the language which had been developed for the purpose, this was spoken of as the confrontation of "virtue" with "fortune" or "corruption."[10]

The call to first principles reappears in the American colonies, most notably in Thomas Paine's exhortations to the New World to regenerate the Old by restoring that republican virtue which had been "eaten out" of the English constitution by crown corruption. In his attack on the English MP Sir William Meredith, in probably the most widely read pamphlet of the revolution, *Common Sense* (1776), Paine takes up the theme. He writes of the difficulties of arriving at "a proper name for the government of England," complaining that although Meredith calls England a republic,

> in its present state it is unworthy of the name, because the corrupt influence of the crown, by having all the places at its disposal, hath so effectually swallowed up the power, and eaten out the virtue of the house of commons (the republican part in the constitution) that the government of England is nearly as monarchical as that of France or Spain. . . . it is the republican and not the monarchical part of the constitution of England which Englishmen glory in.[11]

Paine blames the timidity of the wealthy classes in the face of the Crown's usurpation of parliamentary prerogative on the unprecedented stake they now possess in the financial system controlled by that corrupted body. The massive expansion in commerce thus undermines the "virtue" of the House of Commons. "With the increase of commerce," Paine laments, "England hath lost its spirit."[12] In *The Machiavellian Moment*, Pocock claims that by the eighteenth century "commerce" had replaced "fortuna" ("fortune" or "the circumstantial insecurity of political life")[13] in republican perceptions of "corruption." Invoking Montesquieu's observation in *L'Esprit de Lois* he writes: "Commerce, which makes men cultured, entails luxury, which makes [man] corrupt."[14] It is this stress on the extent to which commercial expansion was seen to undermine—rather than establish—the values of the republic that the principal critics of the republican synthesis were most keen to take issue with. It is to the arguments presented by the most notable of these adherents to a Lockean-liberal interpretation that I will now turn.

The Liberal Critique

Since being self-confessedly awestruck as a young graduate student by the breadth and gravity of J. G. A. Pocock's work, Joyce Appleby has produced a series of essays that rigorously interrogate its more ambitious claims.[15]

An intended effect of this has been something of a restoration of Lock-ean texts to their central position within the canon of American political thought. Appleby, however, does not wish Locke's writings to reassume an earlier unassailable status as the ideological reservoir from which all political thinking in the United States has invariably drawn; she wishes, rather, only to reiterate, in the light of the new historiography, the Lockean premises she remains convinced informed the main body of political thought in the revolutionary and early national periods.

Acknowledging the new thinking and reappraisals generated by what she redescribes as the "republican hypothesis," Appleby commends, in particular, the way in which the methodology of its proponents has served to expose liberalism as one *competing* ideology among others. Treating liberalism as a "cultural artefact" allows scholars "to recognise in [the] self interest [of liberalism] as conceptual a notion as classical republicanism's civic virtue." In a statement reminiscent of Louis Hartz she concludes: "Like fish unaware of water we American writers have moved about in a world of invisible liberal assumptions." She goes on to make clear that her intention is not to refute the revisionist work of Pocock *et alia* in order to "return to the *status quo ante revisionism*."[16] The way such work disentangles republicanism from the political discourse of the era, rather, makes it easier for the historian to identify and trace the emergence of those new Lockean ideas that ultimately displaced it.

Still, for Appleby, the influence of republicanism in eighteenth-century England and America has undoubtedly been exaggerated. In gazing backward so as to link the American republic to the past, she contends, Pocock *et alia* simply fail to discern the *novelty* of many of its underlying principles. The significance of the American republic lay in its modernity and the significance of this modernity for political thought lay in the increasing preeminence of the liberal worldview. At the heart of this worldview was an acceptance of the "revolutionary" fact of "the replacement of the economy for the polity as the fundamental social system."[17] Classical republicanism, Appleby claims, did not have the social grammar necessary to negotiate this shift from *homo politicus* to *homo economicus* in Anglo-American societies. A new grammar, in effect, had to be invented for a

> trading system that had not only moved beyond the confines of political boundaries but had created wealth essential to the conduct of politics. . . . However appealing civic humanism was to English gentlemen involved in

public issues, it did not help persons who sought to understand the private transactions that were determining the shape and direction of the Anglo-American economy.[18]

The idea of liberty, then, began to be recast in economic as opposed to political terms. Consequently, the role of government was perceived on the basis of its capacity to facilitate access to this economic realm of freedom as opposed to its willingness to protect and promote any understanding of the political sphere, classical or otherwise. Appleby relates this oversight to republican historians' perpetuation of an "agrarian myth" in early American history, a notion first advanced in the work of Richard Hofstadter in the 1940s.[19] This ideal, described as that of "the self-sufficient yeoman dwelling in a rural arcadia of unspoiled virtue, honest toil and rude plenty," conveniently reinforces the republican synthesis in its overtones of English "country" republicanism. Appleby, by contrast, contends that the reality behind this myth was of an economic order within which the rewards of large-scale commercial farming—far from being the object of "virtuous" republican suspicion—were enthusiastically seized upon as "a material base for a new social vision."[20] This vision was of a democratic republic premised on a forward-looking, nonhierarchical social organism made up of individuals committed to a market economy. Such commitments were seen to erase Old World social distinctions. Moreover, the abundance of land and natural resources to the west seemed to make this possible on an unprecedented scale.

Crucial within this debate is the figure of Thomas Jefferson, whose historical and philosophical legacy both sides were eager to appropriate. Accordingly, it is to the politics of Jefferson—both in theory and practice—as well as its contested legacy that this study of republicanism and Gore Vidal's novel *Burr* will now turn. The relation between land, economy, and the polity is at the heart of the exchanges prompted by the new republican synthesis in early American historiography. It is within this triad that I will now attempt to situate *Burr*. Republicanism has rightly been characterized by Drew McCoy as something of an "elusive" ideology. Examining this elusiveness within Vidal's *Burr*, however, allows us to negotiate some of the tensions that have made Jefferson's brand perhaps the most elusive of all.

Why Jefferson? Why *Burr*?

Two recently published works, pursuing more openly a phenomenon evident to some degree in nearly all earlier studies, have stressed the ambiguity of the Jeffersonian legacy, one going so far as to characterize Jefferson
himself as an "American sphinx."[21] Any scholar who has devoted serious
time to absorbing both Jefferson's political thought and the historical record of his political career is invariably struck by the complex interface
between the two. The inscrutability of Jefferson's political psyche appears
somewhat at odds with the popular perception of the founding father.
Within the political culture of the United States, Jefferson is widely perceived as the embodiment of an unambiguous, robust sense of liberty most
Americans have come to hold as an article of faith. For this reason, he is
an unavoidable reference point for the intellectual historian of the early
national period. Since Merrill D. Peterson initially charted the vicissitudes
of his posthumous reputation in the early 1960s, Jefferson has increasingly
come to be viewed as a crucial figure within race and gender studies in the
United States. This has served to foreground Jefferson's private life—in
particular his ownership of slaves and alleged affair with a slave servant—
or what, in contemporary political parlance, might be called the "character" issue.[22]

For the traditional intellectual historian, the question of character sits
uncomfortably alongside schemas that—however subtle and receptive to
the nuance of social change—nonetheless tend to assign to ideas a status
independent of the subjects who draw on their tenets. To talk about the
character of Jeffersonian thought is one thing; to talk about the character
of Jefferson himself, quite another. The problems of such an approach are
exacerbated in those rare instances where figures whose thought has exerted long-term influence have also held public office and, thus, exercised
power in a much less oblique fashion. Bearing these two dimensions in
mind, Thomas Jefferson may represent a republican take on Plato's dream
of the philosopher-king: the *philosopher-citizen.*

The question that haunts Jefferson scholarship, consequently, is to what
degree the theory can be said to have informed the practice. Was Jefferson,
in other words, a Jeffersonian? If we follow Pocock and understand
Jeffersonian politics as essentially republican, we might be prompted to
ask: how "republican" was Jefferson's classical republic? Conversely, if we
follow Appleby and interpret Jeffersonian democracy as an early militant

species of liberalism, we might ask: how "liberal" was Jefferson's modern democracy? Gore Vidal's novel *Burr* (1973) asks precisely these questions, albeit in a much less abstract fashion. This is not to say, however, that it fails to represent the complexity of Jefferson. Indeed, in some ways I shall be arguing that the intricate narrative structure of *Burr* conveys a sense of the difficulties in reconciling Jefferson with the ideologies of his day, a reconciliation that has frequently been absent in historical discourse. Although the novel focuses on the life of his contemporary Aaron Burr, it is as much about the founding fathers, and Jefferson in particular, as it is Burr.

A hero of the War of Independence, Burr was one of the founders of the political machine that became Tammany Hall and, by 1800, had become a powerful enough figure in the Republican party to tie with Jefferson in that year's presidential election. There are in Burr's career, like Jefferson's, almost too many fascinating—not to say complicated—episodes to recount here, but to most Americans, if they have heard of him at all, Burr's name is ignominious for two reasons. The first of these is connected with Alexander Hamilton, whom Burr, while still Jefferson's vice president, killed in the most famous duel of the era. The second is the "Burr conspiracy": the allegations of Burr's involvement between 1805 and 1807 in an attempt to invade Mexico, detach the western states from the Union, and establish an empire in the newly occupied territories with himself at its head. Burr was put on trial, where, despite Jefferson's highly irregular attempt to exert executive-branch influence by condemning the accused in advance, he was acquitted of any crime or misdemeanor by a grand jury. Nonetheless, Burr was forced into exile for three years and, largely as a result, the image of a North American Bonaparte determined to break up the Union remains a potent and enduring one. It is certainly not altogether undeserved, although several historians have quite rightly insisted that Burr is a more ambiguous figure than is generally understood.[23] It must also be said that Vidal is perhaps a little *too* smitten by his central character at various points, losing his authorial grip on Burr's voice, letting opinions slip through that sound closer to one of Vidal's own wry political observations. It is not, however, the author's intention primarily to resurrect the tarnished reputation of an unfairly maligned historical figure; it is rather to imagine how a cynical political animal like Burr might have reflected on the first few decades of the American republic.

We might remember here, to take an example from recent U.S. political history, that a similarly tainted figure, Richard Nixon, remained absorbed in his anger at the deification of John F. Kennedy, a man he believed, not without reason, to be as ruthless and corrupt as Nixon himself was perceived to be. So perhaps, Vidal thought, Burr might be made to shed light on the dark side of Jefferson. Both Nixon and Burr, after all, were to remark that they had elections "stolen" from them by an opponent who was subsequently deified (although here, for once, Richard Nixon's accusation seems to have significantly more foundation). In allowing Burr to "speak for himself," Vidal deploys an exclusively *literary* resource: the unreliable narrator, a distorting prism through which we might view the historical personage of Thomas Jefferson. Numerous characters remark upon Burr's penchant for fabrication throughout the novel in the same way that the text faithfully reenacts the accusations of deception and duplicity the founding fathers once hurled at each other. The truth, to Burr, is dull, prosaic, something toward which, like Jefferson's "self-evident" truths of 1776 enshrined later in the Constitution, he remains "equivocal": " 'On with the trial of the century!' Burr held up a large volume. 'This is a précis of my trial. The actual record runs to some eleven hundred pages. If you are ever morbidly disposed, read it. But for the moment, I shall condense the issues, in a way entirely favourable to me!' "24

Time and Narrative in *Burr*

Burr's resentment of Jefferson would not in itself be of much interest if it were not for the fact that the novel situates his robust criticisms in the radically different context of the 1830s. The relation between time and narrative in *Burr* is crucial to an understanding of the ways in which the novel explores the broader themes I am concerned with. The acute sense of historical transition the novel conveys is skillfully achieved via several narrative devices. The overarching narrative is set against the backdrop of Andrew Jackson's presidency. More specifically, it depicts the events leading to the succession of Jackson's vice president, Martin Van Buren, in 1836, the first head of state, we are reminded—lest we overlook the symbolism of the novel's architecture—to be born in the postcolonial era.

The tale is narrated by Charles Schuyler, a young New York journalist who has been assigned the task of procuring politically sensitive information from Burr, now seventy-two years old. By the 1830s, we are informed, the perception of Burr's place in the early history of the republic has become clouded by a widespread and powerful image of him as a traitor to the Union. Combined with this is his notoriety as the slayer of a founding father, one, moreover, whose ideological stock had risen considerably in an age of unprecedented commercialism and increasing political centralization.[25] This latter fact is crucial. Between Schuyler's narrative and the narrative of Burr's political career, recalled via his own memoirs and conversations held with Schuyler, we are able to chart this very process. By the 1830s, the United States is seen to have realized in a fundamental way the Hamiltonian vision of an expansionist republic supported by those modern economic principles that aroused the suspicions of the old Republican opposition during the first Federalist administrations. Furthermore, Burr's commentary on the first Republican administrations from 1800 onward clearly shows the extent to which, once these structures were in place, Jefferson could not dismantle the whole edifice of the "treasurobankites" (*Burr* 242).[26] Equally interesting, however, is the way in which this is in tension with certain *democratic* developments of the Jacksonian era that bear a trace of the Jeffersonian tradition both in its Lockean and classical republican aspects. Most prominent among these are the Jacksonian attack on the National Bank, the appeal to states' rights, and the antielitist character of its rhetoric in general.[27]

The Jacksonian democrats perceived themselves to be at the vanguard of a decentralizing movement that would ultimately place power back into the hands of the people. But what type of power: economic or political? And if the appeals were to Jefferson's principles, then which Jefferson—Appleby's liberal, forward-looking commercial farmer or Pocock's classical republican yeoman? To some extent, the principles of Jacksonian democracy have been subject to the same types of confusion between the roles of the polity and the economy as those of Jeffersonian republicanism. It is quite clear, however, that Jackson's appeal to Jefferson was grounded chiefly in the idea of *democratizing the economy* by breaking up monopoly privilege. Its political features were basically a reflection of this particular Jeffersonian impulse, albeit more nationalistic and mass-oriented in character in an expanding republic with a significantly extended franchise. It is crucial to bear in mind, then, Richard Hofstadter's point that although the age of Jackson is acknowledged as "a phase in the expansion of democracy . . . it is too little appreciated that it was also a phase in the expansion of liberal capitalism."[28]

Vidal's narrative technique foregrounds this notion of political legacy as it manifests itself in a more recognizably modern social context. What was the legacy the founding fathers wished to leave to their descendants, and how might they have wished them to interpret it? And what was the interpretation of that legacy by those descendants in the new social world? Although the United States was still a predominantly rural society in the 1830s, it was nonetheless a society in transformation. Schuyler's New York City, for instance, is beginning its march toward the twentieth century. *Burr* relays how Manhattan Island is about to be occupied by its first commercial buildings, and new penny papers are appearing "that make a fortune by each day giving the public some atrocious novelty" (*Burr*, 522). It is a city in political turmoil where masses congregate, abolitionists trigger riots, and anti-Catholic diatribes lambast the new waves of "papist" immigrants as a threat to American civilization. These were circumstances that could not possibly have been foreseen by the constitution makers, for whom mass meetings were a cause for alarm, slavery an accepted if somewhat troubling component of the economy, and the Protestant faith a cornerstone of the American moral universe. By the 1830s, new patterns were beginning to emerge, and the sense of a gap between past and future they prompted explains the narrative complexity of Vidal's novel.

Imagining Jefferson

Some of these new patterns evident in *Burr* intersect, of course, with those traced by the intellectual historians of liberalism and republicanism discussed earlier. There is an important sense, however, in which *Burr* avoids some of the drawbacks inherent in the approaches of Appleby and Pocock; these, incidentally, are flaws that have, more recently, also been identified by several scholars associated with the "republican synthesis." One of the weaknesses of the "republican synthesis" and the responses to it within early American historiography has been its inability to accept the extent to which both republicanism and, more obviously, liberalism are *ex post facto* concepts. Despite having provided us with trenchant understandings of how Lockean and classical republican concepts entered the mainstream of American political thought, both sides in the dispute have tended to dichotomize these respective theories. The result is that the nascent American republic is seen to be understood unequivocally by its founders as either a modern liberal polity or as a civic-humanist republic. In other words, it is with an either/or as opposed to a both/and formulation that they approach the question. Most pertinently, it downplays the flexibility, or what some including Vidal might view as the expediency, of the founders' politics.

The central problem is one of the selectivity of the historians in question. Decisions as to the appropriateness or irrelevance of material are based on the objectives of rigid interpretative schemas. These schemas are designed to establish a logical pattern that consolidates a thesis. The problem is particularly evident, for reasons I will explore, in those instances where the thought of Thomas Jefferson is under consideration. Both Appleby and Pocock seem to assume a certain *consistency* in the way in which liberal or classical republican ideas shaped Jefferson's confrontation with modernity, but what they fail to take account of is the fact that, although Jefferson was himself undoubtedly aware of such phenomena as an expanding economy, commercialization, property rights, corruption, and so forth, he was not aware in the same way as we are retrospectively. They may have been striking features of American public life to Jefferson, but they were certainly not perceived in the context of the "rise of liberal capitalism" or "the end of classical politics" in the sense we (can only) now understand such developments. Before speaking of the "Lockean" or "Machiavellian" nature of Jefferson's encounter with modernity, then, Gordon Wood has written we might recall that

> For early Americans there never was a stark dictionary of traditions, liberal or classical republican. None of the historical participants ever had any sense that they had to choose or were choosing between Locke and Machiavelli. The categories of "liberalism" and "classical republicanism" into which the participants in the past presumably must be fitted are the inventions of historians and as such are gross distortions of past reality.[29]

In this sense, recent historiography has constructed two Jeffersons out of a wide range of ideas that have only subsequently acquired their own respective coherence. Gordon Wood's *The Creation of the American Republic* was viewed initially as part of a republican *synthesis* with an earlier liberal orthodoxy that perhaps explains his sensitivity to the hybridity of ideas in previous historical circumstances. We might go on to say that what is required if we are to avoid the drawbacks of the approach Wood critiques is an act of *imagination* something akin to that which Vidal offers in *Burr*, that is, an attempt to re-create the way in which Jefferson conceived political problems without drawing conspicuously on any "stark dictionary of traditions."

Filtered through Burr's narration—whose self-serving and evasive dimensions are made explicit in the novel—Jefferson is no longer the strict adherent to a cohesive body of political thought. Burr notes, rather, how "each swift response" of Jefferson's, be it as ambassador to France or as president, is "rich with ambiguities" (*Burr*, 431). The reader is presented, via the persona of Burr, with a radical rereading of Jefferson's character and thought as it responds to a number of unfolding political crises and predicaments. Jefferson's posthumous glory is inexplicable to the elderly Burr, who as the presiding authority in the Senate witnessed Jefferson's attempt to "subvert the Constitution and shatter the Supreme Court" during the trial of Justice Samuel Chase in 1805. "Judge Chase was acquitted," Burr writes in his memoirs, "for the very good reason that there was no true case against him" (*Burr*, 404–405). Burr regards Jefferson's purchase of the Louisiana territories, thereby doubling the size of the United States in one fell swoop, as similarly unconstitutional. Furthermore, compounding this apparent deviation from strict "constructionist" republican constitutional principles was the fact that "Jefferson made it plain that he was in no hurry to extend to the 50,000 souls he had just bought any of those freedoms he had once insisted must be enjoyed by all mankind, or at least by the white inhabitants of the eastern American sea-board at the time of the Revolution" (*Burr*, 342–343).

This remark is foreshadowed in the novel by an earlier episode recalled in Burr's memoirs where Jefferson is recorded as speaking favorably of Montesquieu. The latter's belief, however, that true republican government was only able to exist on a small scale is seen by Burr to prompt a drastic change of opinion in Jefferson after the Louisiana purchase. Perhaps because Burr's career itself, as Stanley Elkins and Eric McKittrick have claimed, is notable chiefly for the *absence* of any consistent adherence to a political philosophy, Vidal can portray him as alert to instances of this shortcoming in the views of his contemporaries.[30] In hardheaded observations like this, he is certainly quick to detect in others manifestations of that imperial impulse associated with his own misadventures: "Certainly this 'ideal' [republican] form of government is not practical for an empire of the sort Jefferson gave us when he illegally bought Louisiana. . . . To justify himself Jefferson turned on his old idol [Montesquieu] and attacked him for (favourite and characteristic Jefferson word) 'heresy.' " (*Burr* 215)

Likewise, Burr is alert to the irony of Jefferson's fiery republican suspicion of executive power throughout the first Federalist administrations in the light of developments during his own presidency. "By the time Jefferson's Presidency ended," Burr claims, "the Executive was more powerful than it had ever been under those two 'monarchists,' Washington and Adams" (*Burr*, 268). Moreover, it is not only Burr who is shown to make such cynical assessments of Jefferson. Vidal is well aware of the frenzied, paranoid climate that characterized politics in the United States after independence, a process that accelerated as the French Revolution polarized Anglo-American political opinion. Defamation and slander disseminated via anonymously published pamphlets dominated the political discourse of the day. Accusations of "monarchism" or "Jacobinism" were flung indiscriminately among the antagonists. Unlikely alliances were forged against mutual enemies and dueling increasingly became a means of resolving grievances originating in the political sphere.[31]

Such chaotic elements help to explain the episode depicted in the novel where Alexander Hamilton meets with his archenemy Burr to persuade him to remain neutral in a Senate vote. We learn, first of all, that "Hamilton and Jefferson spent a good deal of time reading each other's correspondence." Hamilton has discovered that Jefferson "had wrote to advise a Mr Short to invest his money *in the bank*! In the very bank Jefferson is publicly accusing of being a menace to the republic!" Referring to what he regards as the third president's largely self-cultivated image as a peace-loving, frugal farmer suspicious of luxury, commerce, and immoderate wealth accumulation, Hamilton claims Jefferson is "as two faced as Janus." Jefferson's eagerness for a war in Europe, he adds, is based on the opportunity it allows him for personal enrichment via sales of hemp, cotton, and flax. War is, Hamilton quotes Jefferson, "helpful to domestic manufacture." Astutely, Burr goes on to add: "I have no idea if any of this were true. The important thing is that Hamilton believed it to be true" (*Burr*, 224).

It is via such means that the novel acquaints the reader with how the tensions in Jefferson's commitment to republican principles were first received. These are the very tensions that persist in historiographical debates today but are assessed, with hindsight, within the context of an emerging liberal democracy underpinned by a capitalist economy. This, of course, was the economic vision first championed by Hamilton himself and facilitated by his financial policies as Washington's secretary of the Treasury. The siege mentality of Jefferson and Hamilton becomes more comprehensible, however, if we—following Vidal—realize that this eventual path was far from clear to the protagonists themselves. Jefferson and Hamilton believed that at stake in their quarrel was nothing less than the survival of the republic. Whether their respective philosophies were informed by Lockean or Machiavellian values was neither here nor there: they embraced or espoused such values as and when the occasion demanded. As Lance Banning has written in an attempt to bring his fellow historians around to this fact: "Logically, it may be inconsistent to be simultaneously liberal and classical. Historically, it was not."[32]

Burr, Genealogy, and the Jeffersonian Legacy

No era in American history perhaps illustrates Banning's distinction with greater clarity than the period in the early nineteenth century associated with the rise of Andrew Jackson. Indeed, the renaming of the party of Jefferson in 1828 (from the "Democratic-Republican" to "Democratic") can be seen as the Jacksonian pivot that makes visible the lineage connecting Jeffersonian republicanism with the modern-day Democratic party. It also neatly demonstrates the importance attached by this time to associating Jefferson and his supposed heirs primarily with the concept of democracy. It was, ironically, Jackson's opponent, John Quincy Adams, the son of John Adams, Jefferson's old Federalist adversary and fierce critic of the French Revolution, who invoked the republican mantra by running for reelection as a "National Republican." On a broader though certainly not unrelated level, the Jackson era is commonly viewed as the high-water mark in the United States's transition from a modest, agrarian republic to an expansive, increasingly urban democracy supported by a recognizably modern market economy.[33]

Jackson came to power in 1829, with Jefferson's funeral eulogies still ringing loudly in American ears. In many ways, the election of the year before reenacted the bitterly partisan battle of 1800. The specter of monopoly, in the form of a second National Bank, for instance, was once more the subject of fervid political debate. Was the United States, the Jacksonians were asking as Jefferson had in 1800, to be governed by the many or the few, the majority or the minority, the aristocracy or the people?[34] What remained unaddressed was whether such appeals to the people's sovereign will undermined the republican order championed by the founding fathers. As Merrill D. Peterson has written:

> According to the ideology the victory of 1828 was a restoration. But the popular democracy the Jacksonians championed clashed with the republican order they professed to cherish; the party's label in 1828, Democratic-Republican, suggested its ambivalent posture. The proof of Jackson's orthodoxy was to be his adherence to the principles of Jefferson, as if these constituted a fixed and coherent code of government.[35]

Public reaction to Jefferson's death in 1826, then, helped sweep his old party to victory two years later, albeit under a new name. Posthumous tributes to the sage of Monticello undoubtedly would have added resonance to Jackson's professed commitment to "repeat [Jefferson's] revolution of 1800."[36] The reaction to the death of Aaron Burr ten years later was somewhat different. On Burr's death, it was said in one contemporary newspaper, "decency congratulated itself that a nuisance was removed, and good men were glad that God had seen fit to deliver society from the contaminating contact of a festering mass of moral putrefaction."[37]

Gore Vidal is only too aware of the ironies of this discrepancy of reputation by the 1830s. The plot of *Burr* turns on this very theme, subjecting what Vidal believes to be its "fictive" elements to his own unique mode of historical-fictional scrutiny. Such is Aaron Burr's infamy at this historical juncture, the reader learns, that the establishment of any connection, particularly a *political* connection, past or present, with the disgraced former vice president could seriously check the ambitions of any aspiring politician. With this effect in mind, Charles Schuyler's employer at the *Evening Post*, William Leggett, is intent on scuppering Vice President Martin Van Buren's chances of succeeding Jackson as president. This he hopes to achieve by revealing Van Buren as Burr's illegitimate son, conceived during a stay at a tavern run by the Van Buren family in Kinderhook, New York. To support his view, Leggett points to the physical resemblance between the two and the excessive interest Burr took in the young Van Buren who, at an earlier age than was common, managed to find a position in the law firm of a Burr associate. Moreover, on his return from exile and still under indictment for the murder of Hamilton, Burr stayed with Van Buren, then a leader of the Albany regency, the controlling political elite of New York State.

Leggett claims to be acting in the name of democracy, as a supporter of Jackson, whose reforms he believes will be reversed should Van Buren attain office. Unmasking Burr as Van Buren's biological father, however, he intends only as a preliminary strike that will help establish what he perceives to be a more pernicious connection: that of Van Buren as Burr's political heir. "Americans are a moral people," Leggett tells Schuyler, "But even more damaging than his bastardy is his *political* connection with Burr, particularly in recent years. If we can prove dark plots, secret meetings, unholy combinations—then, by Heaven, Van Buren will not be chosen to succeed General Jackson" (*Burr*, 28). This exchange in the novel gives an early signal of the author's interest in playing with ideas of paternity and lineage, in this case by excavating a long-forgotten rumor, powerful at the time, but ultimately lost to history in its failure to ignite a full-blown political scandal. The figurative pull of such genealogical themes is a powerful one within American political culture. If it has been said of Jefferson that "parties do not take sides for or against him, but contend, like children, as to their legitimate descent,"[38] then what, Vidal appears to be asking, might it mean if a whole generation of American politicians could be construed as, in some sense, the "heirs" of Aaron Burr?

Vidal, after all, is not merely interested in gossip for its own sake, although he no doubt takes a certain relish in deflating the more hagiographical accounts of the founding fathers' "virtue." He refuses, for instance, to draw attention to the promiscuity and sexual peccadilloes of historical personages simply to expose any supposed "sexual hypocrisy." The coverage in *Burr* of Jefferson's and Hamilton's indiscretions is likewise unconcerned with the pre- or extramarital nature of such transactions. The point Vidal wishes to extrapolate from the Burr–Van Buren rumor is at once figurative and political: who are the founding fathers and who are their *legitimate* descendants? *Burr* is at pains to stress how virtually every senior politician of the 1830s, including Andrew Jackson, Martin Van Buren, and Henry Clay, were at the very least tacit supporters of Burr during his Mexican misadventure, which was, in constitutional terms, the most serious episode of a career with no shortage of dark corners. William Leggett's attempts to discredit the vice president by raising the specter of Burr are motivated by a refusal to acknowledge Van Buren as the legitimate heir to Andrew Jackson. Vidal, however, ironizes Leggett's efforts in those sections of Burr's memoirs that recall Jackson's own fierce loyalty to Burr in his several hours of need. Here, for instance, is Burr's recollection of Jackson's response to the Hamilton duel: "Never read such a damn lot of nonsense as the press has been writing! All that hypocritical caterwauling for that Creole bastard who fought you of his own free will, just like a gentleman which he wasn't, if you'll forgive me, Colonel! . . . He was the worst man in this union, as you, Sir, are the best" (*Burr*, 416).

Vidal here perfectly captures the voice of Jackson, the "frontier aristocrat," who couches the gentlemanly code of the classical republican elite in the robust language of the emerging democratic order. Both Jackson and Burr entered politics on the back of heroic military exploits, contemptuous of fence-sitting career politicians, preferring to emphasize the importance of "courage," "honor," and other martial virtues as opposed to those less exalted attributes, such as "discretion" and "flexibility," conventionally valued in political life. Furthermore, irony is piled upon irony when Burr records how the great champion of the "common man" was once himself the object of public derision in the aftermath of the Burr conspiracy trial: "A few days later Jackson was nearly mobbed when he addressed an anti-Burr crowd. . . . But he held his ground and with many an oath declared that I was the victim of political persecution. . . . I fear— hard as it is to believe now—that the plebs actually *laughed* at their future idol Andrew Jackson. I at least blessed him for the friend he was" (*Burr*, 483–484).

What, then, are we to make of such affiliations and their bearing on any understanding of the American political tradition? What does it mean when Vidal has Aaron Burr—a figure perceived as *antithetical* to that tradition—announce, "it has been a rule with me to measure people by what they think of Andrew Jackson. Anyone who does not appreciate that frank and ardent spirit is an enemy to what is best in our American breed—by the Eternal!" (*Burr*, 426)? How did a man once perceived by Jefferson as a grave threat to the republic acquire support from Andrew Jackson, later promoted as Jefferson's supposed political heir? Furthermore, how does Burr, marked in political terms as both the Caesar *and* Catiline of the early republic, come to admire the inheritor of the Jeffersonian political tradition?[39] Has the imperialist, we might ask, come to embrace the republic, or has the republic, without realizing it, always secretly embraced the imperialist? These are intriguing questions that finally bring us back to the issues raised by Pocock and Appleby connected with the attitudes toward commerce and expansion, democracy, and empire in the early republic.

Elusive Republicanism

In *Burr*, it might be said, we find a discernible slippage between rhetoric and reality, word and deed, theory and practice in the early republic: a gap prompted by the confrontation between republican discourse and the emerging capitalist economy. For Vidal, this gap gave many of the "republican" pronouncements of the founding generation of American statesmen a contradictory flavor verging on hypocrisy: a flavor too often diluted by deferential historians. Aaron Burr was one of the few members of that generation who consistently refused to countenance the republican claims of the revolution. Burr's eventual fate, the novel implies, is tied to his contempt for such idealistic claims, his refusal to harness new economic impulses and developments to the spirit of 1776, 1800, 1828, or any other alleged republican meridian. Jefferson and Jackson, on the other hand, were always careful to acknowledge the cultural power and importance of such demands, which helped to reassure Americans by connecting past to future.

Vidal's Burr views his own career retrospectively as a premature attempt to embrace new realities, an attempt that was doomed precisely because of its failure to provide a commensurate (and to him no doubt spurious) justificatory political discourse. Burr's inability to legitimate his actions within an acceptable republican rationale resulted in marginalization and obloquy. By contrast, Jefferson and Jackson deftly circumvented this problem by extending the conceptual territory covered by the term. They knew that although "liberalism"—the philosophy best suited to the demands of a broadening capitalist economy—appealed to the heads of Americans, "republicanism" still appealed to their hearts. It is the myriad contradictions involved in this harmonizing strategy, however, that makes the politics of these figures so difficult to compartmentalize. This has led some intellectual historians to speak of a Jeffersonian or Jacksonian *persuasion*, defined by Marvin Meyers as "a half-formulated moral perspective involving emotional commitment,"[40] rather than any more coherent political ethos as such. In this vein, Vidal has a cynical Burr articulate the persuasiveness and sphinx-like qualities of Jefferson in the following passage:

It is amazing how beguilingly [Jefferson] could present [his] contradictory vision. But then in all his words if not deeds Jefferson was so beautifully human, so eminently vague, so entirely dishonest but not in any meretricious way. Rather it was a passionate form of self-delusion that rendered Jefferson as president and as man (not to mention as writer of tangled sentences and lunatic metaphors) confusing even to his admirers . . . when Jefferson saw that he could not create the Arcadian society he wanted, he settled with suspicious ease for the Hamiltonian order . . . he was the most successful empire-builder of our century succeeding where Bonaparte failed. But then Bonaparte was always candid when it came to motive and Jefferson was always dishonest. In the end, candour failed; dishonesty prevailed. I dare not preach a sermon on *that* text.

(*Burr*, 218)

Burr's infamy rests on his capacity for deception, Jefferson's fame on his capacity for self-deception. Burr, incapable of "preach[ing] a sermon on *that* text," like all true villains, revels in his self-awareness, and his candor on such matters allows Vidal an ideal vehicle to pursue these psychological themes. The traditional historical study is always going to be stymied, to some extent, by an overdetermined notion like "persuasion," which hinges on a sense of the subject's "emotional" commitment to a set of ideas. Such psychological factors invariably remain obscure to the probings of the historian. To the novelist, by contrast, such intangibles are the very stuff of artistic representation. Even more avowedly "postmodern" representations than Vidal's, which willfully work against the grain of such "depth models," generally do so in order to endorse the idea of an emotionally withdrawn and psychologically "depthless" modern society.

Jefferson's self-deception was generated by the paradoxical coexistence of a republican philosophy that associated "virtue" with participation in government and a laissez-faire economy where it was transplanted into the social sphere and became associated with participation in *society*.[41] Having never subscribed to any notion of virtue in his public *or* private life, Aaron Burr consequently remained untroubled by this paradox. With virtue banished from the public sphere, the imperial adventurism and political opportunism of a later generation of Americans gives Burr's actions something of a premonitory gloss. "Ahead of the times! That should be on his tombstone," exclaims one character in Vidal's novel. "Aaron Burr always saw the future first. Yet never profited by it" (*Burr* 440–441). *Burr* ends with a depiction of an ageing "embryo Caesar" gambling, one last time, on America's deviation from its republican heritage. In attempting to buy land in Texas to be settled by German immigrants, Burr's prospective investment turns on the United States ultimately annexing the territory from Mexico. He dies, however, before the onset of the Mexican War that would have made his investment good by extending U.S. territories beyond Texas to the Pacific coast. He does not live to applaud the first American imperial conquerors proper, one of whom, Zachary Taylor, will become president on his return, under a Whig party newly committed to the democratic values championed by Jackson.[42]

Vidal's focus on this "prophetic" dimension of Aaron Burr's career, his emphasis on the secret imperial drives that lurk behind the façade of agrarian republican innocence, is a useful corrective to the triumphalist and elegiac notes occasionally sounded in the debates surrounding republicanism in the early national period. *Burr* not only foregrounds some of the destructive effects and legacies of the unrestrained individualism celebrated by Appleby but also questions the tenability of reading "republicanism" as a central guiding ethos in the early national period. Yet the text also remains haunted by the idea of republicanism as a path not chosen, a set of ideas to be invoked against the abuse of centralized power. Republicanism could speak to public feelings of hostility toward certain effects of the new economic forces yet could only beat something of a retreat when given the mandate to tackle those forces in any comprehensive fashion. If classical republicanism dictated that only property holders could participate in civic affairs, it was largely because there had been no historical precedent of a society in which so many individuals *were* property holders. Never before had commerce, in the form of trade and land-acquisition opportunities, held out so great a material promise to so many.

In this sense republicanism was, in the United States—much as socialism and its Jacobin/Chartist antecedents were in Europe—the primary discourse of political opposition to capitalism. If republicanism presented capitalism with its greatest political critique, then socialism can be seen to have subsequently provided a later industrialized capitalism with the missing economic dimension. Neither, however, were able to accomplish *both* these objects. In the same way that Marxism has no conception of the political beyond the economic realm of Necessity, republicanism has no conception of economics prior to the political realm of Freedom. Republicanism then, stands to the economy as Marxism does to the polity: at a considerable distance. This is what gives republicanism its elusive quality. Though capable of galvanizing considerable oppositionist forces, when it is allowed to govern, republicanism fails to achieve its professed ends. Political adjustments and compromises are always to be made in the face of unavoidable economic demands, just as the political implications of radical economic agendas have thwarted governments elected on socialist manifestos.

Thus we see in *Burr* republicanism invoked predominantly by the less powerful as a means of restraining the more powerful. Indeed a key feature of republican "virtue" turns on a certain suspicion of power-wielding per se, most pronounced in the potent, pastoral myth of George Washington as an American Cincinnatus, the reluctant Roman officeholder recalled from the plow to perform civic duties during a "Machiavellian" moment of crisis. As Burr caustically notes, however, evidence of such self-abnegation in the early republic is slim. When Jefferson claims he has no desire to hold office, Burr writes in his memoirs: "I will not record the familiar speech. Washington, Jefferson and Madison gave it in one form or another at regular intervals throughout their political (and they had no other) lives." Again Jefferson is depicted making the appropriate republican noises before taking a more pragmatic approach to the political matters in hand. "The retirement speech done with," Burr writes, "we both continued as if he had not made it" (*Burr*, 276).

In an afterword, Vidal feels obliged to explicitly distance Burr's view of the early republic from his own. "All in all," he admits, "I think rather more highly of Jefferson than Burr does; on the other hand, Burr's passion for Jackson is not shared by me" (*Burr*, 576). This betrays, perhaps, Vidal's sympathy for Jefferson, who, unlike Jackson, understood virtue in still broadly classical terms and, however much in self-deception, sought to keep the United States's republican robe unsoiled by imperial and capitalist enterprise. There was, after all, none of the U.S. *military* imperialism during Jefferson's period in office, which Vidal believes has ultimately led, in the twentieth century, to a tax-devouring military-industrial leviathan and global American empire premised on economic power. Jefferson seems to foresee this latter development in *Burr* when, after his purchase of Louisiana, he remarks: "I do think that we are the first empire in history to *buy* its territory rather than to conquer it" (*Burr*, 430).

Yet Vidal's tardy intervention on behalf of Jefferson is still curious—as if the author doesn't wholly trust the skeptical view of the founders that permeates his own text. In a later nonfiction study of three founding fathers, Vidal offers further repentance for his youthful preoccupation with their hypocrisy (or as he gently recasts it, their "contradictions"). "In my youth," he writes in *Inventing a Nation* (2003), "I was fascinated by dramatic contradictions in character; in age, I am far more interested in those consistencies wherein lie greatness." Washington, whose greatness is evident "throughout his career" (if not much in *Burr*), and Adams (the supposed source of whose greatness, an "overwrought conscience," is thoroughly lampooned in *Burr*) are here invoked as examples of an admirable consistency. The most resonant and interesting of Vidal's retreats here, however, centers on Thomas Jefferson:

> I am now more moved by Jefferson and the Nullification Resolutions . . . where Jefferson's inner consistency about maintaining liberty within a state suddenly turned onerous comes up sharply against the problem of what to do when a heretofore virtuous republican government gets the votes in the two houses of Congress as well as that of a chief executive willing to collude with them in an assault on the Bill of Rights. Inevitably, Jefferson would think that if the States had not the right to nullify the central government's tyrannous acts, they should leave the Union.[43]

It is within this eighteenth- rather than any twentieth- or twenty-first-century context that the strangely "Jeffersonian" cast of Vidal's own "anti-imperialism" becomes apparent. Just as Jefferson loathed slavery for what it did to the slaveowner as much as what it did to the slave, so Vidal objects to colonialism on the basis of its effects on the colonizer as much as the colonized. Vidal's anti-imperialism is not of the modern internationalist variety, designed to demonstrate solidarity with the oppressed abroad, but is rather, in its essentials, consonant with that of a paleoconservative isolationist such as Pat Buchanan. In a perspicacious review of *Inventing a Nation*, Daniel Lazare notes how Vidal's "Old Whig" politics—"a pre-modern Anglo-American type our eighteenth century Constitution has preserved as if in amber"—are rooted in a Jeffersonian view of the American Revolution itself as "a return to some halcyon age in the past when imperial oversight was minimal." As we have seen, however, this had to be accommodated to the economic and ideological imperatives of modern capitalism and liberalism respectively. Thus, as Lazare claims, "America's restorationist revolution led to a looking-glass system of politics in which progress and retrogression, left and right, were jumbled."

It is the fact that Vidal's politics are informed by the "anti-imperialism" of the ideologically "jumbled" American revolution rather than that of, say, Che Guevara or Ho Chi Minh that perhaps explains why they are frequently misinterpreted by those who praise and criticize him alike. The founders, we might recall, originally viewed themselves as loyal British subjects abused by a tyrannical monarch. In trampling so thoroughly and persistently on the prerogatives of parliament and the rights of Englishmen enshrined in the "ancient constitution" (and resuscitated after the Glorious Revolution), George III had effectively dissolved the contract between state and subject.

Lazare's description of Vidal as a "patriot at war with his own country" places him in this tradition. The paradox produced in transplanting the anti-imperial rhetoric of what began as an eighteenth-century family quarrel to the present day does, on one level, help maintain a coherent philosophy still capable of exerting a powerful appeal; hence Lazare's accurate observation that "the more anti-American [Vidal] becomes, the more American he reveals himself to be."[44] Vidal has, since the Vietnam War, been at least as popular as a polemicist and contrarian as he has a novelist—a phenomenon that shows little sign of abating even as he reaches his ninth decade. He remains an angry critic of the recent U.S. occupations of Iraq and Afghanistan, as well as earlier interventions in the Balkans, once again chiefly on the grounds of the ills they inflict on the American republic (a revitalized military-industrial complex, higher taxes, infringements on civil liberties, and so on) rather than those on which intra-left debates are foremost contested—that of the effects on the native populations of these territories.[45]

Beyond the difficulties raised by the idea of using the founders as any kind of touchstone for contemporary U.S. foreign policy, however, there are others more germane to the primarily domestic ambit of this study. Most important perhaps is that the time-warped nature of Vidal's brand of anti-imperialism frequently makes it difficult to distinguish from antistatism or a more generalized opposition to centralized power per se. There can be little doubt that, for Vidal, the most politically meaningful elements of the U.S. Constitution are those initial amendments, demanded by its anti-Federalist opponents, that compose the Bill of Rights. Over the years, this has led Vidal to reappraise the likes of revolutionary-era tax rebel Daniel Shays and, somewhat less explicably, the Oklahoma bomber Timothy McVeigh simply, it would seem, on the basis of their commitment to the Bill of Rights and opposition to "big government."[46] In corollary fashion, it has also led him to produce some less than flattering images, fictional and nonfictional, of figures whose adherence to "rights"—whether those pertaining to the states or the individual—has been tempered by a dedication to other political principles no less American.

Notable among these figures is Abraham Lincoln, who, of course, as president during the Civil War, overrode the doctrines of states' rights and the ancient legal right, enshrined in the Sixth Amendment, of *habeas corpus*. Vidal's novel *Lincoln* (1984) offers a portrait of an American Bismarck, intent on unification at all costs, a president, no less, "who had willed his death as a form of atonement for the great and terrible things he had done by giving so bloody and absolute a re-birth to his nation."[47] Vidal's attitude toward Lincoln, as this passage suggests, is revealing. Summarizing Jefferson's affirmation of states' rights in *Inventing a Nation* the same ambivalent chord is sounded when he notes how a state's ultimate right—the right to "revolution"—was "savagely if not fatally tested by a Civil War in which the abolition of slavery replaced disunion, despite Lincoln's most poetic efforts to the contrary, and any hope of a decentralized Union as the issue has been dead until this day."[48]

Such ambivalence stems from the fact that Vidal seems reluctant to relinquish his antistatist principles even in the face of an issue as morally compelling as the abolition of slavery. Yet the two are, in the context of the grave sectional crisis that confronted Lincoln on his election in 1860, wholly irreconcilable. The perpetuation of the more decentralized state of the antebellum era would unquestionably have left slavery untouched where it existed and most likely even facilitated its extension—too high a price, even for the most ardent contemporary advocate of states' rights, one would have thought. Vidal's anachronistic form of republicanism exposes a certain sentimentality often at the core of the cynic's enterprise—a connection pursued in chapter 3.[49] As Lazare caustically notes, Vidal here "seems to be accusing Lincoln of using slavery as an excuse to ram through a centralized state. ... If only Lincoln had abolished slavery and left it at that, we would have the old Republic back in all its homespun, decentralized glory, purged of its original sin. Imperialism, product of a centralized state, would never have reared its ugly head."[50]

Vidal's novelistic talent combines well in *Burr* with a political sensibility well suited to the age of the founders. This can be explained perhaps by both Vidal's and the founders' shared determination to bracket the question of slavery when faced with political concerns they take to be more pressing. It also explains the unconvincing account of slavery as an expedient issue to be deployed and discarded at will by cynical empire builders in *Lincoln*. Political thinkers associated with the classical republics, of course, also gave little consideration to slavery, labor, the private sphere, or what political philosopher Hannah Arendt usefully gathered together under the rubric of "the social question." Yet the deferment of this question—evident during the composition of the Constitution itself as well as in several notable sectional compromises in the decades prior to the Civil War—would come back to haunt the American polity as the crises it served to generate became more and more acute. Arguably, the most symbolic of these was the attack on the federal arsenal at Harpers Ferry, Virginia, launched by John Brown in 1859. It is to the return of the repressed social question instantiated by Brown—and a novelist far more alert to its moral effects on American liberalism than Vidal—that we will now turn.

2

"OUR DIVINE EQUALITY"

Russell Banks's *Cloudsplitter* and the Redemptive Liberalism of the Lincoln Republic

> Was John Brown simply an episode, or was he an eternal truth? And if a truth how speaks that truth today?
>
> —W. E. B. DUBOIS, *John Brown*

> One cannot think of the long, long story of black bondage and the war that ended it without a shiver of awe. It is the one chapter in American life that brings us back to biblical history.
>
> —ALFRED KAZIN, *God and the American Writer*

> It is not an era of repose. We have used up our inherited freedom.
>
> —HENRY DAVID THOREAU, "Slavery in Massachusetts"

Transcendental Politics

In August 1837, Ralph Waldo Emerson delivered his famous oration "The American Scholar," exhorting the young men of the Harvard Phi Beta Kappa society to free themselves from the dead hand of the past and, more specifically, "the sacredness which attaches itself to the act of creation."[1] This "intellectual declaration of independence," as Oliver Wendell Holmes was later to describe it, has often been viewed as a response to the prevailing European criticisms of early American culture and society as shallow and rootless, impoverished by the absence of tradition. Emerson's confident call for the young nation to seize the possibilities conferred by geography rather than history, his affirmation of nature as the most important index to national character, is rightly seen as a benchmark in the development of American thought.

Yet there is another context for "The American Scholar" that is best understood with reference to internal and political rather than transatlantic and sociocultural antagonisms. By the 1830s, as we have seen in the previous chapter, American political life was a very obvious arena within which a sacred "act of creation" *had*, in fact, established an indigenous tradition. Political ideas in Jacksonian America could be neither advanced nor opposed without first being positioned in relation to a revered heritage. When Emerson states to his contemporaries then, that such a time "like all times, is a very good one, if we but know what to do with it," he might be regarded as demanding something more ambiguous and, perhaps, subversive than the rejection of European social and cultural values. "If there is any period one would desire to be born in," he asks, "is it not the age of Revolution; when the old and the new stand side by side and admit of being compared; when the energies of all men are searched by fear and by hope; when the historic glories of the old can be *compensated* by the rich possibilities of the new era?"[2]

It is fairly obvious that by invoking the idea of "historic glories" proper to an "age of Revolution" Emerson is here conjuring up images of the founders of the American republic. More interesting, however, is the way such ideas are transmitted to a fresh generation whose understanding of individual rights, civic virtue, and modern forms of republican government are being fashioned from the rather different moral and political imperatives of 1837. Emerson's suggestion here that the deeds of the founders require "compensation" is thus revealing. To compensate is to acknowledge a wrongdoing. In a period and regional context marked most conspicuously by the emergence of abolitionism as a political force, talk of a wrongdoing with respect to the Revolution can only refer to one thing: slavery.

Indeed, the broad contours of Transcendentalist philosophy advanced by Emerson in this early address are delineated not only in terms of "the new importance given to the single person" but also by "an *analogous* political movement" that remains unnamed but hardly difficult to identify.[3] Aided by the discovery of previously unpublished material, recent scholarship has facilitated a clearer picture of Emerson's commitment to antislavery politics during this period. Earlier critics' portrayals of a conservative who embraced the cause only belatedly and with some reluctance in the polarized atmosphere of the 1850s are now seen as, at best, partial accounts. Consequently, any notion that Transcendentalism's preoccupation with the sovereignty of the individual somehow precluded meaningful political commitment has also been questioned.[4]

Five months after Emerson had proclaimed the ideals of "The American Scholar" before the Brahmins of New England, Abraham Lincoln, a month short of his twenty-ninth birthday, gave an address before the Young Men's Lyceum in Springfield, Illinois. Lincoln's remarks on "The Perpetuation of Our Political Institutions" can be read fruitfully alongside those of Emerson. On the surface at least, Lincoln would appear at odds here with Emerson's future-oriented sentiments, "The Perpetuation ..." being a plea for moderation and respect for the Constitution and the rule of law in the wake of recent lynchings in the South. Added urgency is given by an event somewhat closer to home: the murder of the antislavery newspaper editor Elijah P. Lovejoy in Alton, Illinois, by an antiabolitionist mob, which had occurred the previous November. What is striking, however, is the language and tone in which the young frontier politician chooses to couch this plea:

> Let reverence for the laws, be breathed by every American mother, to the lisping babe, that prattles on her lap—let it be taught in schools, in seminaries, and in colleges ... let it be preached from the pulpit, proclaimed in legislative halls, and enforced in courts of justice. And, in short, let it become the *political religion* of the nation; and let the old and the young, the rich and the poor, the grave and the gay, of all sexes and tongues, and colors and conditions, sacrifice unceasingly upon its altars.[5]

It is not merely in the explicitness of the call for a "political religion" that one finds here a conflation of the religious and the secular. The lecture as a whole takes something of the Puritan jeremiad form that critics have identified in several of Lincoln's Civil War speeches, most notably the Second Inaugural Address.[6] One finds here a vocabulary of the sacred that—while playing an important role in the ideological shape of the American Revolution—had largely disappeared from national political discourse by the turn of the century. Beyond, however, the calls here for ceaseless "sacrifice" in the name of secular values articulated via such a vocabulary ("pulpits," "altars") lies an ambiguous and, some have suggested, almost prophetic message that has fascinated and perplexed

Lincoln scholars for a number of years. This heavily coded message follows the theme pursued by Emerson a year earlier in "The American Scholar," namely, the desire of the present to establish sovereignty over the past. One passage of the Lyceum speech, in this respect, is worth quoting at length:

> It is to deny what the history of the world tells us is true, to suppose that men of ambition and talents will not continue to spring up amongst us. And, when they do, they will as naturally seek the gratification of their ruling passion, as others have *so* done before them. The question then, is, can that gratification be found in supporting and maintaining an edifice that has been erected by others? Most certainly it cannot. Many great and good men sufficiently qualified for any task they should undertake, may ever be found, whose ambition would aspire to nothing beyond a seat in Congress, a gubernatorial or a presidential chair; *but such belong not to the family of the lion, or the tribe of the eagle.* What! Think you these places would satisfy an Alexander, a Caesar or a Napoleon? Never! Towering genius disdains a beaten path. It *scorns* to tread in the footsteps of *any* predecessor, however illustrious. It thirsts and burns for distinction; and, if possible, it will have it, whether at the expense of emancipating slaves, or enslaving freemen.[7]

Such rhetoric can be read in a number of ways. Again, it might be suggested that Lincoln is here merely calling for republican vigilance in the face of would-be dictators with no respect for the constitutional "edifice" erected by the founding fathers. As we have seen in the previous chapter, Jacksonian America was awash with such opinion, Aaron Burr figuring, by that time, as an "American Bonaparte," and, of course, Andrew Jackson himself (as an "imperial" president) being the major demon within the Whig political culture that shaped the mind of the young Lincoln. But, as Edmund Wilson noted several decades ago, there are also other conclusions that might be drawn.

Wilson famously claimed in *Patriotic Gore* (1962) that in the early Lyceum lecture Lincoln, in actual fact, "has projected himself into the role against which he is warning."[8] Although later critics have gone on to pursue the implicit psychoanalytic meanings of such "projection,"[9] the point to retain here is the less speculative one that Wilson's Lincoln chapter closed on, that is, that Lincoln is "describing this figure with a fire that

seemed to derive as much from admiration as apprehension."[10] John Burt
has substantiated this claim in recent years by outlining a more profound
romantic-religious context for the demonology of the "Address to the
Young Man's Lyceum":

> What Lincoln describes here is not just the tyrant familiar from the civic
> republican literature of the previous century to which we have been intro-
> duced by Bailyn, Pocock and Appleby, or even the Machiavellian man of
> virtú, but the demonic hero familiar to us from the Romantic reading of
> Milton. At least it is clear that the figure Lincoln describes resembles Melville's
> Ahab far more than he resembles Sir Robert Walpole, and Lincoln's own feel-
> ings resemble far more that mixture of fascination and repulsion which Mel-
> ville felt for Ahab than the far simpler disgust the revolutionary generation
> felt for King George or Lincoln's own Whig allies felt for King Andrew.[11]

Burt here usefully takes us beyond the period's routine party political invocations and toward some of the themes I wish to explore in this chapter on
liberalism in the antebellum period. What we might identify here, in both
Emerson's "The American Scholar" and Lincoln's Lyceum lecture, I would
like to suggest, are two points on a spectrum of "transcendental" politics
that would ultimately redefine the meaning of American liberalism by the
time of the Civil War. At one end of this spectrum, I will posit, is the militant abolitionist ideology of John Brown.

What connects figures such as Brown, Emerson, and Lincoln is a near-
spiritual belief in the Declaration of Independence as enshrining a *transcendent* principle removed from historical contingency: the principle that all
men are created equal. Emerson praised the Declaration, in this sense, for
its "blazing ubiquities" and, as we shall see, the document held a significance
for Brown akin to scripture. Lincoln's desire to protect the Declaration from
both the philosophical and the interpretive assaults of his political opponents became a defining feature of his rise to prominence in the 1850s. "All
honor to Jefferson," he wrote to a group of Boston Republicans in 1859,

> to the man who, in the concrete pressure of a struggle for national inde-
> pendence by a single people, had the coolness, forecast, and capacity to
> introduce into a merely revolutionary document, an abstract truth,
> applicable to all men and all times, and so to embalm it there, that today,

and in all coming days, it shall be a rebuke and stumbling-block to the very harbingers of re-appearing tyranny and oppression.[12]

This, however, as historian Garry Wills claims, is a questionable account of Jefferson's intentions in 1776. For Wills, Jefferson "was not like Lincoln, a nineteenth-century romantic living in the full glow of transcendentalism. … He was an eighteenth-century empiricist, opposed to generalizations and concentrating on particulars." The Declaration, Wills asserts emphatically, was no "spiritual covenant."[13] This is probably accurate in the strictly historical sense but, as has been noted in the previous chapter, Jefferson lived for a long time, during an ongoing period of rapid socioeconomic readjustment, and his politics evolved accordingly. Indeed, in the final years of his life Jefferson himself quite self-consciously sought to anchor the Declaration to a civil religion that might help sustain the new nation. In doing so, he wished to stress what Pauline Maier has described as its "redemptive force."[14] Jefferson saw the republication of the Declaration during the 1820s as salutary in this respect, encouraging a further "pledge of adhesion to its principles and of a sacred determination to maintain and perpetuate … [its] … holy purpose."[15]

Such evidence of "romanticism" or, at the very least, a prominent spiritual dimension to Jefferson's thought is not, however, confined to this single sphere. "It is impressive and significant beyond words," Harry Jaffa has claimed, "that Jefferson, who was such a confirmed detractor of revealed theology, and whose works are filled with contempt for it … could not but express himself in the most solemn language of that theology when he contemplated the institution of Negro slavery."[16] It is unsurprising too, we might add, that such an observation should appear in the context of a study of the Lincoln-Douglas debates. It was here, after all, in the tenacious set of arguments advanced by Lincoln during the Illinois senatorial campaign of 1858, that the tensions between the "empirical" and "romantic" strands of Jefferson democracy were finally reconciled.

The Lincoln-Douglas Debates

The Senate election battle between Abraham Lincoln, standing for a still young Republican party, and the incumbent Democrat Stephen A. Douglas in the summer and autumn of 1858 represents a pivotal moment in American history. Not only did the publicity the campaign attracted bring Lincoln to national prominence, but the debates themselves exposed, in graphic fashion, the ideological gulf that would first divide the Democratic Party and ultimately the whole country, resulting in civil war.

Douglas was committed to the idea of a large republic premised on territorial expansion as the nation's "manifest destiny." Such a project, he believed, along Madisonian lines, would help curb the "factionalism" engendered by contentious issues such as slavery. For Douglas, the concept of "popular sovereignty"—allowing local populations to decide these issues for themselves—if implemented in the new territories such as Kansas-Nebraska, promised to resolve the crisis of slavery in the West. Lincoln, by contrast, had already, in the 1840s, denounced such "imperial" enterprises in his criticism of the Mexican War. Above all, however, he objected to slavery on moral grounds—an objection voiced more openly as the campaign progressed—and he feared the opportunities western expansion might afford to extend its influence. Equally important to Lincoln and the Republican Party more generally was the threat posed by the fixed and "dependent" status of the slave to the ideology of "free labor." The presence of a permanently enslaved labor force in the territories would, it was argued, increase the power of slaveholding interests in Washington and undermine the social mobility that energized mid-nineteenth-century American capitalism.[17]

While accepting the fact that the Constitution effectively protected slavery where it already existed, Lincoln firmly believed that the founders viewed the institution as morally unacceptable and therefore ensured that no provision was made for its extension. But although the Constitution undoubtedly remained ambiguous on the question as a whole, Lincoln saw only "eternal antagonism" between slavery and the "perfectionist" credo underwriting the Declaration of Independence. Interestingly, in explaining this relationship during the course of his first reply to Douglas in the campaign, the Declaration is once more elevated to the status of scripture:

The Savior, I suppose, did not expect that any human creature could be perfect as the Father in heaven; but He said, "As your Father in heaven is perfect, be ye also perfect." He set that up as a standard, and he who did most towards reaching that standard, attained the highest degree of moral perfection. So I say in relation to the principle that all men are created equal, let it be as nearly reached as we can. If we cannot give freedom to every creature, let us do nothing that will impose slavery on any other creature.[18]

For Douglas, the Declaration had to be viewed, first and foremost, as a struggle to establish the rights of certain white, middle-class property-owning men at a specific historical juncture rather than the rights of "man" in the abstract. The issue then, in 1776—as during the antebellum period for Douglas—was one of self-determination premised on the rights of a preexisting political community. In one exchange, Douglas seems to taunt Lincoln for his naïve, pseudoreligious understanding of the Declaration, reminding his audience that "no one of [the signers] emancipated his slaves, much less put them on an equality with himself," before asking his adversary whether "every man who signed the Declaration of Independence declared the Negro his equal, and then was hypocrite enough to continue to hold him as a slave, in violation of what he believed to be divine law?"[19] Douglas's chief strategy turned, however, on a wide range of legal arguments symptomatic of what critic David Zarefsky has described as the "constitutionalization of political discourse" that characterized this period.[20] Indeed, the drama of the debates as well as many other sectional crises preceding the war arose from the battle for supremacy between "law," as laid out in the U.S. Constitution (of which Douglas can be seen as representative), and "spirit," or the spirit of that law as embodied in the Declaration of Independence (which might be associated with Lincoln and the "transcendent" turn referred to above).

Several scholars working in different disciplines have identified this bifurcation in American political thought. For the political scientist J. David Greenstone, this opposition constitutes a "liberal polarity," emerging in the 1830s, between "reform liberals ... concerned primarily with the development of the faculties of individuals" and "humanist liberals ... concerned primarily with the satisfaction of preferences of individuals"; for the intellectual historian John Patrick Diggins, religion holds the key to the period as Calvinism once more becomes "the conscience of liberalism," opposing a Machiavellian republicanism that would bracket moral questions from the public realm; for the political philosopher Michael Sandel it is, on the contrary, a republican politics that "cannot be neutral toward the values and ends its citizens espouse" and, rather, a prevailing "minimalist liberalism" accused of the moral abdications evident in American "public philosophy."[21]

Each of these thinkers utilizes the Lincoln-Douglas debates to support their argument and seeks to elaborate what they perceive as the essentially moral foundations of Lincoln's political thought. Greenstone and Diggins stress the positive effects of Calvinism on Lincoln's thought and, in particular, his belief in the idea of America as a new Israel, thus assuring Americans, in Greenstone's words, of their "covenantal status ... as a special people with an 'ancient faith,' a status that imposed solemn responsibilities on them."[22] Sandel, however, is careful to detach this tradition of what we might, following Isaiah Berlin, describe as "positive liberty"[23] from any explicitly religious bearings. Yet even here there is a stray reference that can be seen, perhaps, to somewhat belie this intention. In the broader defense of republicanism undertaken in the conclusion of Sandel's *Democracy's Discontent* (1996), it is with reference to the "soul," that is, a theological rather than political term, that the dangers to liberty posed by the republican emphasis on shaping a common conception of the "good" are acknowledged. The cultivation of virtue among a large and disparate population, he admits, threatens to expose "the coercive face of soulcraft."[24]

It is within this intellectual struggle over the right to assert a place for the transcendent principle within American liberalism—crystallized during the Lincoln-Douglas debates—that the figure of the militant abolitionist John Brown should be understood. Russell Banks's *Cloudsplitter*—a fictional account of the life of Brown and his family—traces this "transcendental turn" in American liberalism. Moreover, in its structure and choice of narrator it presents a context for this process that brings Brown and, to a great extent, the Civil War period itself into sharper intellectual-historical focus.

Cloudsplitter, Religion, and Antebellum America

Cloudsplitter is narrated by John Brown's third son, Owen, who also acted as his principal lieutenant in the Kansas Wars of the 1850s. Owen Brown imparts his recollections to Katherine Mayo, a research assistant to Oswald Garrison Villard, the historian and editor of *The Nation*, whose major biography of John Brown appeared in 1910. The elderly Owen is now, by the

turn of the century, we learn, an *isolato*, an internal exile, spiritually bereft
and struggling to tend sheep in the Californian wilderness. As we shall see,
it is primarily the critical distance afforded via this choice of narrator that
allows the text to map the reshaping of the American political tradition in
the years leading up to the Civil War.

Owen Brown's initial hostility to the Villard project soon gives way to a
sense that this will be a final opportunity to correct the accumulation of
myth and fancy that has gathered around his father's image. More significantly for my purposes here, however, is Owen's admission that this last act
of testimony brings to a close a long and tortuous process of moral and
spiritual reckoning on his own part. Since the infamous Brown raid on
Harpers Ferry in 1859, which resulted in the death of several brothers as
well as the execution of his father, Owen claims to "have been dead these
forty years … I am more the ghost of Owen Brown than I am the man
himself."[25] The visit of Katherine Mayo, however, now holds out the pros-
pect of a form of closure to this "after-life." "It was as if," he confesses,
"your visit had sounded a final knell that drove me into a purgatory which
I had been longing for all these years but had neither the courage nor the
wisdom to seek on my own. As if, now that I am here, there is no going forward or back, no possible ascent to heaven or descent to hell, until I have
told my story" (*Cloudsplitter*, 9–10).

Banks here seeks to place his novel squarely in a tradition of "witness"
literature that runs from the Book of Job in the Old Testament to
Coleridge's "Rime of the Ancient Mariner" and Melville's *Moby Dick*.[26] Such
works depict figures conditioned by "exile" of some description whose
faith in authority, secular or religious, is rendered vulnerable in the face of
the traumatic experience recorded. The resonance of *Moby Dick* is especially notable. The major source of authority for the young Owen is, of
course, John Brown himself, who functions as Ahab to his Ishmael. Like
Melville's creation, John Brown is in the grip of "monomania," obsessed by
a single idea and willing to sacrifice himself and all around him in its pursuit. Brown's all-consuming idea, of course, is the destruction of the "white
whale" of slavery. The theme of "whiteness," moreover—itself the object of
considerable critical scrutiny in recent years—is as important in Banks's
novel as the beguiling chapter "The Whiteness of the Whale" is in
Melville's.

Brown's "monomania" is what we would now understand in terms of
"religious fundamentalism." Calvinism here provides the framework within

which the notions of "sin" and "slavery" fuse—if sin, within this theological schema, is a form of "enslavement," then slavery itself must be regarded as a sin. Thus, for Brown, the American state of the 1850s, in its sanctioning and extension of slavery into the new territories, is nothing less than the Great Satan. "No, for Father," Owen Brown attests, "quite literally, we Americans, white as much as black, Northern as much as Southern, anti-slave as much as pro-, we were, all of us, presently living under the rule of Satan." Yet Banks makes clear that there are also a number of crucial secular questions at stake here. Owen continues:

> It was an inarguable truth to Father that man's essential task while on this earth was to bring both his personal and his civic life into total accord with the will and overarching law of God. And since a republic is a type of state that by definition is governed by laws created and enforced by its citizens, whenever in a republic those laws do not conform to the laws of God, because those laws *can* be changed by men, they *must* be changed by men. And not to change them placed the mortal soul of every one of its citizens in jeopardy. Not to struggle constantly to overthrow the system of slavery was to abandon our Republic, was to surrender our civic freedoms and responsibilities, was to give our mortal souls over to the rule of Satan. We were obliged to oppose slavery, then, not merely to preserve and perfect the Republic, although that alone was a worthy enough task, but to defeat Satan. It was our holy, our peculiarly American, obligation.
>
> (*Cloudsplitter*, 254–255)

Here Banks seeks to restore to the contemporary reader a sense of the tremendous triangular tension between moral, political, and religious conviction during this era. This is what is described by Melville in the famous "Knights and Squires" chapters in *Moby Dick* in republican terms as an "august dignity ... [that] ... is not the dignity of kings and robes, but that abounding dignity that has no robed investiture." Yet this "dignity" is deeply informed by a Protestant Christian absolutism that shares little with the paganism, tepid by comparison, of the classical Roman and Athenian republics: "Thou shalt see it shining in the arm that wields a pick or drives a spike; that democratic dignity which, on all hands, radiates without end from God; Himself! The great God absolute! The centre and circumference of all democracy! His omnipresence, our divine equality!"[27]

The Second Great Awakening and an increasingly vocal abolitionist movement in the North, combined with the emergence of an explicitly proslavery
ideology in the South, were the preconditions of Kansas-Nebraska, Harpers
Ferry, and, ultimately, fratricidal war. For the Brown family, "like some
ancient Hebrew tribe of wanderers and sufferers, burdened by the death of
women and children and by … endless obligations to our father's restless, yet
implacable, God" (*Cloudsplitter*, 32), the interrelationship between the personal pain and political conflict forged by religious faith long predated the
Civil War itself. The tendency of others to posit some prelapsarian idyll, effectively obscuring such tensions, is addressed at the very beginning of the
novel:

> The truth is, for us, the so-called Civil War was merely aftermath. Or, rather,
> it was part of a continuum. Just another protracted battle. Ours was very
> much a minority view, however. It still is. But from the day it began, to
> Northerner and Southerner alike, the Civil War was a concussive trauma
> that erased all memory of what life had been like before it. On both sides
> white Americans woke to war and forgot all the preceding nightmare, which
> had wakened them in the first place. Or they made it a pastoral dream.
>
> (*Cloudsplitter*, 8)

John Brown and Jefferson

The politics of the pastoral, as we have seen in the previous chapter, was
an important source of conflict in the emergence of liberalism as the
dominant ideology in early nineteenth-century America. Yet the meaning
of Jefferson's conception of agrarian democracy, premised as it was on
the right to hold slaves, was even more grievously contested in the years
prior to the Civil War. This, of course, is also evident in the depiction of
1830s New York in Vidal's *Burr*. Banks makes clear in *Cloudsplitter*, however,
that Brown's hostility to slavery—like Abraham Lincoln's—did not lead
him to disavow a Jeffersonian understanding of American democracy.
This is most conspicuous in an episode where Owen and his father journey to Europe on business. The trip is motivated by the elder Brown's
failure to sell wool to the "greedy" and "conspiring" merchants of New
England. English cloth manufacturers, by contrast, John Brown believes,
will be impressed by the comparative quality of American wool and pay a

better price. When asked by his son to explain the superiority of the American product, Brown offers a scathing, republican critique of British society, a critique pitched somewhere between Jefferson's understanding of the independent yeoman and the notion of "free labor" championed by Lincoln:

> "We've *seen* the shoddy goods they try to foist off on us poor colonials, pitching it to us at prices way above our own. Owen that stuff's grown by *peasants*!" he pronounced. The Irish and Scottish peasants were poor and demoralized, he explained. They were practically serfs, a conquered abject population impoverished for generations by a feudal overlordship. They were farmers who couldn't even own the land they worked or the animals they raised, and thus they had no more pride in the products of their labor than did the slaves in the American South.
>
> (*Cloudsplitter*, 338)

Owen Brown is less persuaded by his father's unfavorable "comparison between the products of slave labor and free, quite as if all the cotton being produced in the South by slave labor were not of sufficient quality to control the world market in cotton and make the slaveowners richer than Croesus and their senators and congressmen powerful out of all proportion to their numbers" (*Cloudsplitter*, 338). In his recognition of the formidable political and economic might wielded by the "slaveocracy," Owen Brown here, as he frequently does elsewhere in the novel, offers some pointed criticism of his father's judgment.

The author uses the Browns' trip largely to provide cultural counterpoints that effectively serve to illustrate the extent of their ambivalence toward the United States polity. Early on, for instance, England is praised as a country where "no man could legally buy and sell another" and thus "for that reason alone," despite being an "antique monarchy, not a modern republic," is acknowledged as "a freer country than ours." More pointedly perhaps, at a personal level, England is perceived as a refuge from conscience with the trip, at one point, described as "a vacation from the obligation to be constantly conscious of our national shame" (*Cloudsplitter*, 364). We can see from this that slavery for the Browns (as with Jefferson) is also to be abhorred as much for the psychological effects it imposes on slaveholders and those whose citizenship would seemingly confer a degree of complicity. We also find strong intimations in these passages of Lincoln's regret that slavery undermines the influence in the world of the "republican example" upheld by the United States.[28] It is, however, when the Browns pass through mid-Victorian Manchester that some of the virtues of American society first identified by Jefferson come into full focus. They can view, for example, "the shocking sight at dusk of the sooty mills ... and the blackened hovels of the thousands of laborers whose lives were given over to the mills," with much the same sense of (in Owen Brown's words) "luxurious detachment" evident in Jefferson's tone in *Notes on the State of Virginia* when describing the horrors of nascent industrialization in Europe.[29]

This "detachment" is the privilege that the young Jefferson at least wished to bestow on America, a privilege that would free the young republic from the "crimes" and depredations of modern industrial capitalism:

> The crimes evidenced by these monstrous, huge, prison-like factories were English crimes not American; and the greed that drove the mighty engines of the mills and the owners' callous disregard for the lives devoured in their service were English greed and callousness not American; and the raggedy, exhausted, vacant-eyed men and women and pathetic small children whom we saw wending their way along the narrow streets to their teeming tenements were English, Scottish and Irish workers—not a one of them American.
>
> (*Cloudsplitter*, 366)

We have already seen, however, that as the nineteenth century advanced, the Jeffersonian context for the pastoral became increasingly untenable. For Northerners such as the Browns this vision was adhered to only in an attenuated form, as a reflex reaction against industrialization, urbanization, and, more generally, modernity. Its popularity among proslavery ideologues (many of whom saw "paternalistic" slavery in the South as preferable to European "wage slavery") also rendered the vision problematic. In intellectual terms then, there was a vacuum within which a new understanding of the pastoral might emerge. It was one filled, in large part, by the transcendentalist thinkers of New England, whose substitution of Nature for God and antislavery politics played a crucial role in the intellectual and political life of the antebellum period.

The Significance of Emerson

The meaning of *Cloudsplitter* in the context of the American political tradition that I am interested in here rests primarily on the effects engendered by the use of Owen Brown as the novel's narrator. The self he presents at the beginning of the text is, in several respects, a divided one. This is most explicit, of course, in his attitude to his father, but because of John Brown's antislavery politics and willingness to deploy violence, any Oedipal drama must unfold in the public as well as the private sphere. The complex interrelation between public and private selves, the idea of an internal and external "house divided," is neatly encapsulated in the following passage:

> Ah Father, how you shame me one minute and anger me the next. How your practical wisdom, which at times borders on a love of violence for its own sake, challenges my intermittent pacifism, which borders on cowardice. Your voice stops me cold and then divides me. One day and in one context, I am a warrior for Christ. The next day, in a different context, I am one of His meekest lambs. If only in the beginning, when I was a child, I had been able, like so many of my white countrymen, to believe that the fight to end slavery was *not* my fight, that it was merely one more item in the long list of human failings and society's evils that we must endure, then I surely would have become a happy, undivided man.
>
> (*Cloudsplitter*, 324)

This admission occurs during Owen and John Brown's stay with Samuel Gridley Howe and his family prior to embarking on their journey to Europe. It is here, in Boston, amid the currents of Transcendentalist thought and antislavery agitation, that Owen Brown undergoes what he himself describes as a "transformation" in character. "I realized," he notes,

> I had become, in an important sense, a new man. No more the disgruntled, sulky boy who follows his Old Man around and waited for orders that he could resent. No more the pouting, conflicted ape. This new fellow, who had been a reluctant follower, was now an enthusiast, was a proper lieutenant, was a fellow believer! He might fail here and there—fail to act, fail to believe—but he would no longer question his aspirations or his commitment.
>
> (*Cloudsplitter*, 360)

The process begins as soon as father and son arrive in the city after the Howes have taken them to the Charles Street Meeting House to hear Ralph Waldo Emerson speak on the topic of heroism. The speech that Owen hears Emerson give, "Heroism" (later collected in the first series of essays published in 1841), he comes to view as providing *the* epiphanic experience in the development of his political consciousness. It does so by closing the sense of division previously referred to, that is, by presenting a template for a self no longer "conflicted." Owen—who identifies with Emerson's inability to find spiritual solace in institutionalized religion—can now, paradoxically, reconnect with his father, for whom such "godlessness" is anathema.

The spellbinding quality of Emerson's simple physical presence combined with a masterful oratory style is carefully conveyed. There is no theatricality in the performance. "Instead," we learn, "he spoke simply, directly, in a way that made you feel that he was speaking to you alone and to no one else in the hall. His bright eyes were the colour of bluebells and did not fix on any single person but fixed on the space just above one's own head, as if he were contemplating one's thoughts as they rose in the air" (*Cloudsplitter*, 311). What Emerson offers to his audience is "a freshened way of looking at things" loaded with provocative insight. The talk begins with an early example of this, in the analogy he draws between English culture's obsession with class, in the form of "gentility," and American preoccupations with skin color. Moreover, in examining the "hero" figure, Owen Brown also identifies a crucial subtext in Emerson's "hints and subtle asides," which suggest "that our present national crisis over slavery was the necessary field for such a person" (*Cloudsplitter*, 312). As with the passages from "The American Scholar" examined at the beginning of this chapter, references to slavery are once more carefully encoded in generalities. The allusions, however, do not escape Emerson's impressionable young listener:

Mr Emerson wanted a "tart cathartic virtue," he said, that could contend with the violations of the laws of nature committed by our predecessors and contemporaries. And here he lapsed into language—or should I say he *rose* to language—that, although not once uttering the word itself, excoriated slavery horribly and with great originality. It is a lock-jaw, he said, that bends a man's head back to his heels. It is a hydrophobia that makes him bark at his wife and babes, an insanity that makes him eat grass.

(*Cloudsplitter*, 312)

Emerson then goes on to outline the characteristics he associates with the hero, such as a "military attitude of the soul" and a certain form of "pride" that comes with representing "the extreme of individual nature." Furthermore, he adds, "the hero advances to his own music" and there exists "somewhat that is not philosophical in heroism." "These words," Owen reflects, "struck fire with me, for, of course, they described my father perfectly." Emerson goes on to persuade Owen even further of the relevance of his ideas to the situation and *Weltanschauung* of the Brown family. "Times of heroism," he explains, "are generally times of terror." As was the case in Lincoln's "Address to the Young Man's Lyceum," the death of Elijah Lovejoy is recognized by Emerson in this speech as a sign that such times may well have arrived.

John Brown, however, is, initially at least, less impressed by what he has heard. He departs from the hall before the applause for the lecture has abated and, when joined by his son, complains loudly of the "clouds, fogs, mists of words" that barely conceal the "godless" character of Emerson's thought. "What," he concludes, "does *he* know of terror? Ralph Waldo Emerson has neither the wit nor the soul to know terror. And he surely has no Christian *belief* in him! That's what *ought* to be terrifying him, the state of his own naked soul" (*Cloudsplitter*, 314). Yet this outburst does not prompt, as one might expect, an angry defense of the New England philosopher from his son:

> I followed silently, pondering the meaning and import of his fulmination, even as I nurtured an odd thought which had come to me towards the end of Mr. Emerson's peroration—that Father resembled no man so much as the Concord poet himself. The Old Man was a rough-cut, Puritan version of Ralph Waldo Emerson, it seemed to me that first night in Boston and many years afterward, and even unto the present time, when it matters probably not at all. But it was that night of some personal significance to me.
>
> (*Cloudsplitter*, 314–315)

The final sentence here is another indication that this episode is not to be taken lightly in the context of the narrator's moral and intellectual development. After remarking on a peculiar physical resemblance, their "old-fashioned, hawk-nosed Yankee faces," that might lead one to believe they were brothers, such physical detail is then linked to their force of personality. Both men share the same "pale deep-set eyes" that we are told "looked out at the world with such an unblinking gaze as to force you to avert your own gaze at once or give yourself over to the man's will." Finally, the comparison is extended into the metaphysical sphere: "And just as easily and selflessly as Father believed in his God, Mr. Emerson believed in the power and everlasting truth of what he called Nature. For both men, God, or Nature, was beginning, cause and end, and man was merely an agent for beginning, cause and end" (*Cloudsplitter*, 315).

The episode ends, however, with something approaching concession from John Brown on the matter of Emerson. Sensing a change of mood after walking for some time in silence, Owen notes that his father may indeed have been moved by Emerson's words. "Perhaps," he speculates, "he had been stung by their similarity to his own thoughts and beliefs and had never before heard them so handsomely expressed, and thus his anger had been directed not at Mr. Emerson but at himself." When Brown eventually requests his son's opinion on the lecture, Owen replies that he took the philosopher's words as "high counsel and prophecy." "Very interesting," comes the reply, "High counsel and prophecy. Well, who knows? God speaks to us in unexpected ways. Even in the words of philosophers" (*Cloudsplitter*, 316).

This kind of ambiguity is also evident in the position of Owen himself, who is able to recognize the shortcomings as well as the qualities of both men. If Brown "could not see himself in Mr. Emerson's portrait," then equally Emerson "was probably incapable of seeing my father as the very hero he was calling for." More generally, however, by using a narrator able to reconcile the credos of both Emerson and Brown in this way, Banks allows us to trace the relation of the events depicted in the novel to the broader intellectual culture. What is significant here is the messianic note struck by both men in their public pronouncements during periods of slavery-related crisis. Emerson is clearly calling in both "The American Scholar" and "Heroism" for the emergence of a redemptive disposition, even a redemptive figure, to reinvigorate the young republic by taking up the fight against slavery; John Brown clearly sees himself in that same role.

Such actions, of course, as the Civil War itself proved, might involve the suspension of democratic norms and the temporary convenience of military dictatorship. Lincoln, in the "Address to the Young Man's Lyceum," with this in mind no doubt, was more ambivalent but himself not a little smitten by the aura of such authoritarianism. This increasing willingness to redeem American liberalism with recourse to such methods, however, becomes even more apparent when the Browns visit the battlefield of Waterloo after their stay in England.

Napoleon and Dictatorship

Alongside Napoleon, analogies abound in Banks's novel between John Brown and other historical examples of military dictatorship. Oliver Cromwell, as "Lord Protector" of a Puritan republic, is a continual and, perhaps, obvious point of reference, but the acts and ideas of Brown's contemporaries in Italy—Mazzini and Garibaldi—also feature as sources of Brown's military strategy and political inspiration.[30] The journey to the scene of Napoleon's final defeat is, we are led to believe, motivated only by the former, that is, by Brown's own military plans and, in particular, his desire to learn from Napoleon's mistakes at Waterloo. It is not, he claims, connected with any admiration for the former Emperor of France on his part: " '*Admire* him, Owen? I loathe him! However brilliant a military man he was, he was nevertheless an atheistic monster, an egotistical dictator of the first rank. When he was finally declared dead on his little island of St. Helena, while all over the world people wept, I cheered' " (*Cloudsplitter*, 380).

Earlier, after acknowledging his father's penchant for "passing, erratic distractions," Owen nonetheless notes that the "interest in Napoleon and Waterloo ... had lasted longer than it should have" (*Cloudsplitter*, 378–379). Brown's fascination, we learn, is connected primarily with a famously bold but ultimately foolhardy and hubristic military endeavor undertaken by Bonaparte, one that unfolded over a hundred-day period. It is a sound understanding of this episode, he believes, that may well determine the outcome of his own plans to emancipate slaves in the South. "It was those one hundred days, he explained. One hundred days—from Napoleon's unexpected departure with a half-dozen faithful lieutenants from the island of Elba, where he'd been exiled, to his arrival here at Waterloo three months later with a quarter-million armed men at his command" (*Cloudsplitter*, 381). This is clearly viewed as a template for Brown's own raid on Harpers Ferry in

1859, which was meant to instigate slave insurrection in the South and ultimately mobilize an army of freed slaves to trigger complete emancipation. But the connection between Brown and Napoleon operates on many more levels than that of mere military strategy. Observing his father pace the site of Waterloo, seeing him "track and translate a series of elaborate, invisible runes," searching for clues the past might offer to unlock the future, Owen once more reflects on the increased grip his father's "visions" have come to exert on his own imagination:

> I believed in his visions, that they had occurred, and that they were of the truth—the truth of warfare, the truth of religion. ... He was a man who saw things that I knew must be there but could not see myself, and because I loved him and trusted him, and because of the power of his language and the consistency of his behavior, my belief had swiftly become as powerful and controlling, as much a determinant of my mind and actions, as Father's belief was of his. In this refracted way—though I remained until the end his follower and continued to live with no clear plan of my own and no belief in God—I became during those days for the first time a man of action and a man of religion. The difference between us, between me and my father, is that I would inspire no one to follow me, either into battle or towards God, whereas he had me, and soon would have a dozen more, and finally whole legions and then half a nation, following him.
>
> (*Cloudsplitter*, 384)

The notion of "refraction" invoked here reminds one of the qualities Emerson associates with the "representative man," that is, the way in which the image of an historical era is "refracted" through that of its most imposing personalities. Here, Emerson was famously drawing on Thomas Carlyle's theory of history as best understood via the words and deeds of "great men." Bonaparte himself, of course, was one of the character portraits in Emerson's *Representative Men* (1850). For Emerson, Napoleon was the personification of democracy and the bourgeois revolutions that had engulfed the modern world:

> [Napoleon] desires to keep open every avenue to the competition of all, and to multiply avenues: the class of business men in America, in England, in France and throughout Europe; the class of industry and skill. Napoleon

is its representative. The instinct of active, brave, able men, throughout the middle class every where, has pointed out Napoleon as the incarnate Democrat. He had their virtues and their vices; above all, he had their spirit or aim. That tendency is material, pointing at a sensual success and employing the richest and most various means to that end; conversant with mechanical powers, highly intellectual, widely and accurately learned and skilful, but subordinating all intellectual and spiritual forces into means to a material success.[31]

The distinctive point in the piece more generally, however, is the conflicting sentiments with which Emerson views Napoleon. It is the same ambivalent perception of the leader-dictator figure evident in Banks's portrayal of John Brown and Lincoln's Lyceum speech (for whom Napoleon, we might recall, stands as one such "representative" of the "tribe of the eagle"). This is perhaps because, aside from his image as a dictator, Napoleon can also be seen as a *redemptive* figure, a savior of the French republic, fighting to defend republicanism from the hostile forces of monarchy and aristocracy that, at the turn of the nineteenth century, included Britain, Prussia, and the Austro-Hungarian Empire. Moreover, the image of Napoleon as *liberator*, as the guarantor of national autonomy and democracy, was popular among subjugated populations such as those in Poland previously subject to the rule of the Russian Empire.

Two recent studies of Abraham Lincoln explicitly identify such qualities in Lincoln's own leadership during the Civil War.[32] It is also in this context that the connection between Napoleon and John Brown hinted at throughout *Cloudsplitter* becomes apparent. Brown, of course, as Benjamin Quarles's work has made clear, has consistently been viewed in this less complicated light by African Americans.[33] More specifically perhaps, in terms of character, Emerson's portrait of Napoleon conjures up several more striking similarities.

Bonaparte was the idol of common men because he had in transcendent degree the qualities and powers of common men. There is a certain satisfaction in coming down to the lowest ground in politics, for we get rid of cant and hypocrisy. Bonaparte wrought, in common with that great class he represented, for power and wealth,—but Bonaparte, specially, without any scruple as to the means.[34]

One wouldn't wish, though, to overstate the analogy. After all, in his efforts to align himself with the middle class in his business dealings Brown was undoubtedly a failure; Lincoln, as a successful politician in an era of immense political polarization, was undoubtedly forced to cast a Machiavellian eye on issues from time to time. Yet on the level of personality, the contempt for "cant" and "hypocrisy" as well as the absence of scruple in relation to questions of "means" certainly fit the John Brown profile. Lincoln too, as we have seen, was well versed in exposing the former as features of the arguments of Douglas and other apologists for slavery; likewise, his ruthless prosecution of the civil war was admired—as we shall see in the next chapter—by later revolutionaries such as Leon Trotsky.

Emerson's understanding of Bonaparte's life also mirrors the rationale Owen Brown provides for his father's deeds in *Cloudsplitter*. "Horrible anecdotes," Emerson claims, "may no doubt be collected from his history, of the price at which he bought his successes; but he must not therefore be set down as cruel, but only as one who knew no impediment to his will."[35] The same argument might be made about Lincoln's determination to prosecute the war against the southern states in the face of significant internal opposition, particularly after the substantial initial military defeats endured by the Union army.

The bearing of Emerson's assessment of Napoleon and the broader concerns of this chapter, however, only come fully into view if we examine their relation to the intellectual context of Romanticism from which they emerge. It is Napoleon's appeal to the emotions of men, for instance—to what Emerson describes in terms of "sense," "spirit," and a "universal sympathy" in the following passage—that set him apart as a Romantic figure:

> There is something in the grand talent which enlists a universal sympathy. For in the prevalence of sense and spirit of stupidity and malversation; all reasonable men have an interest; and as intellectual beings we feel the air purified by the electric shock, when material force is overthrown by intellectual energies. As soon as we are removed out of the reach of local and accidental partialities, Man feels that Napoleon fights for him; these are honest victories; this strong steam-engine does our work. Whatever appeals to the imagination, by transcending the ordinary limits of human ability, wonderfully encourages and liberates us.[36]

It is this visionary ability to remain "out of the reach of local and acci-
dental partialities" that also ensures that Emerson, Brown, and Lincoln
occupy important positions in the intellectual history of American liberalism.
The single most important "partialities" that they each ultimately challenged by the 1850s were those wrought by an ideology of what historian
James Oakes, in several important works, has termed "slaveholding liberalism."[37] It is primarily in this capacity that they "transcend[ed] the ordinary
limits" of this earlier form of liberalism and—albeit via the bloody birth of
civil war—effectively brought the United States fully into the modern
world.

From Romanticism to Modernity

The key text in this respect is the Declaration of Independence, the pri-
macy of which emerges clearly in the Lincoln-Douglas debates, Emerson's
doctrine of "self-reliance" and the thought of John Brown as articulated
in the pages of *Cloudsplitter*. As we have seen earlier, Lincoln used the
1858 debates with Douglas to imbue the Declaration with the status of
religious covenant. The biblical injunction to "perfect" oneself as an individual was, in this context, invoked as a model for rejuvenating the Declaration's principle "that all men are created equal." Although, for Lincoln,
slavery as an institution clearly stymied this aim, the struggle to prevent
its extension was a crucial phase in the quest toward the perfection of
that principle. "Let it be," he claimed, given such obstacles, "as nearly
reached as it can."

If Lincoln transplanted this "perfectionist" credo to the political
sphere, then Emerson did so, in a far more sustained and controversial
fashion, to the philosophical sphere. Indeed, more than any other American
thinker, Emerson, in early pieces such as "Self-Reliance" (1841), "The
Transcendentalist" (1842), and his famous "Address Before the Divinity
School" (1838), was responsible for the secularization of such New Testament values in the intellectual history of the United States. The political
implications of Emerson's radical move, however, are more ambiguous.

"To believe your own thought," it is announced at the beginning of
"Self-Reliance," "to believe that what is true for you in your private heart is
true for all men,—that is genius."[38] Here we find an individualism articulated against the grain of Jacksonian, majoritarian democracy. Emerson's

can be seen as a reaction to the stifling social conformity hinted at by his contemporary Tocqueville, in the first volume of *Democracy in America* (1835), as a cultural repercussion of democratic social conditions. "While the majority is in doubt," Tocqueville wrote in this respect of America, "one talks; but when it has irrevocably pronounced, everyone is silent, and friends and enemies alike seem to make for its bandwagon."[39] On the subject of slavery, of course, by the 1850s the majority *had* pronounced to the effect that it *was* tolerable, albeit under prescribed conditions for a proportion of that majority.

The conflict at its sharpest point, then, by this time was between a national, democratic-liberal political culture underwritten by majoritarian precepts and an increasingly strident intellectual culture in the North premised on a "perfectionist" ethos and minority rights. The latter also drew on a residual Puritan emphasis on the importance of acting—in the face of whatever degree of hostility—according to individual "conscience." Perhaps the most famous statement of this position was detailed by Emerson's fellow transcendentalist (and even more vocal advocate of John Brown) Henry David Thoreau. "Any man more right than his neighbor," wrote Thoreau famously in "On the Duty of Civil Disobedience" (1849), "constitutes a majority of one already."[40] *Cloudsplitter* reflects this climate of ideas at a number of points, perhaps most memorably in its depictions of John Brown's evangelical efforts to persuade his followers in Kansas of the righteousness of their cause.

> "The largest majority," he [John Brown] explained, "is often only an organized mob whose noise can no more change the false into the true than it can change black into white or night into day. And a minority, conscious of its rights, if those rights are based on moral principles, will sooner or later become a just majority. What we are building here is nothing less than a free commonwealth promised us by our Declaration of Independence and prophesied and ordained by God in the Bible."
>
> (*Cloudsplitter*, 642)

As well as an expression of the "majority of one," we once again find here an original religious ideal—rooted in the Puritan desire to construct a new commonwealth, a "New England," according to the dictates of conscience—fused with one of the founding documents of secular America.

What brings these elements together most fully is a shared rejection of the materialist thought that was such a feature of American liberalism by mid-century. Such materialism was perhaps most evident in the formalism and constitution-oriented basis of political discourse referred to above, but it was also present in the culture at large, notably so in the sociological arguments put forward by proslavery thinkers such as George Fitzhugh and John C. Calhoun.[41]

The important point in this context is that the materialist basis of this dominant strain of liberalism disavowed the possibility of radical social change premised on "metaphysical" abstractions such as those evident in the Declaration of Independence. If we were to look to political philosophy for an explanation, this, it might well be said, was why the Civil War was fought. It also, interestingly, explains some of the motivation of those later American "pragmatist" thinkers who sought to reconcile the idealist and materialist philosophical traditions in the postwar era. This is a theme I will pursue further in the next chapter.

Russell Banks, however, brilliantly deploys Owen Brown as a means of both illuminating this tension *and* illustrating how various idealist currents—from both secular and religious realms and cutting across class as well as generational lines—came to share a new vision of the American polity. Although, as we have seen, Owen dimly perceives some connection between the ideas of the two men earlier, in his father's ultimately ambiguous response to the Emerson lecture, by the end of the novel he has become fully aware of this process: "Father's God-fearing, typological vision of the events that surrounded us then was not so different from mine. My vision may have been secular and his Biblical, but neither was materialistic. They were both, perhaps, versions of Mr. Emerson's grand, over-arching, transcendental vision, just not so clearly or poetically expressed" (*Cloudsplitter*, 678).

Indeed, *Cloudsplitter* recontextualizes the events it depicts by foregrounding their relationship to both the intellectual culture of Romanticism *and* the more recognizably modern preoccupations that superseded it. This is achieved via the novel's formal narrative structure as well as its thematic concerns. Owen Brown, the *isolato*, tells his tale from out west, a twentieth-century Ishmael imprisoned in his own consciousness, without the solace of community provided by the *Pequod*. In many ways he is also, having "lighted out for the territory" after the Harpers Ferry debacle, living a kind of warped epilogue to *The Adventures of Huckleberry Finn*. This idea is given additional force by the provocative ruminations on the question of race present in the novel and, in particular, an extraordinary episode that concludes with Owen murdering Lyman Epps, a close black companion and underground railroad activist.

Lyman is clearly designated as Jim to Owen's Huck in these sections, their friendship complicated by homoerotic as well as racial tensions—elements that also clearly evoke Leslie Fiedler's famous thesis in *Love and Death in the American Novel* (1960), for which, of course, *Huckleberry Finn* provides a notable primary source. More important perhaps, the complex dynamics of what Owen eventually admits to himself as a "manly love finding itself locked inside a racialist's guilt" (*Cloudsplitter*, 519), as well as its ultimate fate, are designed to foreshadow the trajectory of American race relations from the Reconstruction period to the twentieth century. It is episodes such as this, among others, that ultimately imbue *Cloudsplitter* with such immense contemporary relevance.

A similar level of dramatic force is located in an even greater secret Owen has carried out west with him. Owen's murder of Lyman Epps is in significant part his response to an accusation made by Epps during an argument that "[Owen] ain't half the man [his] father is." Epps's recognition of the degree of disparity between the father's altruism and the son's ambivalence on the question of race forces Owen to acknowledge himself and his fellow countrymen as modern Americans in their "fallen" status. This is the "fall" prompted by the persistence of slavery, a fall that defines American modernity and ultimately ensures that its modern liberal polity is cursed by the issue of race.

One of the achievements of Banks's novel is that it once more foregrounds the *antiracist* basis of John Brown's opposition to slavery. This was first noted by W. E. B. DuBois but later eclipsed by the accounts of more hostile biographers.[42] Given the fact that the overwhelming majority of abolitionists remained deeply skeptical about the possibility of social equality for black Americans, John Brown's position was indeed remarkable. The fact that Banks should foreground this aspect in seizing the fictive mantle of Brown, however, should come as no surprise.[43] Aside from William Faulkner, it is difficult to think of another white twentieth-century American writer who has negotiated the issue of race in as sustained, unflinching, and intelligent a fashion. Both writers focus on the complex place of race within the American political psyche, stressing the idea of "whiteness" as a cultural phantom conjured up to sustain a democracy premised on slaveholding and, subsequently, institutionalized segregation. Subjectivity, as such, is always couched in terms of *intersubjectivity*—Banks, for instance, assigns an extraordinary, Faulknerian degree of significance to the mutually defining nature of his white working- and middle-class characters' relationships with blacks.

Banks's work too flits conspicuously between national and transnational contexts in exploring the idea of "African America"—Jamaica being the backdrop for *The Book of Jamaica* (1980) and *The Rule of the Bone* (1995); Haiti, in part, for *Continental Drift* (1985); and, most recently, Liberia, for *The Darling* (2004). Far from performing an auxiliary thematic role, race is at the center of these novels. For Banks, it is clear, race cannot be represented in all its complexity with only an intermittent twist of the national kaleidoscope; it must, rather, be perceived as the fulcrum upon which the nation depends for any meaningful definition. This implicit recognition of the full transnational, transatlantic range of African American experience serves to foreground contrasting as well as overlapping black histories, societies, and politics. Just as the memory of Haitian slave insurrection might be said to haunt Thomas Sutpen in *Absalom! Absalom!* (1936), so the specter of black agency, past and present, beyond as well as within the borders of the United States, looms large in the fiction of Russell Banks.

Yet while the comparison with William Faulkner is an instructive one in certain important respects, there is one difference, more than any other perhaps, that explains why it would undoubtedly run aground if pursued too ardently. The New England or New York State origins of Banks and most of his white characters are, ideologically speaking, worlds away from Yoknapatawpha County. This is particularly evident in those of his novels such as *Continental Drift, Affliction* (1989), and *The Sweet Hereafter* (1991), which are set in the late twentieth century in the small and midsize postindustrial towns of New England and upstate New York. The secular cultural backdrop of these works is consistently belied by what might best be understood as a kind of residual, cultural Puritanism. Characters frequently exhibit a recognizably early Protestant compulsion to wrestle—often to the point of self-destruction—with matters of conscience. This manifests itself in a number of ways, be it via issues of sexual jealousy, domestic violence, alcoholism, or, moving into more metaphysical territory, those pertaining to bereavement, mortality, or the search for some kind of redemption in an inscrutable, material world. Political action, in these works, is a casualty of the broader forces that help corrode communal values, forcing individuals to retreat into themselves.

In *Cloudsplitter*, however, Banks uses the historical novel to impress upon us the type of radical political vision that once grew out of this cultural preoccupation with "conscience." The most powerful facet of this in the novel is, undoubtedly, the antiracism previously alluded to. John Brown remains compelling to Banks not only for his militant opposition to slavery but also—and this was unusual even among abolitionists—his concerted attempt to break down those racial barriers that continue to engender anxiety and fearfulness in white Americans today. Banks, however, does not ground this sensibility in the pieties of contemporary multiculturalism but in Brown's patriotism, duty, and his sense of anger that America has strayed so far from its professed ideals:

If the country had been made of one race of people, if everyone had been white ... he would not have looked eastward across the Atlantic and loved African Negroes ... or black-skinned people anywhere. No, he loved *American* blacks, and he loved them, I believe, because of their relation to the dominant race of American whites. He saw our nation as divided unfairly between light-colored people and dark. ... Something deep within his soul, regardless of his own skin color, something at the very bottom of his own sense of who he was, of who he was especially in relation to the dominant, lighter race, went out to the souls of American Negroes, so that he was able to ally himself with them in their struggle against slavery and American racialism.

(*Cloudsplitter*, 416)

Yet this struggle to redeem the nation is one that Owen Brown, by the end of his life, comes to see in terms of failure. His own betrayal of his Father thus operates as a metaphor for the failed project of Reconstruction and the segregationist turn in late nineteenth-century race relations. This emblematic quality of Owen's life is made particularly graphic when, alone in his shack, he permits himself the thought that he might once, in another America, have married Lyman's widow, Susan Epps. Raising Lyman's son—the child, of course, of the man he has killed—in the pastoral bliss of an Adirondack wilderness, they could, he fantasizes, have been "one small family free of all the cruel symbolism of race and the ancient curse of slavery, a white man and a Negro woman and child held dear by a family and community that see them and deal with them solely as family and friends and fellow citizens." These we might describe as the "unencumbered selves" of liberal theory and Romantic thought, untainted by social structures and unburdened by history—themes I will return to in subsequent chapters. The image Owen Brown presents here, however, is soon rendered a "fantasy, delusion, dream … a white man's chimera," lasting, he laments, only until "Father comes forward … and places his heavy hands on my shoulders … as if he has settled a yoke upon my shoulders and wishes me to kneel under its weight" (*Cloudsplitter*, 696). By this point, Owen's predicament also brings to mind that of Shakespeare's Hamlet, haunted by the specter of a crime against his father and the corrupted relic of a state that comes in its wake. Indeed, like Shakespeare's creation, Owen's "modernity" manifests itself in "purgatorial" terms characterized by mental instability, suicidal tendencies, and the absence of belief.[44] Indeed, as he himself comes to accept, his final testament to Miss Mayo is motivated by nothing so much as the desire to "become a ghost … so as to replace in purgatory the long-suffering ghosts this confession has been designed expressly to release" (*Cloudsplitter*, 688).

As is the case with Gore Vidal's *Burr*, the issue here is that of the sons' "heresy" with regard to the ideals underlying the founding of the republic. This is what makes the relation between Banks's novel and the politics of patrimony evident in the pronouncements of Emerson, Lincoln, and Douglas such an intimate one. Indeed, Banks tenaciously pursues these themes at crucial moments in the text, situating claims such as those in the following passage from the closing pages of the novel within the religious framework so crucial to any understanding of John Brown and the Civil War. After his father's gang had departed for Harpers Ferry, Owen recollects spreading out some papers, a "mass of incrimination," before the stove, ready to follow an order to destroy them:

It was like listening to a thousand low, choked confessions all at once, as if the voices, mingling and merging with one another, were the sad, accumulated results of a long, unforgiving Inquisition into the heresy and betrayal of their Puritan fathers by an entire generation of sons. I burned none of it. My heretical refusal to play Isaac to my father's Abraham seemed not mine alone: it felt emblematic to me—as if an Age of Heroism had acceded to an Age of Cowardice. As if, in the context of those last days at Harpers

Ferry and the one great moral issue of our time, I had become a man of another time: a man of the future I suppose, a modern man.

(*Cloudsplitter*, 740)

Owen Brown's "modernity," then, is articulated in terms of a republican "fall" from a prior state of grace. *Cloudsplitter* is, in this respect, a republican fable of inexorable "decline and fall." Falling is, in fact, a persistent motif in Owen Brown's memoir. His arm is permanently damaged in a childhood fall; he slumps to the floor of a black church in Boston, overwhelmed by an early spiritual experience; he slips from a tree, an observation point for the Harpers Ferry raid; and finally, he falls in his isolated cabin, alone, in the act of considering this very motif, "a sympathetic act no doubt" (*Cloudsplitter*, 754), just before his confession is complete.

Owen's refusal to die for the cause or carry out the task he has been charged with of destroying a mass of incriminating papers also becomes symbolic in this way. Instead of continuing to confront a corrupt polity in the manner of his father, he heads for the anonymity of the West. It is often overlooked that though the Civil War was fought between the North and the South, it was, also, a conflict very much *about* the West. Were the newly settled territories going to be incorporated as "slave" or "free" states? Tensions as well as ideological fault lines thus shifted and reformed continually with the extension of the frontier. If the Kansas-Nebraska wars that so polarized views can, then, be regarded as a chapter in the story of the frontier as well as that of the war between the states, John Brown can equally be perceived as a character type familiar from the long pageant of fact, fancy, and myth that is the "Wild West."

Nonetheless, while *Cloudsplitter* imbues Brown with the qualities of the alienated outsider redeemed by a moral vision of transracial fellowship and community, his politics of redemption is also presented as one indelibly tainted by violence. Though never quite spilling into the baroque extravaganza characteristic of Cormac McCarthy's countermythologizing Westerns such as *Blood Meridian* (1985), Banks's depiction of the Brown gang's violence is veracious and unremitting enough. More importantly perhaps, the access readers are allowed to Owen's unfolding states of mind ensures that the moral toll extracted by such methods—however virtuous the political goals—can never be simply swept aside.

However, Owen's disillusionment ultimately belongs to something larger than his own betrayal of his father. He, too, has been betrayed. This only becomes fully apparent to him in the West after he "lights out for the territory" in an effort to "become new ... an American without history and with no story to tell," an idea he believed in "then and for many years to come" (*Cloudsplitter*, 757). By the end of the novel, he is disabused of this notion. Contrary to popular mythology, Banks clearly suggests the West is, rather, a land of the fallen. The inference here is that the political culture of mid-nineteenth-century America, in both the North and the South, was too often enraptured by this pastoral vision promising, as it seemed, a retreat from politics and history. America itself, Banks's masterpiece suggests, was a fallen land, stained by the sin of slavery and redeemed only by the singular visions of those like Brown, Emerson, and Lincoln, who saw it as such.

PART II

THE TWENTIETH-CENTURY CONTEXT

3

IDEAS IN MODULATION

Marxism and Liberal Revaluation in Lionel Trilling's
The Middle of the Journey

A feeble logic, whose finger beckons us to the dark spectacle of the
Stalinist Soviet Union, affirms the bankruptcy of Bolshevism, followed by
that of Marxism, followed by that of socialism. ... Have you forgotten the
other bankruptcies? What was Christianity doing in the various catastrophes
of society? What became of Liberalism? What has Conservatism produced,
in either its enlightened or reactionary form? If we are indeed honestly
to weigh out the bankruptcies of ideology, we shall have a long task
ahead of us. ... And nothing is finished yet.

—VICTOR SERGE

He can neither believe nor be comfortable in his disbelief, and he is too
honest and courageous not to try to do one or the other.

—NATHANIEL HAWTHORNE, writing of Herman Melville

Politically New York City ... became the most interesting part of the Soviet
Union. For it became the one part of that country in which the struggle
between Stalin and Trotsky could be openly expressed.

—LIONEL ABEL

Progressives and Reactionaries

There are many historical-contextual factors to be borne in mind
when distinguishing between the respective political agendas
advanced by the Old and New Left. Arguably, the most important
of these is the absence from the latter's historical experience of a politically

and intellectually transformative economic crisis equivalent in magnitude to the crash of October 1929. "The historical context of the Old Left," as John Patrick Diggins has remarked, "was the abundance of poverty; that of the New Left, the poverty of abundance."[1] Indeed, it would be difficult for the intellectual historian to overstate the ultimate effect of the Depression on political thinking and policy making in the United States. As unemployment figures spiraled upward and industrial relations became increasingly fractious during the first half of the 1930s, it became clear that government could no longer look on indifferently as unrestrained capitalism appeared to destabilize American society as never before. Some concessionary form of statism was required as inoculation if Americans were not to develop the full-blown disease of fascism or communism.[2]

The extent to which the Depression had influenced opinion across the political spectrum was clearly evident by the time of the 1944 presidential election. The desire to avoid any similar experience resulted in an unprecedented bipartisan commitment to full employment. Broadly Keynesian policies that promoted stimulation of the economy via deficit spending were, furthermore, advocated as the chief means of attaining this objective. This "New Deal Order" would more or less prevail until the election of Ronald Reagan in 1980 and the subsequent return to laissez-faire economics ideologically framed as a repudiation of the "big government" liberalism of the postwar period. In broader theoretical terms, the consensus prompted by the Keynesian revolution, according to Michael Sandel, also initiated a major shift in U.S. political philosophy, as a "political economy of citizenship gave way to [a] political economy of growth and deliberative justice."[3]

Yet such an understanding of the relation between polity and economy would have been anathema to either main candidate in the first presidential campaign of the Depression. Franklin D. Roosevelt came to power in 1932, much as Bill Clinton did sixty years later, armed with the conventional, time-honored panacea: a promise to balance the federal budget. When John Maynard Keynes visited the White House in 1934, his ideas merely mystified a president committed only to the institutional reform and bureaucratic regulation of economic activity. Such measures were, as most historians have agreed, carefully designed to leave the underlying structure and central premises of American capitalism securely intact. The large-scale federal spending initiatives central to Keynesian economic theory, by contrast, appeared to go against all of its laissez-faire instincts.[4]

So how did American liberalism reconcile the manipulation of aggregate demand with the imperatives of free enterprise, the claims of the collective made urgent by the Depression and a traditional emphasis on individualism? How did it manage to subvert many of its own underlying Lockean principles and still remain a "liberalism," still remain "American," in any meaningful sense? I do not wish to respond to these particular questions directly in this chapter but feel that they are crucial to bear in mind as a broader intellectual context for the remarks that follow. The New Deal undoubtedly helped foster a climate within which the complex attachment of a large section of the 1930s left-liberal intellectual community to Stalin's Soviet Union was made possible. It will be my aim here to use Lionel Trilling's novel *The Middle of the Journey* (1947) to explore this attachment and the complications it engendered for left-liberal political thought. Buried beneath the "common man" rhetoric of this period was what Trilling described in a later introduction to the novel as a "clandestine negation of the political life"[5]—a negation that events in the USSR, by the end of the decade, would make visible to an increasing number of "progressives." *The Middle of the Journey* is well positioned historically to shed light on this development. By composing and publishing his novel in the years immediately following World War II, Trilling was able to articulate a liberal anticommunist position, which was alert to the realities of Stalinism but not yet constrained by the illiberal cultural climate produced by McCarthyism in full swing. In the period after the novel's publication, it became clear that Trilling had based the character of Gifford Maxim on Whittaker Chambers. One unfortunate effect of this association has been to reduce the novel to the status of a cold war curiosity, interesting only for its representation of one of the period's more colorful figures.[6]

The affiliation between certain liberals and the Soviet Union took a number of forms and was accompanied by a complex array of rationalizations. It lasted, however, for the best part of a decade. Indeed, the not insubstantial degree of liberal sympathy for communism in general only began to fully unravel in the wake of the 1936–1937 Moscow Trials and, with less rancor, the 1939 Nazi-Soviet nonaggression pact. This process, after the hiatus provided by wartime alliance, would finally climax, with even greater attendant trauma, amidst the maelstrom of McCarthyist innuendo and recrimination in the 1950s.

The attraction to the Soviet Union can be divided into two phases, the first of which began in the early 1930s largely as a result of domestic economic developments that prompted a major shift in attitudes among left-liberals. The new Roosevelt administration's decision to restore diplomatic relations with the USSR in 1933 can be seen as the culmination of this phase. It was initially triggered, however, by liberal intellectuals associated with such journals as *The Nation* and *The New Republic* who, frustrated by American governmental inertia in the face of economic collapse, had begun following a social experiment many of them had previously written off. In 1930, the first intimations of mass unemployment in the United States stood in stark contrast to reports that stressed the rapid growth of the Soviet economy in the period following the commencement of the first Five-Year Plan. As Frank A. Warren has written: "The Five-Year Plan did not generate excitement until 1930—two years after it had begun. What happened to cause this excitement was 1929 and the depression, the real impetus in turning liberals east towards Russia. ... It was the confrontation of the Five-Year Plan with the depression that served as the catalyst."[7]

What impressed some American observers of the USSR most profoundly was the spirit of experimentalism evident in the construction of a *planned* economy.[8] Planning, of course, had been one of the dominant concepts in the thought of an earlier progressive movement whose ideas still permeated liberal thinking.[9] More abstractly, planning also appealed to a specific strand of American idealism that—alongside a commitment to individual rights and freedom *from* government—stressed equally the duties and responsibilities of those who govern to the governed. It was out of this admiration for planning in the early thirties—which many centrist thinkers could quite readily reconcile with a restructured capitalist economy—that the USSR quickly became a touchstone for self-questioning American liberals. This process, as Richard Pells has noted, was equally facilitated by Russian propaganda itself, which "often emphasized achievements that sounded typically American. Both countries valued the material rewards of mass production, both respected the machine and its power to transform life, both celebrated industrialism and technology, both worshipped bigness as a sign of quality and progress, both preached the virtues of efficiency and physical growth."[10]

Neither did the imperatives of Soviet communism—after Stalin's "pragmatic" turn from internationalism to "socialism in one country"—appear to be especially at odds with those of a pragmatic philosophical tradition which valorized scientific method. Many commentators thus soon became adept at "translat[ing] their praise for the Soviet Union into peculiarly American terms." These were ultimately those that enabled Soviet communism under Stalin to be more easily perceived as "an unfinished test where final judgment could be suspended until all the results were in." Such scientific pragmatism, importantly, "eliminated the need to evaluate or criticize the more unpleasant aspects of the dictatorship."[11] Indeed, by 1935, Walter Duranty, the Moscow correspondent of the *New York Times*, could write on collectivization and socialization in the following terms: "Their cost in blood and tears and other terms of human suffering has been prodigious, but I am not prepared to say it is unjustified. In a world where there is so much waste and muddle it may perhaps be true that any plan, however rigid, is better than no plan at all and that any altruistic end, however remote, may justify any means however cruel."[12]

The warming of such prominent representatives of American liberalism to the Soviet Union generated a number of interesting consequences. Most significant among these, perhaps, was the novel form assumed by a preexisting bifurcation in American political life between "progressives" and "reactionaries." This distinction had its origins in the era of Theodore Roosevelt's presidency, when the term "progressive" had little if any connection with communism or socialism as then understood.[13] However, while the interest of liberal intellectuals in Soviet planning had established some of the theoretical ground for a new "progressive" political alliance, the Communist Party of the United States (CPUSA), following the Comintern line dictated by Moscow, had remained hostile to any organizational links with democratic political groups.

This altered quite dramatically in 1935, when events in Europe caused the USSR to reevaluate its relations with the Western democracies. With the advent of German remilitarization, fascism was now perceived as the chief threat to both Western liberal democracy *and* communism. In response, Moscow retreated from its earlier isolationism, authorizing the establishment of a "Popular Front" in the United States and Europe, to be made up of communist and noncommunist organizations and individuals sharing antifascist goals. The establishment of the Popular Front inaugurated a second phase in the relation between communists and so-called "fellow-traveling" liberals. In the years that followed, this alliance would never be free from division and wrangling given the broad spectrum of disparate, often contradictory opinions it sought to house. In the United States, nonetheless, the widely deployed term "progressive" used to describe those associated with the Popular Front gathered in this opinion to an extent that minimized internecine friction. It did so primarily through its invocation of an ever-improving future that appealed to an Enlightenment-rooted faith in reason and progress prominent in both the liberal and Marxist traditions.

For American liberals culturally programmed to look forward, it had no doubt proved disheartening to be presented with the spectacle of the Soviet Union apparently leading the race to a future they had long taken as their own providential endowment. As a result, by 1935, receptivity and openness to the USSR—as the only means of rejuvenating a seemingly moribund U.S. political tradition—moved from being a touchstone to a cornerstone of "progressive" liberal thought. If the first phase of the liberal attraction to the USSR can be viewed in terms of a drift to the left among centrists, then this second phase should be seen more as the effect of the CPUSA's move to the center under the new Comintern policy. Indeed, so complete was this move that by 1936 CPUSA Presidential candidate Earl Browder could proclaim that "Communism is twentieth-century Americanism." Moreover, his party, by embracing the flag and invoking figures such as Lincoln and Jefferson, was repositioning itself within a far less alien and threatening political tradition. The small groupings of dissident Marxists who only a couple of years earlier had been criticizing the authoritarianism and inflexibility of the CPUSA were astonished by this reversal. "If they saw the party as too uncompromising in 1934," Judy Kutulas remarks in her excellent intellectual history of anti-Stalinism and the Popular Front, "it seemed too accommodationist in 1936."[14]

Within the American Left, however, the progressives linked to the Popular Front wielded significantly more cultural and institutional power than either the CPUSA or the various renegade Marxist groups opposed to it. Indeed, by the mid-1930s, as Kutulas stresses, such progressives *were* the left-liberal establishment. For this reason, dissident Marxists such as Philip Rahv considered them "the real mainstay of Stalinism," giving Stalin's regime an unprecedented degree of legitimacy within the U.S. establishment.[15] Moreover, this cultural power helped dictate the terms of what it meant to be "progressive" as the designation increasingly became premised on how one felt about the foreign and domestic policies of the Soviet Union. The term "reactionary" bestowed upon those who disagreed was, like the term "progressive" itself, drawn from an earlier division in American political life. If this first generation of progressives, however, were focused only on the fate and future of the republic, the one that succeeded was concerned more ominously with the fate and future of mankind. As American progressives increasingly began to look to the international scene, such enlarged ideas of "fate" and "future" became inextricably bound up with the survival of Stalin's Russia.

The Moscow Trials and the Dewey Commission

The "fatalistic" predisposition was at its most conspicuous in the response of CPUSA members and liberal "fellow travelers" to the Moscow Trials, which began in August 1936. In the first of these show trials, several of the October Revolution's most prominent figures were charged with plotting, with Hitler's Gestapo, the assassination of Stalin and other top Soviet leaders. Each defendant signed confessions, with a number of them actually pleading for the death penalty. Furthermore, all the accused named Leon Trotsky, former leader of the Red Army and one of the most senior and respected figures in the Bolshevik Party under Lenin, as the instigator of the plot, competing with one another to denounce him.[16]

The polarizing effect of these events on left-liberal political opinion in the United States was intense. While causing some to renounce or retreat from earlier political positions and allegiances, the trials hardened the conviction of many more who saw the USSR as defending itself from subversion and providing the chief bulwark against the forces of fascist reaction in Europe. The Soviet Union had to be backed at all costs, many claimed, among them a number of liberal sympathizers uneasy with its methods. To withdraw support on the basis of such internal political matters risked jeopardizing the precarious balance of ideological power in Europe and beyond.

Trotsky, an exile since 1929, had been the most vocal Marxist critic of Stalin's regime, protesting the emergence of a new party oligarchy and the abandonment of the Leninist legacy under Stalin's leadership in works such as *The Revolution Betrayed* (1937).[17] Widely recognized as Stalin's most outspoken and intellectually formidable opponent, Trotsky became, in the United States and elsewhere, an inescapable presence for political activists across the left-liberal spectrum during the latter half of the 1930s. Moreover, Trotsky's abiding interest in the relation between politics and aesthetics—which prompted his repudiation of Stalinist philistinism and advocacy of cultural modernism—also made him an equally appealing figure to many artists, writers, and critics, such as those associated with the journal *Partisan Review*.[18] Because of his status as the most ideologically feared critic of Stalin during the crucial period of the Moscow trials, Trotsky thus soon came to dictate the terms of an emergent anti-Stalinist Marxism.

Trotsky, naturally, was scornful of charges brought against him largely on the basis of forced confession. Initially, he demanded that a formal case be made for his extradition—a process that would have forced the Soviet authorities to present firm evidence of his involvement in any conspiracy—but this failed to materialize. The Committee for the Defense of Leon Trotsky was set up by mostly New York–based intellectuals (many of whom were contributors to *Partisan Review*), with the backing of Norman Thomas's Socialist Party. This broader party political support had been acquired via pressure brought to bear by James P. Cannon's Workers' Party, who, under Trotsky's advice, had earlier formulated a policy of "entryism" vis-à-vis the Socialist Party. Designed primarily as a means of securing a forum from which Trotsky could respond to the charges made against him, the committee was also acutely conscious of the opportunity it might provide as an outlet for Trotsky's political views in general.[19]

John Dewey, then perhaps the most highly regarded liberal intellectual in the United States, after discussion with his former pupil and Trotsky Committee member Sydney Hook, agreed to head a commission of inquiry.[20] The Dewey Commission of Inquiry Into the Charges Against Leon Trotsky unfolded in Coyoacan, Mexico, over eight days in April 1937. Despite several attempts to discredit the process in advance,[21] the commission's hearings eventually took place, largely as a result of a powerful intimation among those involved of their historical and intellectual significance. James T. Farrell captured the shared sense of high drama and historical gravitas among the Commission's organizers when he wrote: "It is a spectacle to see, a spectacle rare in history. Imagine Robespierre or Cromwell under such circumstances. Well, this is more, because neither Cromwell nor Robespierre had the intellectual breadth that Trotsky has."[22]

After assessing the evidence offered by the Soviet authorities and witnessing, by all accounts, a remarkable defense testimony from the defendant himself, the Commission announced that Trotsky was innocent of all charges. The importance of this verdict lies in the fact that, initially at least, it was by no means perfectly clear that Trotsky *was* innocent. Fabrication on the scale alleged by Trotsky and his defenders was unimaginable, not only to CPUSA and "fellow-traveling" backers of the Soviet Union, but also, crucially, to liberals with deep reservations about Marxism such as John Dewey. Dewey had always refused to justify or equivocate on the suspension of political freedoms under both Lenin and Stalin while the Soviet system "matured." He had, nonetheless, no reason to believe that this contempt for the political could reach the levels suggested by those on the left who rejected the verdicts of the Moscow Trials. For this reason, Dewey had, in fact, left for Mexico believing Trotsky to be guilty. Like many others, Dewey initially maintained that no court of law anywhere, communist or otherwise, was capable of presiding over deception on such an immense scale. It was only when such certainties began to crumble in the face of accumulating evidence that the implications of liberal commitment to the "progressive" forces embodied in the USSR began to appear more grave.

Liberals with communist sympathies maintained a somewhat pragmatic position of "agnosticism" on the trials, claiming, with some justification, that the truth was difficult to ascertain under such historically unprecedented circumstances. The pragmatism of others, however, took a more troubling form. The CPUSA, following the Comintern line, saw the trials as "necessary," an unavoidable process that would keep the revolution on course by cleansing the party of "reactionary" and "subversive" elements. Many of their fellow-traveling liberals did not dissent significantly from this position. To liberals with a greater degree of moral and political investment in the Soviet Union, Stalin's high-level purge was also "necessary," if "regrettable." It was to be understood as an unfortunate phase within an otherwise progressive series of developments, a phase that could not be explained with reference to the political culture of liberal democracies such as the United States, which emphasized civil liberties and the rights of the individual. The trials' credibility, furthermore, many such progressives argued, should not hinge on normative legal criteria that demanded evidence of Trotsky's "guilt" or "innocence." Such factors had to be subordinated to more urgent political imperatives.

This position implicitly affirmed Stalin as the practical and pragmatic leader intent on making History—much in the way that some early nineteenth-century radicals had viewed Napoleon. Trotsky's criticisms seemed, by contrast, to undermine antifascist solidarity, with Trotsky himself appearing to American progressives as an "ineffectual intellectual trapped by his theoretical dogma."[23] The preservation of the Popular Front against fascism, then, justified the means deployed to silence those who disturbed its harmony. This was ultimately the liberal input into a reading of the trials as the inevitable triumph of the "objective" Law of History over the merely "subjective" fantasies of the theorist. Maurice Merleau-Ponty was later to characterize the trials, in this respect, as "a drama of subjective honesty and objective treason."[24]

The Means and the Ends

The central irony of this apologia for Stalinism is that it did not diverge significantly from Trotskyist orthodoxy, which held with similar obstinacy to the view that the ends justify the means. Trotsky's quarrel with Stalin, however, did not turn on the morality of this strategy per se. It centered, rather, on the fact that Stalinism did *not* bring about the end it purported to. As opposed to the liberation of mankind by means of the advancement of class struggle, Trotsky argued that Stalin espoused Marxist-Leninist philosophy while in actuality reimposing oligarchy through a new form of "state" capitalism. Thus it might be said Trotsky did not recoil so much in moral horror from Stalinist means but in political horror from Stalinist ends. He himself, notoriously, had not hesitated in deploying severe means to subjugate the Kronstadt rebels during the civil war, because he believed that such rebellion would ultimately lead to counterrevolution. Accordingly, many anticommunist liberals as well as Soviet-supporting "progressives" believed that the democratic good faith of liberals such as Dewey—who were prepared to give Trotsky's grievances a hearing—was being abused by a revolutionary whose theoretical writings held such sentiment in open contempt.

For Trotsky, the most important achievement of the hearings in Mexico had been their exposure of the motivation behind Stalin's purges: the consolidation of his own power by means of a ruthless state bureaucratic apparatus. This, in turn, had allowed Trotsky as defendant to present himself as the persecuted hero and legitimate heir of a Marxist-Leninist tradition that stood in opposition to such developments. In short, the commission had been notable primarily, for Trotsky, in allowing the consideration of these competing ideologies. To this extent, Trotsky's view coincided with those of the trial's critics, who equally perceived the hearings in terms of an "ideological struggle"; they differed only in so far as Trotsky believed the hearings to have afforded the crucial historical occasion for a *balanced* consideration of such matters. John Dewey, on the other hand, subscribed to neither of these positions. For him, the commission's work was "one of evidence and objective fact, not of weighing theories against each other."[25] Accordingly, Trotsky's guilt or innocence had to be established without reference to the inexorable law of human history advanced by both the "progressives" and Trotsky himself. It was from within this climate of divergent opinion that Trotsky and Dewey were to debate the relationship between means and ends in the pages of the *New International* in the summer of 1938.

Dewey and Trotsky had parted company with a keen sense of their political differences but also, as I have explained, a new mutual respect for each other's moral integrity.[26] In some ways, the *rapprochement* between Dewey and Trotsky is just as puzzling as that which occurred between the pro-Stalin CPUSA and "fellow-traveling" liberals. Dewey was later to describe the events in Mexico as "the most interesting single intellectual experience of [his] whole life."[27] Trotsky himself claimed that the Dewey Commission hearings had given his "faith in the clear, bright future of mankind ... [an] indestructible temper," praising Dewey as "a man of unshakeable moral authority" and the "personification of genuine American idealism."[28] This convergence is all the more surprising when considered in the light of their philosophical exchange only a year later.

Trotsky's piece "Their Morals and Ours" was prompted by the widespread criticism of Marxist doctrines as "amoral" in their adherence to the "Jesuitical" maxim of "the ends justify the means." The former Bolshevik leader responded by requesting that such critics outline the basis of—rather than merely assert—their own moral positions. Close examination of the bourgeois critic's moral precepts, Trotsky claims, reveals that morality is always socially constructed and hence *never* independent of the social relations Marxism foregrounds. Such supposedly transcendental "supraclass morality," Trotsky writes,

> inevitably leads to the acknowledgement of a special substance, of a "moral sense," "conscience," some kind of absolute, which is nothing more than the cowardly philosophical pseudonym for God. Independent of

"ends"—that is, of society—morality, whether we deduce it from eternal truths or from the "nature of man," proves in the end to be a form of "natural theology."[29]

The rejection of the "ends justify the means" maxim also, Trotsky points out, fails to acknowledge its manifestations in Anglo-Saxon utilitarian philosophy. In a similar vein, the "pollution" of Stalinism is counterposed to the abstraction "democracy"—an ahistorical maneuver that fails to recognize that anti-Stalinists such as Trotsky "in order to characterise Soviet bureaucracy ... have borrowed the terms of 'Thermidor' and 'Bonapartism' from the history of bourgeois democracy." This, he adds emphatically, is because *"democracy came into the world not at all through the democratic road."*[30] Aware that he is writing for an urban, predominantly Northern U.S. readership, Trotsky then skillfully reiterates this position in a more pointed context:

> Lincoln's significance lies in his not hesitating before the most severe means, once they were found to be necessary, in achieving a great historic aim posed by the development of a young nation. The question lies not even in which of the warring camps caused or itself suffered the greatest number of victims. History has different yardsticks for the cruelty of the Northerners and the cruelty of the Southerners.[31]

John Dewey's response to Trotsky's typically bold, if carefully pitched, argument was equally deft and can be seen as something of a blueprint for the combination of "pragmatism" and social-democratic values that have furnished much of the American philosophical response to Marxism in the postwar era. Dewey notes that the "transcendental" morality criticized by Trotsky in "Their Morals and Ours" is actually reinscribed via Trotsky's dependence on the class struggle as "the law of all laws." Far from means and ends being involved in a relationship of interdependence, therefore grounding Trotskyite praxis, means (in the form of "class struggle") are invoked without reference to alternatives or any view to their consequences. Hence, they soon assume at best a semidetached relationship to the ends ("the liberation of mankind"), that is, if they do not overwhelm those ends completely. Dewey is here attempting to highlight the flawed "science" that underwrites this central axiom of orthodox Marxism: "Since the class struggle is regarded as the *only* means that will reach the end, and since the view that it is the only means is reached deductively and not by an inductive examination of the means-consequences in their interdependence, the means, the class struggle, does not need to be critically examined with regard to its actual objective consequences."[32]

Bearing in mind this failure of critical examination, Dewey adds later, "it is conceivable that the course actually taken by the revolution in the USSR becomes more explicable when it is noted that means were deduced from a supposed scientific law instead of being searched for and adopted on the ground of their relation to the moral end of the liberation of mankind."[33] Dewey's position, however, does not presuppose the rejection of a scientific approach to social theory in itself. It is rooted, rather, in a scientific methodology that refuses to derive ends from *laws*, natural or social, be they those promoted by Trotsky or the political forces of all types who oppose him.

I have focused on this broad intellectual context and, more narrowly, Dewey and Trotsky as important intellectual figures within it in order to facilitate my critical reading of Lionel Trilling's novel *The Middle of the Journey*. Trilling's work is an attempt to reconstruct in fiction the political and intellectual choices forced upon middle-class liberals and radicals in the aftermath of the Moscow Trials. Perhaps because of its concern with moral, political, and intellectual life, *The Middle of the Journey* has been either ignored or given cursory treatment in most surveys of postwar American literature. It can be viewed, however, as a self-conscious attempt to depart from the fantasies of a prepolitical state of nature that characterize the "classic" American novel or romance, an interesting effort to integrate politics and fiction in a manner more readily associated with the European novel. In spite of the *deus ex machina* of Susan Caldwell's death, which ultimately provides the novel with thematic and artistic resolution, *The Middle of the Journey* remains noteworthy for both the ambition and incisiveness with which it maps the political psyche of a generation. This thematic is more familiar in another strand of the European tradition represented by works such as Conrad's *Under Western Eyes* (1911) and Dostoevsky's *The Possessed* (1871)—a novel, incidentally, that Trilling's central character begins but fails to finish reading. More specifically, *The Middle of the Journey* delineates the origins of a retreat from Marxism among liberal intellectuals, a retreat that continues to inform American political thought today.

The Middle of the Journey:
The Politics of Death and the Death of Politics

Trilling's novel tells the story of John Laskell, who, recovering from an illness that brings him close to death, visits Nancy and Arthur Croom, two married friends who have recently moved to a Connecticut farmhouse. The author of a book entitled *Theories of Housing*, Laskell, we learn, is the kind of New Deal liberal who "had committed himself to the most hopeful and progressive aspects of modern life, planning their image in public housing developments, defending them in long dull meetings of liberals and radicals" (*TMOTJ*, 30). Laskell finds that his own liberal views, which appear to have undergone a crisis of reorientation in the time since his illness, are now increasingly at odds with the "progressive" politics espoused by the Crooms. The resulting confrontation forces Laskell to accept the need for some degree of political and philosophical revaluation. The process is both accelerated and complicated by the appearance of a mutual friend, the former communist Gifford Maxim, who believes himself to be in physical danger after breaking with the party.

At the heart of the matter, Laskell believes, is the very fact of his illness itself, mention of which the Crooms appear to scrupulously avoid. This engenders frustration on the part of their visitor, who comes to regard their reluctance to raise the issue as the sign of an overinvestment in the "progressive" political vision. This commitment

> was expressed in their youth, their vigor, their unquestioning attachment to each other, the child they had and the child to come; but it did not stop there as Laskell knew—it went beyond, expressing itself in their passionate expectation of the future, an expectation that was at once glad and stern, in their troubled but clear sense of other people all over the world, suffering or soon to suffer. Life could not reach further, could not pitch itself higher, than it had in these young Americans.
>
> (*TMOTJ*, 17)

To discuss the past in any depth or to acknowledge the reality of death in the Crooms' presence, Laskell discovers, is to risk undermining their faith in this "affirmative life." It is, in some profound sense, he comes to believe, also to question the politics that anchors that faith. Such intimations finally find open expression when an exasperated Laskell turns to Nancy and says, "You talk about morbidity and living in the past—as if you thought that death was politically reactionary" (*TMOTJ*, 116).

At this point, Laskell has not disclosed the news of Gifford Maxim's break with the party. Later, however, he realizes that his decision to withhold this information is bound up with his feelings about his illness. After acknowledging an element of revenge for the Crooms' reluctance to discuss these feelings with him, we learn that "more decisive than this was his determination that the only way he could tell the story of Maxim was to make it part of the story of his illness. Without the account of what he had felt during those weeks in bed, the story of Maxim would lack the particular force it had in his mind" (*TMOTJ*, 80).

Laskell's brush with death and his subsequent existential crisis force him to take stock of his relation to past, present, and future. He is struck by an overriding sense of the radical *contingency* of existence and the extent to which a life lived in and for the future, a life lived on the basis of promises, is akin to the airless life of the "well-loved middle class child." This is the life symbolized by the Crooms and their childlike faith in the future, a life cushioned by the "progressive" promise of growth and change. After his illness, however, Laskell no longer feels able to make this "distinction between what he now had and was and what he expected to have and be." The passage from childhood to maturity should be conditioned, rather, by a recognition that "the future and the present [are] brought together, that you lived your life *now* instead of preparing and committing yourself to some brighter day to come" (*TMOTJ*, 144).

Maxim's break is linked to such musings in the sense that it forces Laskell to face some of the grave consequences that can flow from a ruthless commitment to the future. The concrete historical backdrop articulated alongside this break, accordingly, gives Laskell's new sense of life's contingency an important set of political implications. The means/end question raised via the discussion of Gifford Maxim's actions while a communist can thus be informed by a broader set of considerations than is common. If nothing else, *The Middle of the Journey* can be read as a rare and striking example of a novel that establishes death as a force with a complex but formidable bearing on the political sphere.

This complexity manifests itself on a number of levels, most obviously in the aftermath of Laskell's own illness, when his exposure to the tragic, conditioned nature of human existence forces him to reappraise his friends' vision of the political future. However, although the narrative is constructed around several dramatic events that touch upon the novel's concern with death and tragedy (Laskell's illness, Maxim's abandonment of the party), one event in particular is made to bear most of the weight of these themes. This is the death of a young girl, Susan Caldwell, whom Laskell befriends and whose mother, Emily, he has become emotionally entangled with after an initial sexual encounter. Susan dies after being struck by her father, Duck, who is ashamed at her inability to perform during a school concert. She is unable to read William Blake's famous "Jerusalem" lyric with any assurance, as a result of Laskell's overelaborate guidance—a product of the rarefied literary sensibilities generated by a middle-class liberal education. The matter is complicated, however, and the tragic dimensions further accentuated by the fact that Susan was born with a weak heart—a fact concealed from her father but revealed to Laskell by Emily Caldwell.

As already noted, this particular episode seems a somewhat melodramatic means of ensuring that the novel's plot services its themes—no doubt a less incongruous method might have been contrived. However, it is not in the action but in the dialogue, the exchange of political-philosophical opinion—in the sense in which it both explains and is explained by this tragedy—that *The Middle of the Journey* comes into its own. A striking feature in this respect is the work's implicit and explicit intertextuality. Trilling's novel, as one might perhaps expect from such a celebrated literary critic, is littered with allusions to a plethora of philosophical and literary sources, from the title itself (a reference to the opening lines of Dante's *Inferno*) to Spinoza, the *Iliad*, and a whole host of other texts.

My aim here will be to focus on two specific instances of the novel's intertextuality in order to illustrate the ways in which *The Middle of the Journey* engages with the type of questions broached by Trotsky, Dewey, and, more generally, U.S. left-liberal opinion after the Moscow Trials. It might be argued that by focusing on what are, strictly speaking, "secondary" texts I will be subtracting from the primary material, Trilling's novel itself. However, it is my belief that *The Middle of the Journey* invites no such approach, given the notable extent to which its central characters, as *intellectuals*, are understood to be the products of their reading as much as their "environment" or "experience" in the more mundane sense. Indeed, Trilling's literary criticism itself disavows the types of division between literature and "experience" that more orthodox approaches often presuppose—a materialist dimension to his work frequently overlooked. Trilling regards readers' engagement with literature, primarily, as *experience* in its own right. When composing prefaces to classic works, for example, he writes, his design is "to make it more likely that the act of reading will be an experience, having in mind what the word implies of an activity of consciousness and response. They try to suggest that the work of literature is an object that might be freely touched and handled, picked up, turned over, looked over from this angle and that, and, at least in some sense, possessed."[34]

Most of the characters in *The Middle of the Journey* then—even the undereducated Emily Caldwell, whose (mis)reading of Spengler's *Decline of the West*, for instance, helps define *her* to Laskell and the Crooms—can be said to "possess" texts in this respect. Perhaps more provocatively, it might be said that Maxim is, in his commitments to first Marx and then Christianity, possessed *by* (Marxist and Scriptural) texts. With such factors in mind then, I will commence by demonstrating how Trilling brings "The Grand Inquisitor"—Dostoevsky's dark and brilliant meditation on good and evil—to bear on the pressing political and moral issues raised during the "Red Decade."

Stalinism and "The Grand Inquisitor"

After Gifford Maxim explains his fear that breaking with the party may have placed his life in danger, Laskell, to give Maxim a "public" existence, secures his friend an editorial post at *The New Era*, a liberal journal of politics and culture owned by another of his friends, Kermit Simpson. By the time Maxim and Simpson pay a visit to Connecticut a few weeks later, Laskell has told Arthur and Nancy Croom of Maxim's break. Laskell is surprised, however, to learn that Nancy had once agreed to receive secretly marked letters for Maxim related to clandestine party activity. This was agreed without her husband's knowledge and after Arthur had turned down an earlier request from Maxim for him to do the same. Arthur Croom, unaware of his wife's actions, responds to Maxim's break by attributing it to a moral failing on Maxim's part, as though, Laskell thinks, the party were somehow "a fixed point from which all deviation implied something wrong with the person deviating" (*TMOTJ*, 156). It is only when a deeply agitated Nancy, realizing the possible danger she has placed herself and her family in, attributes Maxim's decision to "insanity" that Laskell gets his first intimation of her involvement—a fact she confirms when later confronted on her own. Laskell's general ambivalence toward the rigid frameworks of guilt and innocence within which his friends seek either justification or absolution for their actions is captured when he reflects during this episode that "he did not know whether he was frightened for Nancy or by her" (*TMOTJ*, 155).

The compulsion within many strands of modern political thinking to apportion guilt and innocence indiscriminately is forcefully taken up via the character of Gifford Maxim. Maxim functions as what might best be described as a "grand inquisitor" of the secular messianic political values of the 1930s progressive. In a preface to "The Grand Inquisitor" (a chapter from Dostoevsky's *The Brothers Karamazov* [1880] published, in this instance, as a self-contained parable), Trilling claims that "it can be said almost categorically that no other work of literature has made so strong an impression on the modern consciousness or has seemed so relevant to virtually any speculation about the destiny of man."[35]

"The Grand Inquisitor" retells the story of Jesus Christ's temptation in the wilderness, the original Gospel account of which was given in the New Testament (Luke 4:1–13). For forty days, Satan offers Jesus all the earthly kingdoms in return for his worship. Jesus, of course, resists, choosing freedom over the temptations of temporal power and, famously, Satan, in the face of such divinity, departs "for a season." Dostoevsky's tale, however, relocates events to the court of Seville during the Counter-Reformation. In his "infinite mercy," Jesus, once more, walks among the poor, dispensing miracles. This occurs, we are told, at the height of the Inquisition, the day after "the burning of nearly a hundred heretics ... *ad majorem Gloriam dei* in 'a magnificent auto-da-fé.'"[36] The Cardinal of Seville, the Grand Inquisitor of the title, assumes the role of Satan when Jesus is arrested as a false prophet by the authorities. In Dostoevsky's retelling, however, the Inquisitor asks Jesus not to exchange freedom for "bread" and his own personal gain, as Satan did originally, but to exchange freedom so that bread might be available for the whole of *mankind.* "But you did not want to deprive man of freedom," claims the Grand Inquisitor,

> for, you thought, what sort of freedom is it if freedom is bought with loaves of bread? You replied that man does not live by bread alone, but do you know that for the sake of that earthly bread the spirit of the earth will rise up against you and will join battle with you and conquer you. ... Do you

know that ages will pass and mankind will proclaim in its wisdom and science that there is no crime, and therefore, no sin, only hungry people?[37]

As Trilling writes in his preface, the "surrender of freedom" requested of Jesus here is precisely that which the modern totalitarian state has demanded of its citizens. Moreover, in the mass societies of the West, increasing conformity and social passivity testify to the emergence of an at least broadly similar impulse in the development of modern liberal-democratic political cultures. The increased stress on the claims of Necessity over those of Freedom—a stress that has defined the political terrain of modernity—makes us alert to the higher stakes of the choice faced by Jesus in Dostoevsky's prescient tale. To embrace the claims of Freedom over those of Necessity in such circumstances is to burden individuals with what Emmanuel Levinas has described as a "difficult freedom."[38] But, as Trilling points out, the idea of Adam's *felix culpa*, his "*happy* sin [my emphasis]" in eating from the Tree of Knowledge and "the *fortunate* fall [my emphasis]" that followed, stems from the fact that it "made the occasion for Jesus to bring about the redemption and salvation of man, bringing him to yet a nobler condition than before his loss of innocence." In this respect, Trilling continues, "it is not necessary to accept the religious implications of this idea to respond to what it says about the nature of man—that man is not all he might be unless he bears the burden of his knowledge of good and evil, and the pain of choosing between them, and the consequences of making the wrong choice."[39]

Given the importance Trilling attaches to "The Grand Inquisitor" for the light it casts on the politics of modernity, it is unsurprising that the tale's presence should be felt in a novel of his that sought to explicitly engage with this theme. When Gifford Maxim announces to his friends that, in the twentieth century, "we are all of us, all of us, the little children of the Grand Inquisitor," he is surely referring to the *secularization of heresy* that has played such a significant role in the revolutions of the modern age.[40] This development, however, has meant that any "auto-da-fé" is now administered in the name of Man rather than God. At the heart of Trilling's novel is the desire to address the question of how projects designed to eradicate human suffering, to eliminate the specter of *les misérables*, have invariably degenerated into dictatorship and terror. "Why is it," Maxim asks, "that as we become more sensitive to the sufferings of mankind we become more cruel? ... the more we plan to prevent suffering the more we are drawn to inflict suffering. The more tortures we think up. The more people we believe deserve to be tortured. The more we think people can be ruled by fear of suffering" (*TMOTJ*, 223–224).

Maxim marshals all his own inquisitorial skills, acquired from his immersion in radical politics, to attack what he regards as the moral evasions that mask such realities. This leads him to mercilessly compound Laskell's agony over his role in Susan Caldwell's death. The terrible unintended consequences of Laskell's own "good intentions," in this case, cause him to examine the ways in which questions of individual and collective responsibility manifest themselves more generally. For Maxim, an ex-Marxist now turning to Christianity, the imperative is to acquire "company in guilt" for his past. Maxim's Calvinist doctrine of universal guilt provides the moral framework for his reactionary turn, driving his efforts to make Laskell feel responsible for Susan's death. Yet if this collective burden defines the human condition, then what, Laskell is understandably led to ask, becomes of *individual* responsibility? It is obvious, in this way, that Maxim is motivated as much by a desire to diminish the blame he must bear for his own actions while in the party. This amounts, however, only to an inversion of an earlier worldview.

To Laskell, Maxim, as a party member, could once be characterized by his efforts to involve those around him in his virtue. Now, seeking salvation elsewhere, he is trying to implicate everyone in his guilt. Maxim's interrogation of Laskell, then, indicates to his friend that even after this ostensibly drastic conversion he "was still quite the inquisitor, just as good as he had ever been" (*TMOTJ*, 271). Indeed, the zeal of Gifford Maxim's *anti*-Marxism—to the degree that it is nourished by religious preoccupations—cannot but help recall Trotsky's characterization of all "bourgeois morality" as, at root, "theological." For the reborn Maxim, heaven is, quite literally, as Trotsky sardonically claimed, "the only fortified position for operations against dialectical materialism."[41]

Yet Maxim and the Crooms also might be said to share precisely that predisposition that John Dewey identifies with Trotsky and Marxism more generally at the close of his "Means and Ends" article. "Orthodox Marxism," Dewey concludes in that piece, "shares with orthodox religionism and with traditional idealism the belief that human ends are woven into the very texture and structure of human existence."[42] Trotsky, we might recall, was criticized by Dewey for subordinating moral questions to an absolute ("the class struggle") without reference to consequences. Maxim and the Crooms have their own absolutes—the "corruptibility" and "perfectibility" of man—their own certainties as to the ends "woven into the very texture and structure of human existence." Both are drawn to their respective systems by a clear vision of humanity divided in terms of good and evil, guilt and innocence. "Analogously speaking,"one critic of the novel has commented along these lines, "the Crooms posit grace without nature, while Maxim asserts nature without grace."43

For Laskell, however, both of these positions spell disaster. "An absolute freedom from responsibility," he responds to his friends, "—that much of a child none of us can be. An absolute responsibility—that much of a divine or metaphysical essence none of us is" (*TMOTJ*, 307). Laskell is tortured then by a sense of the carnage such "absolutism" wreaks in the political sphere. It is a major paradox to him that questions of responsibility have assumed such immense proportion in an age whose theoreticians have continued to assert, with greater and greater force, the effect of environment and socialization upon human behavior. Indeed, Trilling points to a revealing instance of this clash between the will to moralize and the will to undermine prevailing moral assumptions when he has Laskell recall:

> It was an apparent contradiction in Marx's *Capital*, that would some day be worth putting his mind to, that in the great chapters on the working day the industrial middle class was denounced on moral grounds, although in a preface the writer had explicitly exempted individual industrialists from moral censure, saying with an almost gracious reassurance that it was not they but the historical process that must be blamed.
>
> (*TMOTJ*, 150)

The stunned incomprehension with which Laskell meets Susan Caldwell's death, in this respect, has a much broader application. "When something involved so many things so tenuously," he despairs in the period following this tragedy, "then it was ridiculous to think about it as responsibility" (*TMOTJ*, 273). How, then, given such circumstances, Trilling is also implying here, should we think through the meaning of political action where complex social organisms, on a much greater scale, ensure that consequences assume an even more opaque and overdetermined form? Within the terms I have begun to outline here, how can judgment be passed in such a way that the Grand Inquisitor's demand for stability and order might be reconciled with the freedom (Dostoevsky at least believed was) embodied in the person of Jesus Christ?

Herman Melville, marked as his Christianity was by a concern with human "corruption," did not share his Russian contemporary's preoccupation with the corruption of Rome.[44] Perhaps because of this, when he began to write *Billy Budd* in the years immediately preceding his death in 1891, Melville saw the increased scope for speculation an explicitly secular context might provide for such themes. Gifford Maxim's first publication in Kermit Simpson's magazine is a review of *Billy Budd*. The responses this review provokes establish the theoretical ground for the exchanges that follow, when Maxim himself reappears later in the novel. By having Maxim—*The Middle of the Journey*'s own "grand inquisitor"—interpret this brilliant meditation on the competing claims of Law and Spirit, Trilling is able to bring Melville's formidable political acumen to bear on his own characters' very specific historical predicament. Interestingly, the political philosopher Hannah Arendt, who was working on her monumental *Origins of Totalitarianism* (1951) at around the time Trilling's novel appeared, herself chose precisely these two texts to support some central arguments in a later work, *On Revolution* (1963). It seems more than appropriate, then, to compare the use made of these two works in Trilling's novel to the meanings attributed to them by this important and influential political philosopher.

Judging *Billy Budd*

In *On Revolution* (1963), Hannah Arendt invokes both "The Grand Inquisitor" and *Billy Budd* to explore the thought underwriting the revolutions of the modern age. Melville and Dostoevsky are important, Arendt believes, in so far as they recognize "the tragic and self-defeating enterprise the men of the French Revolution embarked on almost without knowing it."[45] For Arendt, the French Revolution signaled a catastrophic turning point in Western political thought and history. With the appearance of poverty on the political scene in the aftermath of 1789, "necessity" displaced "freedom" as the chief category of political and revolutionary thought.[46] Thus "compassion" for the poor and a belief in their innate "goodness" became the hallmark of revolutionary zeal, a process that reached its zenith when the Jacobins came to power, as Arendt explains, "not because they were more radical but because they did not share the Girondins' concern with forms of government, because they believed in the people rather than in the republic and 'pinned their faith on the natural goodness of a class' rather than on institutions and constitutions."[47]

It is this belief in the "natural goodness" of man that prompted the shift from the republic to the people as the locus of sovereignty. Arendt is drawn to "The Grand Inquisitor" and *Billy Budd* for the way both stories tease out the implications of Rousseau's and Robespierre's innate belief in the "goodness" of man. They do so by reconsidering the person of Jesus of Nazareth, whom Arendt describes as, prior to the French Revolution, "the only completely valid, completely convincing experience Western mankind ha[s] ever had with active love of goodness as the inspiring principle of all actions."[48] In her reading of "The Grand Inquisitor," Arendt correctly identifies Dostoevsky's desire to portray Jesus as "hav[ing] compassion with all men in their singularity, that is, without lumping them together into some such entity as one suffering mankind." The "pity" of the Grand Inquisitor, by contrast, she adds, "like Robespierre ... de-personalized the sufferers, lumped them together into an aggregate—the people *toujours malheureux*."[49]

Yet Arendt's reading also oversimplifies matters a little here. Recognition of Dostoevsky as a great *artist* might be said to turn as much on his capacity *not* to wholly alienate the reader from a character in this way. The argument put forward by the Grand Inquisitor, it surely must be accepted, is *also* compelling, much more so, in fact, than Arendt suggests in her few brief observations. "The greatness of the story," she concludes, "lies in that we are made to feel how false the [Grand Inquisitor's] idealistic, high-flown phrases of the most exquisite pity sound the moment they are confronted with compassion."[50] But are we? The strength of the tale might equally be said to rest, on the contrary, in the *persuasiveness* of these "idealistic, high-flown phrases," which the reader cannot help but respond to despite the countervailing presence of no less a figure than Jesus Christ. To write so trenchantly against the grain of Christian morality, to play so well the part, quite literally, of "Devil's advocate," might be said to be Dostoevsky's real artistic achievement. As Trilling comments in his preface to the story, "the choice, as we confront it ... is by no means simple, for the Inquisitor argues his case with the force of rationality and humaneness very much on his side."[51] Trilling attempted to harness some of this very force when he created Gifford Maxim in the Grand Inquisitor's image.

There is more ambiguity here, then, than Arendt's definitional objective in this section (to distinguish "compassion" from "pity") can accommodate. Useful as it may be, this distinction is not as unambiguously supported by Dostoevsky's story as Arendt seems to imply. Both Trilling's preface and the expression given to similar themes in his novel, for instance, suggest an alternative understanding of "The Grand Inquisitor." Trilling's is a more complex "totalitarian" reading built simultaneously around notions of both the Grand Inquisitor's "idealism" *and* his "practicality." For Trilling, Dostoevsky's character anticipates the emergence of the totalitarian dictator whose destruction of the political sphere can be justified as much as a "practical" or "pragmatic" measure as it can in the "idealistic" terms Arendt criticizes. Nonetheless, irrespective of the sense in which they are understood, the actions of the totalitarian dictator, like those of the Grand Inquisitor, are also invariably explained in terms of the "rationality" and "humaneness" Trilling points to in his reading of the tale.

The Crooms and Maxim, in a similar way, can be viewed as embodying this coexistence of the "idealistic" with the "practical." As discussed earlier in relation to Trotsky, it is not just "revolutionary" or "radical" politics (represented in *The Middle of the Journey* by the Crooms and communist Maxim) but also politics labeled "counterrevolutionary" or "reactionary" (represented by the Christian Maxim) that have been associated at various points with "idealism" and "high-flown phrases." Likewise, defenses of "the ends justify the means" doctrines can be seen in exactly the same way: "practical" in so far as they involve being "realistic" (aware of the need for sacrifice) yet also "idealistic" (in their promise of a world worth making sacrifices for). Hannah Arendt allows for no such ambivalence in her reading of the character of the Grand Inquisitor. In *On Revolution*, the complexity of this figure is elided in order to substantiate Arendt's views on the meaninglessness of "pity" in the political sphere and the excesses of revolutionary ardor. The three or four sentences in which she attempts to summarize the meaning of the story are not enough, finally, to seriously rival Trilling's deeper understanding of the light cast on the politics of revolution by Dostoevsky's creation.

Arendt does, however, give more attention to Melville's *Billy Budd*, bringing some of her highly original political thinking to bear on a notoriously ambiguous text. This tale of a "foundling," a young sailor of no known origin, places a character seemingly representative of Adamic "goodness" in a "Man-of-War" vessel that, as in much of Melville's fiction, stands as a microcosm for society.[52] The "society" of the *Indomitable*, however, unlike that of Budd's earlier ship, *The Rights of Man*, is marked by plurality, by the presence of men rather than "Man" (Arendt's "lumped together aggregate"). Such plurality also, however, allows for the presence of "radical" or "natural" evil. On the *Indomitable*, this takes the form of John Claggart, the master-at-arms whose "evil," in this way, we are informed, is "a depravity according to nature." Claggart's former life, of which, like Budd's, "nothing was known," is an indication of the author's desire to reveal the "natural" dispositions they represent as similarly—in so far as they are not those of men—destructive of the "lasting institutions" of the political sphere.[53] Billy Budd, by virtue of being "one to whom not yet has been proffered the questionable apple of knowledge," is unable to recognize Claggart's malevolence in his efforts to link him with mutiny.[54] The shock of this discovery, when the accusation is finally made to his face, renders Budd—already afflicted by an impediment in moments of anxiety or distress—speechless. This speechlessness, itself an expression of prelapsarian innocence, causes Budd to strike Claggart in frustration.

After Claggart's death from this blow, the full moral orientation of the story comes into view. Captain Vere, the source of final authority on board the *Indomitable*, must pass judgment on Billy Budd. After convening a meeting with several of the frigate's petty officers, Vere ultimately overrules the attempts made to save Budd from the punishment prescribed for such an offense under martial law. The drama of *Billy Budd*, the tension it exposes between Freedom and Necessity, Spirit and Law, is rooted in Vere's exclamation—made, incidentally, not following deliberation but in the instant immediately after Budd's deed: "Struck dead by an angel of God! Yet the angel must hang!"[55] Vere, then, instinctively recognizes the claims of Necessity over Freedom, Law over Spirit, authorizing Budd's execution in the name of Law.

Melville's tale is set at the end of the eighteenth century, in the early years of the Napoleonic wars, when Britain's naval power had been seriously undermined by mutinies. With this development foremost in mind, Vere, in articulating the reasoning behind his decision, appeals ultimately to "the practical consequences to discipline, considering the unconfirmed tone of the fleet at the time, should a man-of-war's man's violent killing at sea of a superior in grade be allowed to pass for aught else than a capital crime demanding prompt infliction of the penalty."⁵⁶ If Budd and Claggart are meant, initially, to appear as emblematic characters, Vere functions, by contrast, as the focal point for the tale's complex relation to questions of judgment. In actual fact, however, this complexity is centered on the *inversion* of good and evil, guilt and innocence that the text constructs: Budd, the personification of goodness, is guilty of murder; Claggart, the personification of evil, dies a victim.

Since its discovery in the 1920s, *Billy Budd* has divided critical opinion fairly evenly into two camps. To some, Budd's hanging, and, in particular, his cry, immediately prior to his death, of "God bless Captain Vere!" to the onlooking crew of the *Indomitable*, marks the text as Melville's final "testimony of acceptance," the author's conclusive acknowledgement of the claims of Law over Spirit. To others, however, the manner of Budd's execution can only be understood as an expression of a dark and lacerating irony. Such a grotesque spectacle, they propose, could only be conjured up by a mind deeply troubled by such claims.⁵⁷ In *On Revolution*, Hannah Arendt's reading of the story clearly adheres to the former interpretation. Arendt seizes, in particular, upon Vere's contempt for political ideals "incapable of embodiment in lasting institutions" to bolster the series of careful discriminations between the American and French revolutions that organize her thesis. Unfortunately, in doing so, she conflates the position of Vere with that of Melville himself. Although Melville would undoubtedly affirm Vere's Burkean recognition of Law as passed down via "lasting institutions," it is far from clear that he would regard Budd's execution as a straightforward means to this end. Unlike Machiavelli and Arendt, Melville was much troubled by the idea of banishing "goodness" from the political sphere.

The secular, Machiavellian understanding of "virtue," which, in a number of persuasive observations, Arendt associates with Vere, is not nonetheless, as her reading suggests, the only one to be derived from the text. The idea of "virtue" in *Billy Budd* is equally informed by the author's own powerful albeit complicated relationship to Calvinism. As John Patrick Diggins has argued, the work of Herman Melville, in this sense, like the political vision of Abraham Lincoln, can be seen as evidence of a "return of the sacred to political thought." Those values endorsed by Jesus Christ, as the ultimate embodiment of goodness, are thus not treated with Machiavellian suspicion but embraced as an example of, to invoke Melville's own description of Budd, "certain *virtues* pristine and unadulterate,"⁵⁸ which can ultimately *inform* political action. When Melville, in a lyrical passage, has Budd "ascend" against clouds of "vapory fleece hanging low in the East ... with a soft glory as of the fleece of the Lamb of God seen in a mystical vision,"[59] it is clear, Diggins writes, that he

> is asking us, the readers, to ponder the Christlike nature of innocence and love as exhibiting benevolence and forgiveness. In political terms these qualities may be fatal; yet without "the pristine virtues," without the values that are sanctioned by the religious imagination, politics alone can never be virtuous. The good man may go to his death along with those who are not good, as Machiavelli warned, but from the death of goodness radiates the resurrection of life.[60]

Although Arendt reads *Billy Budd* as embracing the fundamentally *secular* vision of the political advanced by Machiavelli, which involves learning "how not to be good," Diggins establishes the text, just as convincingly, as an attempt to *desecularize* the classical notion of virtue in a "synthesis of religious sentiment and political obligation."[61]

Perhaps most notable in Arendt's reading of *Billy Budd* is her sudden receptiveness to the idea of "necessity," which, at least in the context of her broader argument, is held responsible for the impasse in political thinking she associates with modernity. Despite lamenting the "absolutes" that surrender Freedom to Necessity in the work of Marx and others, Arendt nonetheless affirms the validity of Vere's decision, which, as Diggins notes, is itself "unqualified, irrevocable, absolute."[62] There is, then, something of a slippage in meaning between the context in which "necessity" is invoked here and its deployment elsewhere in *On Revolution*. Arendt appears to discriminate between what might be described as political necessity, the "lasting institutions" that function as Vere's "absolute,"[63] and biological necessity, a preoccupation with which under Marxist and Jacobin regimes has wreaked havoc as an "absolute" in the political sphere.

In *On Revolution*, Arendt offers a brilliant critique of biological necessity as the millstone around the neck of modern political thought, but it is again questionable whether her choice of literary text can be marshaled to this particular effect. A strong sense of inconsistency, if not contradiction, remains in her reading of "necessity" in Melville's tale as it stands in relation to the far more critical understanding of the term evident elsewhere in her study. What distinguishes, we might ask in this respect, the "necessity" championed by Captain Vere in the name of the existing order from that upheld by Stalin or Trotsky, for supposedly radical ends, that is, for the sake of "lasting [albeit communist] institutions"? In a line of inquiry we might well imagine John Dewey pursuing, we could ask: why do Vere's ends justify *his* means? What other consequences might his "unqualified, irrevocable, absolute" decision entail? It is far from clear in *Billy Budd*, as Arendt suggests, that Melville discerns the idea of necessity in the same way as she herself does.[64] By contrast, the range of responses among the characters in *The Middle of the Journey* to Melville's work—shaped by the trials in Moscow, which dramatized so many of the issues later explored in *On Revolution*—cover some of the possibilities Arendt closes off in her own analysis.

When confronted by Maxim's review article "Spirit and Law," both Laskell and the Crooms are taken aback by its contents. Maxim's reading of *Billy Budd* is deeply informed by his own personal experience and its changing relation to the prevailing political and intellectual climate of the times. Accordingly, he commences by dismissing "the modern mind in its most vocal part, in its radical or liberal intellectual part," which, in its limited impression of Billy Budd as a "weakly acquiescent ... oppressed worker" and Captain Vere as "a conscience-ridden bourgeois," is thus "not really capable of understanding the story." *Billy Budd* should be viewed, rather, as "a political parable, but on a higher level than we are used to taking our political parables." For Maxim, Melville's design is to convey "the tragedy of Spirit in the world of Necessity, the tragedy of Law in the world of Necessity, the tragedy that Law faces whenever it confronts its child, Spirit" (*TMOTJ*, 160).

Maxim then, like Arendt, falls into the "acceptance" rank of critics. But for him the relation between Spirit and Law is not antithetical but *dialectical*. Maxim may have jettisoned his Marxism but his religious *Weltanschauung* retains a Hegelian vision of opposing historical forces unfolding toward the reign of absolute Spirit. *Billy Budd* is read by Maxim much as the young Marx read Hegel, that is, as an acknowledgement of the fact that "Spirit and the Law that is established in the world of Necessity are kin, yet discontinuous." Melville draws on the Old Testament, which establishes this structure in the tale of Abraham's sacrifice of Isaac. "It is not merely," Maxim writes, "that Vere understands that Billy is his son, the Isaac to his Abraham; it is that Billy understands that Vere is his father and blesses him in his last words. Spirit blesses Law, even when Law has put the noose around his neck, for Spirit recognizes the true kinship." The modern progressive, by contrast, disavows this kinship, according to Maxim, by believing "that

Spirit should find its absolute expression at once," in defiance of Law, with anything less than this full and final expression of Spirit worthy only of dismissal as an "ignominious moral inadequacy" (*TMOTJ*, 161).

The way in which Trilling charts how progressives such as the Crooms might respond to this interpretation exposes some oversight in Arendt's reading. The Crooms are struck by the extent to which Vere can be seen to represent "progressive" forces as much as those of the status quo. In particular, Nancy Croom, perhaps because of her greater commitment to those forces, quickly sees the analogy with the Moscow trials—a point of comparison that, given her intellectual background as a historian of totalitarianism, surprisingly escapes Arendt. Speaking of Stalin's purge of senior party figures, Nancy Croom claims:

> Even if those men were subjectively innocent—I mean even if they had good motives for what they did, like Budd—I don't believe that's so, but even if it were so—they may have had to be executed for the sake of what he calls Law in the world of Necessity. And you remember how they all concurred in their punishment and seemed almost to *want* it. Certainly before they died they had a proper appreciation of Law. They realized that the dictatorship of the proletariat represented Law.
>
> (*TMOTJ*, 163)

Again, what is striking here is a commitment to Law that overrides all other considerations, sanctioning sacrifice, even of innocents, to a future kingdom of God or some secular substitute. As Nancy admits of the trials: "Of course God wasn't mentioned, but it was the same thing" (*TMOTJ*, 163). Arthur Croom's qualified praise for Maxim's article, on the other hand, stems less from the "idealism" that has increasingly attracted Nancy to communism than it does from a Burkean sensitivity to "circumstances," to politics as "the art of the possible." "The great danger to the progressive movement," he claims, "is that [liberals] ... see economic democracy developing over there and that doesn't satisfy them—they begin shouting for immediate political democracy, forgetting the realities of the historical situation" (*TMOTJ*, 164). These are something close to the terms in which the French Revolution is characterized in *On Revolution*, except "political" and "economic" should be transposed and Arendt, of course, identified the clamor for change as originating with "the people" rather than an intelligentsia of "liberals."

My argument here is not presented as a wholesale rejection of the broader case Arendt makes in *On Revolution,* which is, after all, built around more than a few short forays into nineteenth-century literature. But it is meant to show that draining the ambiguity from complex fictions can significantly undermine the claims of the political philosopher. Arendt would take Melville's sympathy for the predicament of Captain Vere without his recognition of Billy Budd's virtue, Melville's respect for Law without his appeal to Spirit, and, more generally, she divorces the author's politics from its important religious referents. But for Melville, the sacrifice involved in taking sides in this way *is* the tragedy of politics in the modern age. As Nancy Ruttenburg has written:

> To propose that Melville is here choosing sides—between "acceptance" and "resistance," good and evil, God and the Devil: mutually exclusive alternatives that Billy and Claggart are imagined unambiguously to represent— obscures the pathos of *Billy Budd* as Melville's "last will and testament" as it underestimates its achievement as literary art. Most regrettably, it celebrates the sacrificial logic that Melville strives to hold at bay.[65]

Trilling, by contrast, foregrounds the ambiguity Arendt overlooks in Melville's story by having a multiplicity of voices articulate a range of interpretation. Laskell's response is a counterpoint to the closed sacrificial logic espoused by Gifford Maxim and the Crooms. For Laskell, his friend's transformation not merely into "disaffected revolutionary" but "the blackest of reactionaries" generates feelings of both disbelief and disgust. After hearing the responses of the Crooms, the chapter closes with Laskell playing with the idea of rereading Maxim's review. Yet the ultimate significance of Melville's tale as a crucial source of meaning within Trilling's novel is beautifully suspended when Laskell tells himself that at some point he must also "consider why Arthur had looked at him with a special, personal intensity as he made that rather long speech of his and a certain stubbornness that his whole body was expressing" (*TMOTJ,* 164).

Liberalism in Modulation

The refusal to establish the meaning of *Billy Budd* as a fixed entity in *The Middle of the Journey* is further evidence of what Mark Krupnick has described as Trilling's "continuing irresolution, or what might be called his allergy to closure."[66] As Krupnick, among other critics, has noted, Trilling is a dialectical thinker who never seeks to neatly resolve those tensions he regarded as crucial in his critical project: between mind and reality, life and death, will and idea.[67] If the strength of Arendt's work can be located in her willingness to make and support distinctions (between the political and the social, the private and the public, and so forth), the strength of Trilling's might be said to lie in its refusal to do so. Both saw the rise of liberal capitalism as destructive of particularity and contingency in its dependence on the organizational impulse. Karl Marx's work in this respect was, again for both, symptomatic of this development, with its vision of a society cut adrift from politics altogether and a static, functionalist state responsible for the mere "administration of things." Trilling saw his critical task, in this way, as an attempt to redefine liberalism so as its adherents might, while acknowledging the indispensability of organization at some level, also, at the same time, understand that

> organization means delegation, and agencies, and bureaus, and technicians, and that the ideas that can survive delegation, that can be passed on to agencies and bureaus and technicians, incline to be ideas of a certain kind and a certain simplicity: they give up something of their largeness and modulation and complexity in order to survive. The lively sense of contingency and possibility, and of those exceptions to the rule that might be the beginning of the end of the rule—this does not suit well with the impulse to organization.[68]

It was from within this broad understanding of modernity that Trilling cultivated his criticism and sought to outline its relation to society. The importance he attaches to literature as a means of countering such tendencies, to the same degree, was attributed to its status as "the human activity that takes the fullest and most precise account of variousness, possibility, complexity, and difficulty."[69] In *The Middle of the Journey*, however, Trilling's commitment to these ideas takes on a more Arendtian cast, as his concerns turn to its meaning in the political sphere. In terms very similar to Arendt's, Trilling's focus is on the negation of political life in the modern age, which he associates with those revolutionaries whose "only political purpose was to express their disgust with politics and make an end of it once and for all ... [and] ... do away with those defining elements of politics that are repugnant to reason and virtue, such as mere opinion, contingency, conflicts of interest and clashes of will and the compromises they lead to" (*TMOTJ*, xx). These are precisely the tensions underlining the confrontation between Dewey and Trotsky, who discovered that, while a common basis for truth claims might be established within the confines of a commission of inquiry designed to perform a strictly circumscribed task, the moral imperative for action in a *democratic* political realm defined by pluralism becomes infinitely more difficult to agree upon.[70]

Trilling can also be seen then as an early advocate of the type of agonistic understanding of the political reprised by Arendt in the following decade. Furthermore, the "disgust with politics" exhibited by revolutionaries was regarded by him as no more than "a bitter refusal to consent to the conditioned nature of human existence" (*TMOTJ*, xx). Again, this is how Arendt seeks to reorient our sense of the political in her most famous work, *The Human Condition* (1959), where, as in *The Middle of the Journey*, politics is seen as demanding an *ontological* reconceptualization.[71] This stress can also be found in the political fiction of Dostoevsky, whose novel *The Possessed*, dismissed by many 1930s Marxists as "reactionary," nonetheless attracted words of praise in a 1938 *Partisan Review* essay by Philip Rahv. Foregrounding a similar "ontological" focus, Rahv perceives Dostoevsky's achievement in his understanding of revolutionary politics in terms of *metaphysical* failure, that is, its inability to reconceive values previously articulated within a religious framework. Notions of sin, of individual conscience and responsibility, were dismissed as "bourgeois morality" when they had, in actual fact, a fundamental bearing on political questions.[72]

Toward the end of *The Middle of the Journey*, Laskell undergoes a minor epiphany when he realizes why, during the course of yet another exchange of opinions, his friends seem to have grown suddenly angry with him. "It was the anger," he realizes, "of the masked will at the appearance of an idea in modulation" (*TMOTJ*, 308). Again, this returns us to Trilling's sensitivity to the process by which ideas, unless continually reinterrogated, can fossilize into an extension of the will. The central paradox of liberalism, in this sense, is that "in the very interest of affirming its confidence in the power of the mind, it inclines to constrict and make mechanical its conception of the nature of mind."[73] Liberalism, Trilling suggests, requires a conception of itself as a political philosophy perpetually in modulation in order to prevent the forms of moral collapse it entertained in the 1930s.

It is, however, a long road, in intellectual history terms, from there to here. Since the 1980s, considerable anger has been directed at Trilling from within the academic left in the United States. For many, Trilling has come to stand as a neoconservative talisman or, at the very least, for much that was oppressive about cold war liberalism.[74] However, at least one leftist critic has attempted to forestall the troubling, slow-burn process of Trilling's critical legacy being appropriated by the neoconservative opponents of the Cultural Left.[75] The closing chapter of Harvey Teres' study of the New York intellectuals asks "What's Left of Lionel Trilling?" Teres here deftly repositions Trilling in what might be regarded as a republican tradition of criticism with both ancient and modern antecedents. "He belongs," he claims, "in the line of the worldly citizen-critics, which extends from Plato and Aristotle to Hazlitt and Arnold, critics who gave pronounced attention to literature's connection to the well-being of the polity, and who portrayed that connection, as well as the nature and interests of the polity, with unusual specificity and insight."[76]

Trilling's most important accomplishment within this role involved a vital revaluation of post-Depression American liberalism—a crucial juncture in the republic's history. His anxiety was registered at a number of levels, drawing him, for instance, to certain works of modern literature because, as Teres points out, "liberalism seemed incapable of sustaining a culture autonomous and imaginative enough to produce incisive self-critique." It is precisely this commitment to self-critique that accounts for the more arresting moments in *The Middle of the Journey*, where political thinking is conveyed as a vibrant ongoing process, part of a journey, as the title suggests, with no terminus. Laskell, rejecting the "consummation" inherent in the notion of Adamic pasts or futures, like Ishmael, nonetheless survives. It is, in this way, a very *American* political novel, concerned, as Trilling himself wrote of E. M. Forster, with "man in the world without the sentimentality of cynicism."[77]

4

LIBERALISM BETRAYED

Neoconservatism and the Postwar American Left in Philip Roth's American Trilogy

America would remember the sixties as a decade of the left. It must be remembered instead as a decade when the polarization began. "We must assume that the conservative revival is *the* youth movement of the '6os," Murray Kempton wrote in 1961, in words that would sound laughable five years later. Forty years later, these are words that are, at the very least, arguable.

—RICK PERLSTEIN, *Before the Storm*

I will go to my grave being proud of what I had fought for in the impeachment battle, my last great showdown with the forces I had opposed all my life—those who had defended the old order of racial discrimination and segregation in the South and played on the insecurities and fears of the white working class in which I grew up ...

—BILL CLINTON, *My Life*

I Married a Communist: Liberalism and the Old Left

If Lionel Trilling's *The Middle of the Journey* offers invaluable insights into the relationship between liberals and radicals at the time of the Moscow trials, then it also, in some quite striking ways, seems to foreshadow the unraveling of this relationship during Senator Joseph McCarthy's meteoric rise to national prominence in the early years of the cold war. Trilling based the character of Gifford Maxim on Whittaker Chambers, a CPUSA member and acquaintance of his in the 1930s who by the end of that decade had exchanged communism for Christianity. Most famously, after the war, Chambers was to expose a prominent official in the Roosevelt administration, Alger Hiss, as a Soviet spy and, in the process, help create the climate in which McCarthy could emerge as American anticommunism's very own Grand Inquisitor.

Trilling's novel also projects Maxim into this role by anticipating a moment of liberal crisis when this character's Manichean worldview might acquire greater currency. As Douglas Tallack has noted, it is the carefully honed intellectual response of John Laskell that allows Trilling here to appear "*so* prophetic of the McCarthy era in his study of Maxim":[1]

> [Laskell] was thinking that Maxim ... would not religiously retire from the world but would go where worldly power lies waiting for men to pick it up. He had been seeing the great executive force that lay behind Maxim's expression of his view of the nature of guilt and responsibility. It seemed to him that the day was not very far off when Maxim's passions would suit the passions of others.[2]

It is, in fact, tempting in retrospect to "read" Arthur and Nancy Croom through the historical experience of the Hiss trial, transposing their "fellow-traveling" liberal identities on to those of Alger Hiss and his wife (who was also implicated during the trial). It is important, however, to remember the major geopolitical transformation that had occurred as a result of the outcome of World War II. In the early 1940s, the domestic context was determined by a war economy that helped normalize government economic intervention and thus strengthen an emerging liberal consensus organized around the values of social democracy. By 1950, however, the context was one of cold war anticommunism and an incipient national security state. The cold war also brought to a halt those expressions of antifascist solidarity with the Soviet Union that had played an important role in prewar and wartime U.S. foreign policy.

Any understanding of liberalism during this latter period, then, must be attentive to such national and supranational developments. We have already seen, in the previous chapter, how many American liberals involved in the establishment of an antifascist "Popular Front" in the 1930s—notwithstanding the events of the Moscow trials—held to the view that the Soviet Union was an ultimately "progressive" force. The signing of the Nazi-Soviet pact in 1939 would be the next event to add to the ranks of disabused liberals. As Hitler and Stalin cynically divided swaths of Eastern

Europe between them like the colonial powers of yore, forces previously designated as "progressive" were now more or less indistinguishable from those long-maligned forces of "reaction."

Yet a significant portion of liberal sentiment in the United States would remain ambiguous toward communism in the immediate years after World War II. The Soviet Union was, after all, a wartime ally and its guiding creed could hardly metamorphose into the stuff of ideological *bête noire* overnight. Events, nonetheless, moved quickly after 1945, as Czechoslovakia came under the Soviet orbit, tensions mounted in Berlin (which ultimately prompted Moscow to mount a blockade of the city), and the influence of communist parties significantly increased in France and Italy. The defining domestic event, however, in terms of shaping the contours of postwar liberalism in the United States, was the election of 1948, when Henry Wallace ran against incumbent Democratic president Harry Truman from the left.

Wallace had been a longstanding member of Roosevelt's cabinet and, after the war, had been appointed secretary of commerce in the Truman administration. He rejected Truman's hostility to the Soviet Union and soon became, as one intellectual historian has characterized him, "the last remaining spokesman ... for the New Deal and the preservation of the wartime alliance." These views led Wallace to give increasingly vocal expression to his differences with other cabinet members on matters of foreign policy. Such outspokenness appealed to many disenchanted liberals, who identified him as "a man with a mission."[3] The schism was publicly acknowledged in September 1946, when Wallace was fired by Truman.

From that point on, Wallace sought to build a left-liberal coalition that would challenge the liberal status quo on everything from U.S.-Soviet relations to issues of economic and racial equality within the United States itself. The result was the establishment of the Wallace-led Progressive Party, which threatened to split the Democratic Party vote at the 1948 presidential election. However, the Progressive Party, from its inception, was plagued by accusations that it was a mere front for communist and far-left elements.[4] Related to this was Wallace's own failure to overcome his image as the archetypal naïve, "fellow-traveling" liberal. The fact that on the eve of the election Whittaker Chambers testified before the HUAC, portraying the New Deal as an ideological haven for subversive leftists such as Alger Hiss (whom Wallace himself had once employed when he was secretary of agriculture under Roosevelt), only reinforced this impression.[5] Such factors—combined with an astute Truman campaign reiterating the administration's firm anticommunist credentials while outlining the need for progressive social and economic reforms—effectively neutralized the Progressive Party as a political force. Wallace ultimately took only 2.4 percent of the popular vote and no electoral college seats.

Henry Wallace's presidential candidacy in 1948 features prominently in Philip Roth's *I Married a Communist* (1998), which, alongside *American Pastoral* (1997) and *The Human Stain* (2000),[6] has been described by the author himself as part of "a thematic trilogy, dealing with the historical moments in postwar American life that have had the greatest impact on my generation. I'd say the greatest impact on me, except I don't believe my response is singular."[7] It is clear from this that Roth perceives these works and the characters therein as representative in some sense relating to the ideological ethos of postwar America.

We will return to the idea here of Roth's central characters' lives as representative in a way similar, perhaps, to that identified in the novels previously examined. I would like to begin, though, with an analysis of *I Married a Communist* (the "first" novel in terms of the trilogy's narrative chronology). Each of the novels in the trilogy deploys Nathan Zuckerman, an authorial alter ego familiar from Roth's earlier fiction, as a narrator, to establish a greater sense of narrative as well as thematic continuity. Of the three works, however, this is the one in which Zuckerman is himself most directly involved in the events he narrates. As will be proposed here, *I Married a Communist* can be read as the tale of Zuckerman's (and to some degree at least, by inference, Roth's own) early political and intellectual development. This occurs against the backdrop of the Wallace campaign, which cements the relationship between the young Zuckerman and the novel's "hero," communist activist Ira Ringold; it also offers a set of reference points within which Roth chooses to outline the ideological ethos that is American liberalism in the early postwar years.

The full story of Ira Ringold's representative life is told by Ira's brother Murray, who, as Nathan Zuckerman's former high-school English teacher, introduces them to each other in October 1948. A chance encounter has now brought the aging Murray Ringold to the porch of Zuckerman's isolated home in present-day Connecticut, where the narrative unfolds over a couple of long summer evenings. Ira's life is both epic and emblematic, a story of American dichotomies particular to a specific midcentury historical moment. One of Roth's major triumphs here lies in his unusually complex depiction of the political radical—a figure that might easily be reduced to the level of caricature in the hands of a lesser novelist. Ira Ringold is a man of Whitmanesque multitudes and contradictions. He is the self-reliant, independent American who hoboes around the nation taking various manual-labor jobs during the Depression before serving in the military after America enters the war, yet he also represents the second-generation, working-class, Jewish autodidact, whose ability brings him fame and wealth as an Abraham Lincoln impersonator and as the popular radio actor "Iron Rinn" in the postwar years.

Ira is a big man in every sense, muscular in physical and intellectual terms, as passionate about the life of the great outdoors as he is about that of the mind. Ira is as equally at ease with the country folk who inhabit the area near an isolated shack he keeps as he is in the Manhattan apartments of the writers and actors of the New York radio world. It is little wonder then, that the young Zuckerman, a gifted student himself, is dazzled by this Jewish American role model. As an older man, however, Zuckerman, on learning of Ira's tragic fate from Murray, comes to recognize an element of hubris in Ira's restless pursuit of himself:

> I had never before known anyone whose life was so intimately circumscribed by so much American history, who was personally familiar with so much American geography, who had confronted, face to face, so much American low life. I'd never met anyone so immersed in his moment or so defined by it. Or tyrannized by it, so much its avenger and its victim and its tool. To imagine Ira *outside* of his moment was impossible. For me, on those nights up in the shack, the America that was my inheritance manifested itself in the form of Ira Ringold.
>
> (*IMAC*, 189)

Ira's tragedy is brought about by the publication of a schlock memoir entitled *I Married a Communist*, written by his former wife, Eve Frame. This, of course, brings him to the attention of HUAC investigations into the question of "subversive" activity in the entertainment industry. Frame, a radio actress, plays the role of the assimilationist Jew in thrall to the mores and values of the dominant WASP culture. She is encouraged to publish her memoir by Bryden and Katrina Van Tassel Grant, a gossip columnist and author of popular romances, respectively, who represent the epitome of reactionary WASP "pampered privilege" and for whom, Murray recalls, "the Ringolds were the Rosenbergs" (*IMAC*, 7).

When Roth's novel first appeared in 1998, several reviewers approached it as an all-too-thinly coded act of revenge for a memoir published by the author's ex-wife, the actress Claire Bloom, which revealed intimate details of the couple's marriage.[8] It is certainly the case that Eve Frame and her daughter Sylphid are unmistakable portraits of Bloom and her teenage child and that Ira's volatile relationship with Sylphid mirrors Roth's with his own stepdaughter. If this were not enough, *I Married a Communist* also depicts a sexual relationship between Ira and a friend of Sylphid's along with all of its disastrous repercussions (Bloom too alleged that Roth attempted to seduce a friend of her daughter's).

Such seemingly personal preoccupations, at least in part, contributed to an overall impression among reviewers that *I Married a Communist* was a less successful work than its widely praised, Pulitzer Prize–winning predecessor *American Pastoral.* Yet the theme of betrayal is much broader than these readings allow, hinging, as it does, on far more than that of marital and familial relationships. Betrayal, in fact, is central to the novel's understanding of ideology and the idea of political commitment as they find expression within the story's historical context. In this sense, as Murray Ringold attests, the personal and the political are interlocked in unprecedented ways in the United States during this period, reflecting, to some extent at least, the condition of totalitarian societies where the distinction between the two is erased:

> To me it seems likely that more acts of personal betrayal were tellingly perpetrated in America in the decade after the war—between '46 and '56—than in any other period in our history. . . . Eve's behavior fell well within the routine informer practices of the era. When before had betrayal been so destigmatized and rewarded in this country? It was everywhere during those years, the accessible transgression, the *permissible* transgression that any American could commit. . . . Betrayal is an inescapable component of living—who does not betray?—but to confuse the most heinous public act of betrayal, treason, with every other form of betrayal was not a good idea in 1951.
>
> (*IMAC,* 264–265)

The idea of betrayal, moreover, is essential to an appreciation of the emergence of the young Nathan Zuckerman's political consciousness as he falls under the sway of various adult influences only to "betray" them for others. Once more, both the literal and figurative role of "fathers" as well as related notions of cultural patrimony and political legacy loom large. We have already seen this process at work in Nathan's admission that "the America that was my *inheritance* [my italics] manifested itself in the form of Ira Ringold." On the national party political canvas, this "inheritance," for Ira and Nathan, is personified in the liberalism of Henry Wallace that causes the split with Truman. Both Wallace and Truman, after all, sought to position themselves at this time as the "legitimate heirs" to FDR and the New Deal. Such "filial" tension, furthermore, is paralleled in the Zuckerman family. "This division within the Democratic Party," Nathan recollects, "was reflected in the split within my own household between father and son" (*IMAC*, 29).

Nathan's father, "who had admired Wallace when he was FDR's protégé," opposes the Wallace third-party candidacy on the pragmatic grounds that it will divide the Democratic vote and thus pave the way for a Republican victory. "I was terrifically disappointed," Nathan confesses, "to hear my father flatly refuse to vote for the candidate who, as I tried to convince him, supported his own New Deal principles." Wallace stands for "a national health program, protection for unions, benefits for workers"; he opposes, Nathan adds, "Taft-Hartley and the persecution of labor [and] the Mundt-Nixon bill and the persecution of radicals." The latter he describes to his father as "the first step to a police state. ... [Wallace] called it 'the most subversive' bill ever introduced in Congress." However, Nathan is most impressed by Wallace's refusal to address segregated audiences: "the first presidential candidate ever to have that degree of courage and integrity" (*IMAC*, 30).

Nathan's influences by this time also include the novels of Wallace supporter Howard Fast. He is drawn, in particular, to the vivid Old Left appropriation of Thomas Paine's politics offered in Fast's *Citizen Tom Paine* (1943). Paine is here, Zuckerman recalls, the "common man" to Jefferson's aristocrat, "savagely single-minded and unsociable, an epic, folkloric belligerent" (*IMAC*, 25). The parallels with the personality of Ira Ringold are unmistakable. The book, of course, is recommended to him by Murray. For Nathan, then, the influence of the Ringold brothers serves as a "one-two punch promising to initiate me into the big show, into my beginning to understand what it takes to be a man on the larger scale ... compel[ling] me to respond at a level of rigor that felt appropriate to who I now was. Be a good boy wasn't the issue with them. The sole issue was my convictions."

Remembering, however, the fact that he ignored his father's request that he refuse Ira's invitation to attend a downtown Wallace rally, Zuckerman in late middle age is now able to look more sympathetically on the conflicting demands placed upon others. The responsibility of the Ringolds, he reflects, was of a different order to that of the father's,

> which is to steer his son away from the pitfalls in a way the teacher doesn't. He has to worry about his son's conduct, he has to worry about socializing his little Tom Paine. But once little Tom Paine has been let into the company of men and the father is still educating him as a boy, the father is finished. Sure he's worrying about the pitfalls—if he wasn't, it would be wrong. But he's finished anyway. Little Tom Paine has no choice but to write him off, to betray the father and go boldly forth to step straight into life's very first pit.
>
> (*IMAC*, 32)

Nathan's father also points to Eleanor Roosevelt's and (former secretary of the interior under FDR) Harold Ickes's failure to endorse Wallace. Likewise, the CIO too, he claims, has withdrawn its funding and support for the same reason: communist infiltration of the Progressive Party. Roth here indicates that his novel is not to be read simply as a hindsight-heavy, liberal tirade against the HUAC's persecution of individuals such as Ira Ringold. A sense of betrayal was felt too by other progressives (whose politics were equally defined by the New Deal era) toward liberals such as Wallace who refused to take the antidemocratic realities of communism seriously. Of the infiltration of the Progressive Party, the senior Zuckerman believes, Henry Wallace was ultimately "either too naïve to know it or—what was, unfortunately, probably closer to the truth—too dishonest to admit it" (*IMAC*, 33).

The situation is resolved only when Nathan's father asks to meet Ira Ringold after his son requests permission to visit Ira at his Zinc Town shack. He wishes to establish, once and for all, whether Ira is in fact a member of the Communist Party. Before doing so, however, he relays to his son and Ira how, in 1930, "disgusted with the ... anti-Semitism and anti-Negro prejudice ... with how the Republicans scorned the unfortunate and with how the greed of big business was milking the people of this country to death," he himself knocked on the door of the Newark Communist Party offices only to receive no reply:

Luckily, that door was locked. And in the next election Franklin Roosevelt became the president, and the kind of capitalism that sent me down to the Communist Party office began to get an overhaul the likes of which this country had never seen. A great man saved this country's capitalism from the capitalists and saved patriotic people like me from Communism. Saved all of us from the dictatorial regime that *results* from Communism.

(IMAC, 102–103)

When asked, Ira claims not to be a member of the party and professes his admiration for Nathan, who, Ira promises, will spend his time at Zinc Town in outdoor pursuits such as "swimming and hiking and fishing." Nathan recalls being relieved that the meeting had concluded without acrimony although, he is only now aware, this was "largely because Ira was not telling the truth" (*IMAC*, 105).

The episode ends very powerfully, with Nathan remembering "the wound inflicted on his father's face" after he unthinkingly departs with Ira to celebrate the forthcoming vacation, leaving his father alone in his office. It is a look "of resigned disappointment, his kind grey eyes softened by—distressfully subdued by—something midway between melancholy and futility," a look that would enter Nathan's consciousness at future moments spent with other mentors such as Ira, the communist Johnny O'Day, and, later, his tutor at the University of Chicago, Leo Glucksman: "His face with that look on it was always looming up, superimposed on the face of the man who was then educating me in life's possibilities. His face bearing the wound of betrayal" (*IMAC*, 106).

Ideas of betrayal as they relate to both literal and figurative understandings of fatherhood or the notion of maintaining a legacy more generally are established in a number of other ways in *I Married a Communist*. Ira Ringold, for instance, is first brought to Nathan's attention when, in his capacity as a Lincoln impersonator, he is invited by Murray to read Lincoln's Second Inaugural and Gettysburg addresses before the high-school students. The brothers then go on to recreate the Lincoln-Douglas debates for their young audience. Any *modern* liberal credentials that might be attached to Lincoln are only mildly hinted at here but, in the years immediately following the war, we learn Ira had been much more explicit in situating communist ideology within the mainstream political tradition represented by Lincoln. It is while working at a record plant in Chicago with his friend Johnny O'Day (who had recruited Ira to the CPUSA during the time they spent together in a poverty-stricken Tehran during the war) that Ira first impersonates the "father" of the modern American nation. Here, we learn, Ira had received "a big hand for giving to the word 'slavery' a strong working-class, political slant" (*IMAC*, 44). By the time he is spotted by the radio writer Arthur Sokolow (who goes on to make Ira the "common man" star "Iron Rinn") the act has been cultivated yet further:

> Ira was [now] onstage for a full hour as Lincoln, not only reciting or read-ing from documents but responding to audience questions about current political controversies in the guise of Abraham Lincoln, with Lincoln's high-pitched country twang and his awkward giant's gestures and his droll, plainspoken way. Lincoln supporting price controls. Lincoln condemning the Smith Act. Lincoln vilifying Mississippi's Senator Bilbo.
>
> (*IMAC*, 45)

Moreover, Roth builds upon this theme of paternity via the ominous figure of Johnny O'Day. This tough Irish American activist stands, albeit temporarily, as more than a mere mentor to Ira and Nathan as a result of their respective encounters with him. The sense in which O'Day assumes the role of the father with regard to Ira, for example, is brought into focus by a prior stress on the fact that Ira has grown up without parents. As such, Zuckerman reflects, "the orphaned Ira was the perfect target for O'Day." However, it is only when Nathan himself, "anything but an orphan" (*IMAC*, 43), several years later in his first months at the University of Chicago, falls under his influence that the full significance of O'Day's ideological com-mitment to communism becomes apparent. Interestingly, a single meeting with O'Day is enough to produce within Nathan an overwhelming desire to break inherited ties—both parental and otherwise:

> By the time I got back on the train that evening, the power of O'Day's unrelenting focus had so disoriented me that all I could think about was how I was to tell my parents that three and a half months was enough: I was quitting college to move down to the steel town of East Chicago, Indiana. ... I wasn't asking them to support me financially ... I could no longer justify continuing to accede to bourgeois expectations, theirs *or* mine, not after my meeting with Johnny O'Day, who, despite all the soft-spokenness

concealing the passion, came across as the most dynamic person I had ever met, more so even than Ira. The most dynamic, the most unshatterable, the most dangerous.

(IMAC, 232)

Once more we are also confronted here with evidence of the Ahab-Ishmael dynamic delineated in Russell Banks's *Cloudsplitter.* Nathan's "disorientation" in the face of O'Day's personal (and political) magnetism here mirrors that of Ishmael's and Owen Brown's in the face of the charismatic power of Ahab and John Brown respectively. The description of O'Day that precedes the above passage, for example, offers a neat précis of this political archetype:

> Perhaps because there was nothing contradictory in O'Day's aims ... because the speech was a pretext for nothing else, because it appeared to rise from the core of the brain that was *experience,* there was a tautened to-the-point quality to what he said, the thinking firmly established, the words themselves seemingly shot through with will ... in every utterance, a wily shrewdness and, however utopian the goal, a deep practicality, a sense that he had the mission as much in his hands as in his head.
>
> *(IMAC, 231)*

Unlike Ira, who must reconcile his radical politics with his emotional and creative needs for the bourgeois worlds of the family and the theater—needs that effectively prohibit any long-term withdrawal from that world—O'Day "live[s] the life he proselytize[s]." This takes the form of an ascetic existence in a single rooming house "cell" with only a typewriter, two chairs, a table, and a single bed for company. "It was as though," Nathan claims, "everything that wasn't in that room had vanished from the world" (*IMAC,* 227). O'Day, like Ahab and John Brown, is here seen as locked in his own interiority, physically and mentally isolated in self-imposed exile. O'Day's obsession with ideology in this novel assumes the thematic position occupied by the idea of "monomania" in the pages of *Moby Dick.* O'Day's room, like his speech, is an effort to generate "the tang of the real," yet it is also a room without color, gaiety, or a sense of human presence, just as his own speech is "also the speech of someone in whom nothing ever laugh[s]. With the result that there [is] a kind of madness to his singleness of purpose" (*IMAC*, 231–232). With this perception in particular, the analogy with Ahab and Brown could not be more clear—all possess what Nathan terms at one point "a heart without dichotomies" (*IMAC*, 238).

The last we hear of Johnny O'Day in the novel is when Murray tracks him down several years later in an effort to help Ira recover from a mental breakdown. O'Day refuses to visit Ira in the hospital as a result of his anger at Ira's "betrayal" of the Party, which he "used ... to climb to his professional position." For O'Day, Ira's fate at the hands of his McCarthyite inquisitors is no tragedy either in personal or broader political terms. He is, rather, to be held in what seems even greater contempt himself as "a fake and ... a dope and ... a traitor. Betrayed his revolutionary comrades and betrayed the working class. Sold out. Bought off. Totally the creature of the bourgeoisie. Seduced by fame and money and wealth and power" (*IMAC*, 288).

Nonetheless, only shortly after meeting up with O'Day in Chicago, Nathan Zuckerman finds himself pulled toward the intellectual territory inhabited by his college tutor Leo Glucksmann, whose approach to the world stands in sharp contrast to that of O'Day. This ultimately leads Nathan to "betray" his allegiance to the Old Left. Reflecting on the shift in influence from Ira to O'Day to Glucksmann, Nathan offers his most explicit statement of the paternity and patrimony themes that underwrite *I Married a Communist*:

> All were remarkable to me in their own way, personalities to contend with, mentors who embodied or espoused powerful ideas and who first taught me to navigate the world and its claims, the adopted parents who also, each in his turn, had to be cast off along with their legacy, had to disappear, thus making way for the orphanhood that is total, which is manhood. When you're out there in this thing all alone.
>
> (*IMAC*, 217)

Leo Glucksmann is the final of these "adopted parents" that we meet in the novel. The "new recruitment phase" overseen by this young professor begins after Zuckerman solicits Glucksmann's opinion of *The Stooge of Torquemada*, what might best be described, in the parlance of the times, as an "anti-anti-communist" drama Nathan has written in the leftist-progressive mode. Glucksmann, recollected by Nathan as a "foppishly overdressed boy genius" aesthete, offers a withering critique of the work, describing it as "crap … awful … crude, primitive simple-minded propagandistic crap." More pointedly, he adds, "it reeks to high heaven of your virtue." It is the broader theoretical impetus propelling such criticisms, however, that leads Nathan to ultimately question many of his prior convictions, in particular, no doubt, the relationship between politics and art:

> "Art as a weapon?" he said to me, the word "weapon" rich with contempt and itself a weapon. "Art as taking the right *stand* on everything? Art as the advocate of good things? Who taught you all this? Who taught you art is slogans? Who taught you art is in the service of '*the people*'? Art is in the service of *art*—otherwise there is no art worthy of *anyone's* attention. What *is* the motive for writing serious literature, Mr. Zuckerman? To disarm the enemies of price control? The motive for writing serious literature is *to write serious literature*. You want to rebel against society? I'll tell you how to do it—write *well*."
>
> (*IMAC*, 218)

Here we acquire our first intimation of Roth's interest in probing a key area within the ideologies of both the Old and New Left—their focus on the politics of culture. This interest is at its most explicit, as we shall examine, in *The Human Stain*, the final installment in the trilogy. Yet by the end of the novel it is not Leo Glucksman, Johnny O'Day, or Ira Ringold who have had the most lasting effect on Zuckerman. It is, rather, Murray Ringold whose influence seems the most profound. Even as a man in his sixties, Zuckerman is forced to reflect upon the path his own life has taken as a result of his former teacher's words of counsel. Observing Zuckerman's ascetic, solitary existence in rural Connecticut, Murray reminds him not to delude himself about the repercussions of effective withdrawal from human society—whether it be via a Zinc Town shack, a Chicago rooming house, or a university campus. When Zuckerman claims that he merely "prefer[s] it this way," Murray replies:

> No, I watched you listening. I don't think you do. I don't think for a moment that the exuberance is gone. You were like that as a kid. That's why I got such a kick out of you—you paid attention. You still do. But what

is up here to pay attention to? You should get out from under whatever's the problem. To give in to the temptation to yield isn't smart. . . . Beware the utopia of isolation. Beware the utopia of the shack in the woods, the oasis defense against rage and grief. An impregnable solitude. That's how life ended for Ira, and long before the day he dropped dead.

(*IMAC*, 315)

Murray fears the notion of retreat in this sense as it presents what he describes at one point, in explaining his dislike of Johnny O'Day, as a "moral pass." If politics requires a morality premised on "worldly" consciousness, that is, in the first instance, a moral commitment to engagement with the world beyond one's own doorstep, then Zuckerman too seems aware that he may have acquired his own form of "moral pass." Preoccupied now with "worlds" beyond this one, he follows the "wheeling logic" of the planets and stars with the aid of a stargazers' map from the Sunday *New York Times*, "chuck[ing] out the four pounds of everything else." Moreover, he recognizes that "soon I was chucking out the daily paper as well; soon I had chucked everything with which I no longer wished to contend, everything but what was needed to live on and to work with. I set out to receive all my fullness from what might once have seemed, even to me, not nearly enough and to inhabit passionately only the parts of speech" (*IMAC*, 321). It is also apparent, however, that Murray Ringold has paid a heavy price for his own determination to remain engaged with society. Refusing to leave his home and job teaching mostly black children in inner-city Newark—despite already being mugged twice himself—Murray's wife Doris is killed after being attacked on the street. Earlier in the novel, Murray has already alerted Nathan to the omnipresence of betrayal as a theme in human history. As a high-school teacher of literature, he feels he has "no excuse for finding betrayal anywhere but at the heart of things. ... It's a very big subject, betrayal." After citing Othello, Hamlet, and Lear as examples, he then moves to the most influential text of all:

Just think of the Bible. What's that book about? The master story situation of the Bible is betrayal. Adam—betrayed. Esau—betrayed. The Shechemites— betrayed. Judah—betrayed. Joseph—betrayed. Moses—betrayed. Samson— betrayed. Samuel—betrayed. David—betrayed. Uriah—betrayed. Job—betrayed.

Job betrayed by whom? By none other than God himself. And don't forget the betrayal of God. God betrayed. Betrayed by our ancestors at every turn.

(*IMAC*, 185)

Perhaps inevitably, Murray perceives his wife's death in terms of betrayal. "Myself with all my principles," he reflects, "I can't betray my brother. I can't betray my teaching. . . . And so who I betray is my wife. I put the responsibility for my choices onto somebody else. Doris paid the price for my civic virtue." More pointedly, Murray tells Nathan of the extent to which Doris's death has forced him to reevaluate his long-held liberal values: "Do you know what I realized? I realized I'd been had. It's not an idea I like but I've lived with it inside me ever since" (*IMAC*, 317). It may be mere coincidence that Roth here illustrates Murray's self-questioning with resort to the motif of "mugging," but nonetheless it cannot help but bring to mind Irving Kristol's famous definition of a neoconservative as "a liberal who has been mugged by reality."[9] Indeed, the exploration of such themes as the politicization of culture (via popular radio drama in the 1940s and 1950s) and the relationship between race and urban decline (via the depiction of Newark in the aftermath of the 1967 riots) indicates, at the very least, a concern with items regularly placed at the top of the original neoconservative political agenda.[10] These and other common topics of neoconservative discourse receive more sustained coverage in *American Pastoral* and *The Human Stain*, books in which the 1960s as well as the political and cultural repercussions of that decade come under greater scrutiny. The broader philosophical context for neoconservatism, however, is set up at the close of *I Married a Communist*, when Nathan ponders Murray's "betrayal" of Doris: "You control betrayal on one side and you wind up betraying somewhere else. Because it's not a static system. Because it's alive. Because everything that lives is in movement. Because purity is petrifaction. Because purity is a lie. Because unless you're an ascetic paragon like Johnny O'Day or Jesus Christ, you're urged on by five hundred things" (*IMAC*, 318). This is the chastened liberalism that finds expression in Trilling's *The Middle of the Journey*, the emphasis on "movement" and disavowal of the "static system" paralleling Trilling's "allergy to closure." As we have seen, in its depiction of Gifford Maxim and via its intertextual embrace of Melville's *Billy Budd* and Dostoevsky's "The Grand Inquisitor," Trilling's novel is equally suspicious of such "ascetic paragon" figures.

Yet this branch of liberal thought itself, in its traumatic encounters with the ideologies of both the Old and New Left in the postwar era, did not remain cohesive and divided into several strands. This is, no doubt, the reason why the "neoconservative" appellation, while still useful in charting the development of liberal resistance to authoritarian forms of leftism, nonetheless remains a slippery one. The entry for the term in a recent *Companion to American Thought*, for example, reads:

> This highly charged label indicates the worldview or ideological stance of conservatives who were once liberals, but who turned to the right during the late 1960s and early 1970s. From the start neo-conservatism has been largely a reactive phenomenon, defining its own positions in relation to the leftward drift of American liberalism—within the Democratic Party, the news media, the universities and the cultural and literary worlds.[11]

For the intellectual historian in particular, an important distinction should be drawn here. Some to whom the label has been applied, like Lionel Trilling—while far less indulgent of the "illiberal egalitarianism"[12] of the hard left than earlier liberals such as John Dewey—undoubtedly remained faithful to a Deweyan commitment to the role of the liberal intellectual and, to take another Deweyan stress, the importance of the university in American public life. Others, more closely associated with the term perhaps, such as Irving Kristol and Norman Podhoretz, feel that in its failure to confront the illiberal authoritarianism of the left, the broader intellectual culture that dominates the universities has effectively betrayed the liberal tradition.[13]

One consequence of this is that within the work of this latter group we find what Peter Steinfels has astutely described as a "counter-intellectual" impulse.[14] It is toward this line, finally, that Nathan Zuckerman seems to lean when he summarizes Murray Ringold's predicament in a way that brings together the trilogy's themes of betrayal, revenge, and generational conflict:

> This was the existence that America had worked out for him—and that he'd worked out for himself by thinking, by taking *his* revenge on his father by cri-ti-cal think-ing, by being reasonable in the face of no reason. This was what thinking in America had got him. This was what adhering to his

convictions had got him, resisting the tyranny of compromise. *If there's any chance for the improvement of life, where's it going to begin if not in the school?* Hopelessly entangled in the best of intentions, tangibly, over a lifetime, committed to a constructive course that is now an illusion, to formulations and solutions that will no longer wash.

(*IMAC,* 318)

The phenomenon of neoconservatism is one of the most prominent features of the unraveling and transmutation of American liberalism since World War II. It is hardly surprising, then, that works, such as Roth's, that take as their subject the ideological ethos of postwar America should explore many of the areas and raise a number of ideas familiar from a now extensive corpus of neoconservative literature. Questions, however, pertaining to Roth's own understanding of postwar liberalism and the political orientation of his late work with regard to the American left and the neoconservative movement can only be fully examined in the context of Roth's own early critical and commercial success as a writer in the 1960s and, most revealingly of all, with reference to *The Human Stain*, the final novel in the trilogy.

American Pastoral: Liberalism and the New Left

Writing in 1998 in *Commentary*, the house journal of American neoconservatism, the critic Norman Podhoretz reviewed the career of Philip Roth. Claiming to have discovered Roth the writer as a newly hired assistant editor of *Commentary* in the 1950s, Podhoretz then proceeds to chart what he regards as the high and low points of the novelist's subsequent output. Although not without moments of notable critical acuity, the assessments that follow generally tell the reader at least as much about the phenomenon of neoconservatism and Podhoretz's own personal political journey as they do about the merits or otherwise of Philip Roth's fiction.

The neoconservative impulse is reflected in Podhoretz's description of his own steady disillusionment with Roth's work through the 1960s and 1970s. At first, this was prompted by his gradual realization of the legitimacy of certain criticisms made by Jewish organizations for what they perceived as Roth's "negative" representation of the Jewish community in his early fiction. Despite agreeing to publish Roth's equally controversial rebuttal of these criticisms, "Writing About Jews," as a still left-leaning editor in 1963, Podhoretz now claims that he did so despite "an uneasy (if largely hidden, as much from myself as others) sympathy for the Jewish nervousness over Roth's work."[15] It became clear to Podhoretz, however, after his own neoconservative turn, prompted by the cultural effect of the New Left in the 1960s, that Roth's anger could not be attributed simply to the "self-loathing" of the assimilationist Jew, as many of his critics accused.

Long before the appearance of the bitter satire on the Nixon presidency *Our Gang* (1973), Podhoretz claims to have noted how, from the publication of his first stories, collected in *Goodbye, Columbus* (1959), Roth's contempt had been, in almost equal measure, directed at gentile WASP America. By the 1970s, Roth was now, to a Podhoretz repudiating what he perceived as liberalism's subordination to the values and morality of the counterculture, the "laureate of a new class," of an elite liberal intelligentsia, "in the sense," he describes, "that everything [Roth] wrote served to reinforce their standard ideas and attitudes, to offer documentary evidence for their taken-for-granted view that America was a country dominated by vulgarians, materialists, bores and criminal political leaders."

For this neoconservative critic, the young Philip Roth became something of a totemic figure within a new radicalism that had redefined liberalism and finally destroyed, in the process, what remained of the postwar political consensus. This consensus, of course, had been rooted in an understanding of liberalism Podhoretz himself had once embraced. Indeed, it was liberalism's alliance with new sociopolitical forces hostile to fundamental American values, Podhoretz believes, that accounted for the considerable commercial success of Roth's work in the late 1960s and early 1970s. "More and more people," he recollects, "had come along who were in tune with the disgust for Americans and American life that had been expressed in Roth's work from the beginning and who hence had increasingly come to recognize him as their own."[16] It is for these *political* reasons, Podhoretz claims then, that his early enthusiasm for Roth began to wane. Although he goes on to say that he has continued to devote much time to reading the subsequent output, he adds dolefully that "not all of it turned out to be well spent."

This, however, was about to change. While discerning a more sympathetic tone in a number of mid-period Roth works eventually anthologized in *Zuckerman Bound: A Trilogy and Epilogue* (1985)—what he describes as "a touch of tenderness ... extended towards the Jews he had so relentlessly and exuberantly ridiculed in the books that once brought him fame"— Podhoretz is even more surprised by Roth's *American Pastoral* (1997). Here, he is delighted to detect nothing less than "a born-again Philip Roth whose entire outlook on the world had been inverted."[17] So why the change of heart? How had one of neoconservatism's foremost cultural critics—the author of *Breaking Ranks* (1983), one of the movement's definitive political memoirs—suddenly come to champion a figure whose earlier work comes close to embodying, by his own admission, everything he presumably felt the need to "break ranks" with? Is *American Pastoral*, as Podhoretz suggests, an ambiguous expression of *mea culpa*, that is, a repudiation of liberalism, a guarded neoconservative "breaking ranks" narrative? Or are there elements of continuity evident that enable it to be situated within a more conventionally liberal framework?

It will be my argument that Podhoretz is far too eager to attach a particular type of neoconservative agenda to *American Pastoral* and— despite the validity of some of his points—the argument as a whole fails to properly consider the full breadth and range of a novel that represents several contrasting positions on questions of American culture and politics. Before proceeding to this argument, however, it is worth pausing to note how such selective reading is also evident in Podhoretz's critique of *I Married a Communist*—a novel he admits to receiving with considerable disappointment. After the "delighted astonishment" with which *American Pastoral* is greeted, what is described as the subsequent novel's "reassuring declaration of solidarity with [Roth's] old comrades within the liberal establishment" obviously comes as an anticlimax. Explaining his reaction, Podhoretz claims that in this work Roth effectively

> signs a loyalty oath (as one might put it) to the old-time liberal religion from which he seemed to have defected in *American Pastoral.* And I mean old-time. Every liberal cliché about America at the height of the cold war is resurrected here—that its fear of the Soviet Union and its hostility to Communism were paranoid, that the Communists at home posed no threat worth taking seriously, and that the congressional investigations and the blacklists were cynical ploys aimed not at quashing communist influence but at discrediting liberals and Democrats.[18]

The somewhat anachronistic terminology in which the above criticisms are couched betrays the extent to which the neoconservative politics espoused by Podhoretz are deeply rooted in the anticommunism of the early 1950s. Even in 1998—almost fifty years after McCarthyism and nearly a decade after the collapse of the Soviet Union itself—Podhoretz is reaching for the "loyalty oath" metaphor (a strategy even he seems somewhat self-conscious in deploying—"as one might put it") and is still capable of imagining a "liberal establishment" whose cohorts regard each other as "comrades."

Examining some of the novel's features, one would think too that Murray Ringold's political journey in particular—given his feelings about the deterioration of Newark and the death of his wife—might strike a chord with a neoconservative critic. The isolated figure cut by Nathan Zuckerman at the very end of the story, furthermore, is closer to the jaundiced liberalism of Trilling's John Laskell (Trilling was one of Podhoretz's tutors at Columbia University in the 1950s and was, for a time at least, something of an intellectual model). It might also be added that the communist Johnny O'Day is surely the most disturbing character in the novel (although the right-wing Grants admittedly are not too far behind). Finally, Podhoretz might at least give some credence to the important historical point Roth makes here, namely, that "the iron pole of righteousness" (*IMAC*, 318) could be destructive and self-serving in the hands of communists such as Ira Ringold and Johnny O'Day as well as anticommunists such as Bryden and Katrina Grant.

Podhoretz's essay ends with the same strange combination of self-regard, condescension, and almost paternal forbearance with which it opened. The critic who originally "discovered" the artist as a young man—after an all-too-brief meeting of minds—is now disillusioned once more with the artist as an older man. "After all these years," he regrets, "and after a brief interlude in which I thought my troubles with Philip Roth had finally been resolved, I find myself disturbed by them yet again." Roth must, it is suggested in conclusion, "finally summon the courage to 'let go' altogether of the youthful habits of mind and spirit from which he seemed to be freeing himself for a while but which, on the evidence of *I Married a Communist*, are still putting up a strong fight."[19]

Podhoretz *is* accurate, nonetheless, in so far as he identifies the presence of a certain "*old-time* [my italics] liberal religion" in this work—but it is not one from which, as he goes on to suggest, "[Roth] defected from in

American Pastoral." One of the central flaws of Podhoretz's analysis lies in his failure to note the many *continuities* between these two texts—continuities crucial to those questions pertaining to the postwar liberal political tradition under consideration here. As a neoconservative, Podhoretz is too eager to uncover evidence of *discontinuity,* that is, of an author "breaking ranks" with liberalism, via the type of dramatic political self-questioning he himself once underwent.

While Roth in *American Pastoral* is merciless in his assault on certain forms of liberal compromise that came to the fore in the 1960s, he also gives significant expression to liberal values, many of which predate the confrontation between liberalism and the New Left during this era. These are, for the most part, in line with the "old-time liberal religion" Podhoretz condemns in his remarks on *I Married a Communist.* The figures through which this position finds expression in the respective novels are Murray Ringold and Lou Levov. Moreover, Lou Levov's son, the central figure in *American Pastoral,* Seymour "the Swede" Levov—whose quiet patriotism, commitment to the work ethic, and postethnic perspective Podhoretz would presumably admire—is himself the object of criticism as well as sympathy, particularly when interrogated by his outspoken brother Jerry.

American Pastoral portrays the rise and fall of a New Jersey Jewish family. Although the story commences with narrator Nathan Zuckerman's description of a mysterious encounter in 1985 with the Swede (named so for his light, distinctly non-Jewish features), it only begins to unfold properly after a high-school reunion dinner ten years later. Here Zuckerman meets his old school friend Jerry, the Swede's younger brother, and learns of the tragic events of the Swede's life. In his vivid recollection of his boyhood hero, the blond-haired Jew who effortlessly embodies ambitious, energetic, American manhood via his athletic, military, and business success, and the subsequent delineation of his ultimate downfall, Zuckerman imbues the Swede with the tragic, mythic status of Fitzgerald's Jay Gatsby. Roth's character, moreover, also simultaneously shares and extends Gatsby's symbolic historical significance by representing an assault on ethnic in addition to class barriers to the pursuit of happiness. The Swede, he notes, was

> the boy we were all going to follow into America, our point man into the next immersion, at home here the way the Wasps were at home here, an American not by sheer striving, not by being a Jew who invents a famous

vaccine or a Jew on the Supreme Court, not by being the most brilliant or the most eminent or the best. Instead—by virtue of his isomorphism to the Wasp world—he does it the ordinary way, the natural way, the American-guy way.

(AP, 89)

The Swede personifies a very specific, powerful, and predominant notion of American virtue. He represents the goodness, responsibility, and hard work inherent in the wholesome postimmigrant dream of the Eisenhower era. Unlike his father and immigrant grandfather, the Swede has never had to work in tannery sweatshops but, notwithstanding this, is fully cognizant of the drive and sacrifice required so that his forebears might bequeath a Levov-owned glove factory to him as his own American inheritance. The passages describing both the skill of the traditional glovemaker and the immense physical and mental exertion required to harness these skills to the demands of mass production are as intricate and powerful as any in the novel.

Yet such feelings toward previous generations are tempered by a sense of alienation. Men like Lou Levov, the Swede's father, Zuckerman recalls in this vein, were "limited men with limitless energy." They are energetic capitalists but not parasites, driven by pride rather than naked materialism, men whose intimate acquaintance with poverty, hardship, and the excesses of the free market during the Depression made of them lifelong New Deal liberals. This was the generation who embraced an American work ethic by means of a new sense of social justice that served to redefine the meaning of liberalism in the Roosevelt era. The sense of distance between such men as Lou Levov and their Americanized white-collar, professional, and college-educated sons is apparent when Zuckerman writes that Lou was of a generation

for whom everything is an unshakeable duty, for whom there is a right way and a wrong way and nothing in between … whose compound of ambitions, biases and beliefs is so unruffled by careful thinking that he isn't as easy to escape from as he seems … for whom the most serious thing in life was *to keep going despite everything*. And we were their sons. It was our job to love them.

(AP, 11)

As is the case in *I Married a Communist,* the role played and influence exerted by the father figure generates troubling questions. Early on, for example, we are told of the Swede that "nothing permeated more of his life than his father's expectations" (*AP*, 38). Later, the Swede is forced to acknowledge this "problem of the father," that is, the problem "of maintaining filial love against the onslaught of an unrelenting father" (*AP*, 361). Once more, this does not represent purely personal, emotional bonds and tensions but is also intimately connected with the sense of cultural belonging and political allegiance that the Swede is born into. The Swede's understanding of his own national identity, for instance, is defined to a notable extent alongside that of his father's. Their respective ideas of what it means to be an American are shown as both a basis for a shared set of values and yet also sources of ideological tension and cleavage. In this respect, the fact that the Swede has been "bequeathed" an "American nickname" is regarded as significant, setting him apart from those Levovs that preceded him in America: "He carried [the nickname] with him like an invisible passport, all the while wandering deeper and deeper into an American's life, forthrightly evolving into a large, smooth, optimistic American such as his conspicuously raw forebears—including the obstinate father whose American claim was not inconsiderable—couldn't have dreamed of as one of their own" (*AP*, 207–208).

In political terms, a symbolic moment arrives during a visit to Hyde Park, New York, when the Swede is on leave from the Marines. Here, "stand[ing] together as a family looking at FDR's grave ... [the Swede] silent, proudly wearing his new summer uniform," it is now clear that "something meaningful was happening" (*AP*, 208). The liberalism of Roosevelt and the New Deal are, then, signposted as the key political reference points for the Levovs and World War II, the defining historical event. That World War II should provide such an important backdrop is not simply a product of the Swede's decision to join the Marines or, for that matter, the fact that the Levovs are Jews; it is, rather, viewed as both the occasion of and catalyst for an unprecedented period of national unity and an emergent sense of transethnic solidarity.

While serving in the military, the Swede for the first time meets and ultimately comes to share a camaraderie and sense of purpose with men raised on Texas farms and others from Italian, Irish, Polish, and Slovak backgrounds. Moreover, the immediate postwar climate in which the Swede reaches adult maturity is seen to enlarge this process of collective reinvention. Zuckerman, a few years younger than the Swede, recalls: "Our class started high school six months after the unconditional surrender of the Japanese, during the greatest moment of collective inebriation in American history. And the upsurge of energy was contagious. ... The Depression had disappeared. Everything was in motion. The lid was off. Americans were to start over again, en masse, everyone in it together" (*AP*, 40). This mood permeates the novel's first section, entitled "Paradise Remembered." Interestingly, the Jewish neighborhood of the immediate postwar period is then compared to an earlier society similarly prone to moments of republican "rebirth." "Am I wrong," asks Zuckerman, "to think we delighted in living there? No delusions are more familiar than those inspired in the elderly by nostalgia, but am I completely mistaken to think that living as well-born children in Renaissance Florence could not have held a candle to growing up within aromatic range of Tabachnik's pickle barrels?" (*AP*, 42). "Paradise Remembered" ends ominously, however, after we learn of how the Swede's life is thrown into disarray by his daughter, Meredith "Merry" Levov, whose mounting alienation from her family and the values they represent culminates, finally, in a decision to "bring the [Vietnam] war home to America" by bombing the local post office in February 1968, an act that results in the death of a local doctor.

The middle section of the novel, "The Fall," provides greater context for the political gulf between father and daughter but also documents the Swede's drift from the political and moral views held by his own father. We learn that while dutifully rejecting a professional baseball career to take over the Newark Maid glove factory, the Swede nonetheless confounds other expectations. Most prominent among these is his rejection of the middle-class suburban life of upwardly mobile Jewish Americans advocated by his father in favor of the greater freedom the Swede imagines an alternative "non-hyphenated" America can bestow. This is made clear, for example, in his decision to marry the Irish American Catholic Dawn Dwyer, a former Miss New Jersey, with similar assimilationist aspirations. Zuckerman's earlier image of the Swede as a *parvenu* Moses leading the Jews into an American Israel is further accentuated along these lines with the young Levovs' purchase of a stone house in Old Rimrock, situated in the heart of rural and affluent WASP New Jersey.

"The Fall" also deals with the aftermath of the bombing, beginning with the appearance of Rita Cohen, a political radical who claims to be able to put the Swede in touch with his daughter, who is now on the run.

Subsequently, he discovers Merry living in a poor inner-city area of Newark, adhering to a rigidly antimaterialistic religious faith that forbids her from harming any living being. Indeed, from this point in the novel, with the onset of the latter half of the 1960s, Newark, New Jersey, is itself regarded as a symbol of postlapsarian, liberal crisis and can be read as providing a deeper, historical context for Murray Ringold's vivid description of the urban blight of late twentieth-century Newark in the closing pages of *I Married a Communist.* In *American Pastoral,* the urban "battlefields" engendered by the Newark riots of July 1967 are constructed as a domestic counterpoint to those in Southeast Asia. This, of course, is very much in line with the growing unease among liberal intellectuals by this time that the war—as a result of its enormous expense as much as moral factors—was undermining progressive reform projects at home.[20]

The Swede's inner-city factory—staffed with mostly local black residents—comes under siege, but after the riots and to the immense frustration of his father, he refuses to relocate. The Swede's father's anger—again, like Murray Ringold's anger at the continued decline of Newark—is racially charged and rooted in a sense of not only personal but political betrayal. Lou Levov is a liberal committed to racial equality and, more generally, the idea of the state as a facilitator of education, social mobility, and, ultimately, self-reliance. Rapacious manufacturers and shortsighted unions, in his view, are held equally responsible for Newark's ills. As a supporter of the New Deal order in its most recent manifestations—Johnson's civil-rights legislation and Great Society program—Lou Levov, too, like Murray, feels that he's been betrayed or "had," claiming that

> they took this city and now they are going to take that business and everything that I built up a day at a time, an *inch* at a time, and they are going to leave it *all* in ruins! And that'll do 'em a world of good! They burn down their own houses—that'll show whitey! ... Oh that'll do wonders for a man's black pride—a totally ruined city to live in! ... And *I* hired 'em! How's that for a laugh! *I hired 'em!*
>
> (*AP,* 163–164)

The quest for full racial equality in the 1960s played a major role, of course, in the redefinition of American liberalism during this time and, by the end of the decade, was equally a central focus of the emergent neoconservative critique of this transformation. In 1963, Norman Pod-horetz published a hugely controversial essay that in many ways set the agenda for white, liberal discussions of the race question in the years that followed. "My Negro Problem—and Ours," published in 1963 in *Commentary*, hit a nerve within Northern liberal intellectual circles by identifying a slippage—within Podhoretz's (then still liberal) worldview as well as that of his peers—between politics and experience. Like Lou Levov and Murray Ringold, Podhoretz saw himself as atypical in so far as he was a liberal who had had personal contact with blacks. By contrast, he claims, "everywhere we look today ... we find the curious phenomenon of white middle-class liberals with no previous personal experience of Negroes—people to whom Negroes have always been faceless in virtue rather than faceless in vice—discovering that their abstract commitment to the cause of Negro rights will not stand the test of a direct confrontation."[21]

Podhoretz in this piece also points to what he regards as the many broader consequences of such liberal bad faith, which include white residents' abandonment of inner cities and public schools, opposition to redistricting, and the annexation of suburbs (thereby weakening city tax bases). These are, ironically, developments later liberal historians would draw attention to in accounts of the Newark crisis.[22] For neoconservatives, on the other hand, the relationship of such phenomena to problems of urban decline and racial inequality would be understood as symptomatic rather than causal. The Swede, however, in this respect, is hardly as selfless, by comparison with his father, as he might appear. Pressured, generationally speaking, from "above" by the hard-headed liberalism of a father desperate to preserve the family business, the Swede is equally pressured from "below," so to speak, by the New Left radicalism of his daughter:

> Whatever it cost him to deny his father relief from his suffering, stubbornly to deny the truth of what his father was saying, the Swede could not submit to the old man's arguments, for the simple reason that if Merry were to learn ... that Newark Maid had fled the Central Avenue factory she would be all too delighted to think, "He did it! He's as rotten as the rest! My own father! Everything justified by the profit principle! Everything! Newark's just a black colony for my own father. Exploit it and exploit it and, when there's trouble, fuck it!"

(AP, 165)

Merry Levov, of course, bears comparison with a number of characters encountered in earlier chapters. Like Gifford Maxim in Trilling's *The Middle of the Journey*, Merry is depicted as in thrall to a series of obsessions and beliefs or "improbable dream[s] of purification" (*AP*, 95). As a child, her attention shifts from Catholicism to an infatuation with Audrey Hepburn; as a young adult, the same type of "perfectionism" that underwrites John Brown's militant antislavery and personal asceticism leads her, in a similar manner, to political violence and then on to "Jainism." Indeed, in a remarkable fantasy sequence in which the Swede prays to black militant Angela Davis for his daughter's safe return, the latter analogy is made explicit. Here, in communion with "St. Angela," the Swede is told that "the disobedience of oppressive laws ... including violent disobedience, goes back to abolitionism—his daughter is one with John Brown!" (*AP*, 160). Drawing on the same religious vocabulary Trilling makes use of in his novel, Roth also has the radical Rita Cohen remark of Merry: "We can only stand as witnesses to the anguish that sanctifies her" (*AP*, 176).

The idea of a "sanctifying anguish" equally recalls *Billy Budd*—in fact it is not too much to say that Rita Cohen's above characterization might itself have been pulled from the final execution scene in Melville's story. Like Billy Budd, Merry is afflicted with a stammer that frustrates communication and is seen to predispose her to violence. She shares with Budd and John Brown a "radical innocence" and sense of virtue that ultimately proves destructive. Melville's Billy Budd and Banks's John Brown, however, are far more ambiguous characters whose actions cannot be interpreted simply in terms of psychopathology. As Robert Boyers has noted in one of the few dissenting reviews amid the effusive critical praise heaped on *American Pastoral*, in this way, Roth "sets up as representative figures of disorder and 'reality' persons who are mad and whose attachment to disorder is so pathological that they make it impossible for us to consider seriously the actual sources of discontent in American society."[23]

This is a fair criticism in so far as it goes. The "pathology" of the New Left as configured in *American Pastoral* certainly serves to misrepresent a diverse movement that incorporated many democratic elements. Such a relatively constricted and reductionist depiction of sixties radicalism also, no doubt, explains the novel's appeal to a neoconservative critic such as Podhoretz. If, however, we focus primarily on the central figure of the Swede, we find that the mainstream values of bourgeois liberalism and the affluent society of midcentury America do not go unchallenged. The association of the

Swede with the concept of the "pastoral" is at the very heart of the novel's political and moral concerns. Within the American context, furthermore, this idea of the pastoral is intimately connected with the nation's political foundations in Lockean liberalism. It is to this relationship, then, that we need to turn, in order to make full sense of the essentially political basis of the powerful criticisms leveled at the Swede by other characters in *American Pastoral.*

The narrative structure of *American Pastoral* previously alluded to is important in this respect, as it immediately establishes a loaded literary as well as political-historical context against which the meaning of the Swede's story might be deciphered. The text to return to here is *Paradise Lost* rather than its Old Testament source material. Like John Milton's epic poem, Roth's novel deploys the pastoral in order to evoke a *secular* vision of Eden and a fall from innocence that must be attributed to the intrusion of History. The United States—as the work of the "myth" critics previously referred to demonstrates—offers a particularly pertinent modern context for the reenactment of the Fall myth. The crucial connections between this defining cultural characteristic and a specific tradition of political philosophy, however, as already discussed, remain largely unexamined.

The prominence of the philosophy of John Locke within America's dominant liberal political tradition, in this respect, is worth attending to. For Locke, the economy and not the polity, nature and not the public sphere (or the *agon* of classical politics) is the arena of freedom. Consequently, as Vidal traces in the pages of *Burr*, the modern age demanded a new political philosophy—liberalism—which acknowledges this "natural law." When Locke comments that "in the beginning all the world was America" in his *Second Treatise on Government*, he is, as John Diggins has observed, "implying that liberal man was born of his primal encounter with nature." Such primal encounters form the backbone of the classic American literary canon, where political freedom is conceived of in terms of man's ability to master the natural environment. This mastery affords a distance from the state and the political realm by carving out a zone untouched by History or what Diggins breaks down into "time, custom and Old World memory."[24]

The idea of such a flight from history is a crucial component of what we might better understand—following William Empson, Leo Marx, and Lawrence Buell—in terms of the pastoral mode as (liberal) ideology.[25] In Roth's novel, the idea of the pastoral as ahistorical informs the reader's perception of the hero's plight. The Swede has geared his whole life toward the evasion of conflict and, accordingly, acquired no understanding of the political, no inclination of the storm clouds gathering to sweep History into his carefully demarcated world. The family home in Old Rimrock, in this way, provides the novel with its Garden of Eden, that is, a primary pastoral context within which the tragic dimensions of this intrusion might be fully gauged. "How had the Swede," in this sense, writes Zuckerman,

> come to be history's plaything? History, American history, the stuff you read about in books and study in school, had made its way out to tranquil, untrafficked Old Rimrock, New Jersey, to countryside where it had not put in an appearance that was notable since Washington's army wintered in the highlands adjacent to Morristown. History which had made no drastic impingement on the daily life of the local populace since the Revolutionary War, wended its way back out to these cloistered hills and, improbably, with all its predictable unforeseeness, broke helter-skelter into the household of the Seymour Levovs and left the place in a shambles.
>
> *(AP, 87)*

The Swede's own retreat from the political—tied as it is to Old Rimrock's status in the novel as refuge from History—is also made more explicit on occasions. This is evident, as we have already seen, in his reasons for refusing to close the Newark Maid factory, but it also manifests itself in other ways. A decision to join a political group, New Jersey Businessmen Against the War, for example, is motivated by anxieties surrounding his own deteriorating relationship with his daughter rather than any major misgivings about the war itself: "The Swede had never belonged to a political group before and would not have joined this one and volunteered for the steering committee and paid a thousand dollars toward their protest ad in the *Newark News* had he not hoped that his conspicuous involvement might deflect a little of her anger away from him" (*AP*, 100).

It is, appropriately enough, at the end of "The Fall" section of the novel where the full ramifications of the Swede's Lockean preoccupation with the private sphere and the "economy" at the expense of ever-impinging political and social currents is made manifest. This emerges after the Swede discovers that not only were later acts of political violence on Merry's part responsible for three additional killings but that she herself, in subsequent years, has been raped twice while in hiding in inner-city Newark. It is only now, on turning to his brother Jerry for advice, having failed to persuade his daughter to leave an infested slum, that the Swede must confront the full range of his own limitations and the extent of his "fall" into what, else-where in the novel, is described in terms of "the fury, the violence and the desperation of the counter-pastoral ... the indigenous American berserk" (*AP*, 86).

Jerry is relentless in his criticism. He begins by castigating his brother for refusing to take Merry away from Newark against her will, viewing this as merely another manifestation of the Swede's capacity for "acces-sion," his inability to make difficult choices that disrupt "appearances." This ultimately explains the "unrevealed" nature of the Swede's character, which eludes the type of sharp definition that, for Jerry, can only emerge as a result of directly confronting the realities of personal and/or politi-cal conflict. This too, Jerry adds, has a deleterious moral effect on those around the Swede by prompting in them either frustrated, implacable opposition or the type of compromise premised less on mutual respect than on an overly refined sense of propriety. Hence, in Jerry's view, the Swede's "choice," for example, to marry an Irish Catholic against his father's initial wishes, should be seen as no such thing.

> If Dad had said, "Look, you'll never get my approval for this, never, I am not having grandchildren half this and half that," then you would have had to make a choice. But you *never* had to make a choice. *Never*. Because he let you slide through. Everybody has always let you slide through. And that is why, to this day, nobody knows who you are. You are unrevealed—that is the story Seymour, *unrevealed*. That is why your own daughter decided to blow you away. You are never straight about anything and she hated you for it. You keep yourself a secret. You don't choose *ever*.
>
> (*AP*, 276)

If such indecision leads to a kind of ethical paralysis, it also engenders a lack of self-knowledge. This is itself, Jerry goes on to suggest, a prod-uct of a fundamentally "false image" of those social and economic rela-tions within which that self must be situated. The Swede is imprisoned by the WASP illusion of pastoral family life; his identity and, in Lockean terms, his understanding of "freedom" is determined by the narrowly circumscribed economy of glove making. "You have no *idea* what this country is," his younger brother reminds him, "all you know is what a fucking glove is" (*AP*, 276). Yet it is in this respect, Jerry notes, that is, to the extent that the world of glove making itself constitutes a lost, pastoral order, that the Swede most resembles his father: "you're still in your old man's dream-world, Seymour, still up there with Lou Levov in glove heaven. A household tyrannized by gloves. ... Oh where oh where is that outmoded America, that decorous America where a woman had twenty five pairs of gloves?" (*AP*, 277).

Yet, ironically, it might equally be said that Jerry's somewhat unforgiving, overassertive outbursts along with his undoubtedly inflated sense of self-worth also make him resemble no one so much as his father, Lou Levov. Both, in their own ways, are proponents of a "strong" liberalism that champions a morally premised commitment to "intervention." The aggressive liberal individualism of the son, with its minoritarian emphasis on the "rights" of the self or "minority," here overlaps with the robust New Deal liberalism of the father, with its majoritarian emphasis on the broader "rights" of society as a whole or the "majority." It is precisely this overlap, it might be said, that has ensured that they have remained at loggerheads. Such disagreements range from that which his mother recalls concluding with a fifteen-year-old Jerry "scream[ing] ... at his own father, his 'rights,' his 'rights'" to later furious rows connected with Lou's interference in his younger son's divorce arrangements.

It is also this "strong" liberalism that serves to differentiate them from the Swede, whose "weak" liberalism, by ultimately positing no more than a politics of disengagement, thereby generates a moral vacuum. Both the Swede's brother and father criticize him, in this respect, for what they regard as his naive embrace of the American pastoral. "Out there playing at being Wasps," Jerry exclaims, "a little Mick girl from the Elizabeth docks and a Jewboy from Weequahic High. The cows. Cow society. Colonial old America. And you thought all that façade was going to come without cost. Genteel and innocent. *But that costs, too, Seymour. I* would have thrown a bomb. *I* would become a Jain and live in Newark" (*AP*, 280).

Lou Levov's objections, meanwhile, while similarly suspicious of the dominant WASP culture, can be situated within a historical context that even more forcefully undermines the Swede's attachment to the idea of Old Rimrock as a depoliticized pastoral idyll. "You're dreaming. I wonder if you even know where this is," Lou asks the Swede. "The Klan thrived out here in the twenties. … This is rock-ribbed republican New Jersey, Seymour … this place was Republican when Roosevelt was *living*. Republican during the New Deal. Think about that." When his son suggests that this was merely party political (Republicans disliked FDR "because he was a Democrat"), Lou is quick to remind him of the less consensual cultural context within which New Deal values were once sharply contested: "No, they didn't like him because they didn't like the Jews and the Italians and the Irish—that's why they moved out here to begin with. They didn't like Roosevelt because he accommodated himself to these new Americans. He understood what they needed and he tried to help them. But not these bastards. They wouldn't give a Jew the time of day" (*AP*, 309).

Needless to say, both Lou and Jerry Levov believe that the Swede has completely mishandled the situation with his daughter. For his closest male relatives, the Swede has come to occupy the type of moral no-man's land many neoconservatives would later identify as the defining feature of midcentury liberalism. This is the "devitalized" center of post-Vietnam American politics. "Refusing to give offence," Jerry says, "Blaming yourself. Tolerant respect for every position. Sure, it's 'liberal'—I know, a liberal father. But what does that mean? What is at the *center* of it? Always holding things together. And look where the fuck it's got you!" (*AP*, 279).

It might be surmised then, at this point, that such characters represent a certain "distancing" from mainstream liberalism insofar as it can be said to find expression in the Swede's position. Yet before identifying such "distancing" too explicitly with neoconservative political values, it is perhaps instructive, once more, to note another example of the type of continuity overlooked by Norman Podhoretz in his analysis of Roth's novels. The final section of *American Pastoral*, "Paradise Lost," which immediately follows Jerry's tirade, begins in the summer of the Watergate hearings, the recorded proceedings of which the Levovs tune into on television each evening. During this period, Lou Levov's preoccupation with the corrupt Nixon administration verges on the obsessive. This involves the writing of numerous letters to various figures who rose to prominence over the course of the Watergate scandal.

The Swede is here reminded of those occasions during the previous decade when his father would send Merry copies of the letters he mailed to Lyndon Johnson voicing his opposition to the war in Vietnam. Lou Levov would attempt to present such acts as an alternative avenue of democratic opposition to the war to a granddaughter whose political views he believed were becoming "out of control." Moreover, some of the more extreme views of the New Left—such as Merry's facile equation of American foreign policy with fascism—are undermined by her grandfather's invocation of his own historical experience as a liberal during the New Deal and McCarthy eras. A recent past that was regarded by the New Left generation as at best remote and at worst irrelevant—incorporating Father Coughlin ("that son of a bitch"), the Dies committee ("isolationist, bigoted, know-nothing fascists"), and Roy Cohn ("A disgrace. A *Jew* and a disgrace") (*AP*, 289)—is here recalled by Lou Levov in order to revive those historical moments when the notion of "homegrown" U.S. fascism was perhaps more tenable.

Unlike the Swede, then, Lou Levov is only too willing to challenge Merry's views. This is yet another instance of the disparity between the forms of liberalism Lou and his elder son might be said to represent. For the Swede, Merry is not to be argued with or confronted but only to be "left alone," her radicalization and increasingly unstable behavior dismissed as a "phase," but for Lou, the imperative of assuming personal responsibility for a member of his family is the overriding factor: "No, I will *not* leave her alone. This is my granddaughter. I *refuse* to leave her alone. I refuse to lose a granddaughter by leaving her alone" (*AP*, 291).

This, of course, echoes the later frustration and anger directed at the Swede by Jerry for his refusal to take Merry out of Newark by force. Indeed, the strength of Lou Levov's views, views that underwrite his disdain for passivity—in the realm of the political as well as the personal—come to the fore as a consequence of the Watergate scandal. The Swede is unable to comprehend passion of any description in such a context. "It is as though," he reflects of his father, "in his uncensored hatred of Nixon, Lou Levov is merely mimicking his granddaughter's vituperous loathing of LBJ" (*AP*, 299). But Lou's contempt for Nixon in *American Pastoral* is rooted in the historical experience of McCarthyism. For Lou Levov, Nixon will always be the "Tricky Dicky" he became in the aftermath of his initial rise to national prominence as the young congressman instrumental in securing the conviction for perjury of Alger Hiss. In the immediate years after this, Nixon rode the wave of McCarthyism all the way to the vice presidency, his electoral strategy based primarily on the dissemination of anti-communist innuendo at various Democratic opponents.[26]

Nixon's victory in the 1968 presidential election was premised on an ostensibly broad appeal to a "silent majority" alienated not only by New

Left radicalism but, more generally, by the way in which values such as self-reliance, the work ethic, and the cult of the American "self-made man" had been undermined by a New Deal order that had outlived its usefulness. It was, as one historian has asserted, Nixon's "career-long populist conservatism [that] rhetorically associated government activism with an effete, out-of-touch, and profligate Democratic party" that provided "a formula for future republican triumphs."[27] More than any other figure, it was Richard Nixon who capitalized on the "devitalized" center ground explored in *American Pastoral.*

However, as Garry Wills describes in *Nixon Agonistes: The Crisis of the Self-Made Man* (1970), the principles to which Richard Nixon himself was committed belonged to a pre–New Deal consensus that united figures such as Herbert Hoover and Woodrow Wilson. These were the principles of "classical liberalism" and "market competition" first established in the early national period and consolidated in the decades following the Civil War. As Wills notes in an introduction to a new edition of his study: "These were far from what people were calling liberalism by the 1960s—big government, compassion for the poor, tolerance of dissent. [Nixon] was not a liberal in that sense. His liberalism was that of the Social Darwinians, and he was as dated as those obsolete specimens."[28]

Thus Wills recognizes in Nixon a symptom (rather than spokesperson) of the "weak" liberalism the Swede might be said to represent in *American Pastoral.* This liberalism of "self-deceptions," Wills identified at the time, has "an air of pusillanimity about it, of flight from pursuing truths. It refuses to take uncomfortable realities into account, whether these be in the realm of social theory, of political fact or of psychological challenge. Its symbol is Nixon's refusal even to deal with blacks or dissident students, as if the 'silent majority' were the whole of society."[29] The Swede too, we might add, notwithstanding his less reactionary politics, refuses to "deal" with such elements in any meaningful way. As Wills claims elsewhere in *Nixon Agonistes,* it was precisely this disengagement from "uncomfortable realities" that ensured that a great degree of New Left ire was directed at supposedly liberal institutions such as the media and the academy.

This same "crisis of the self-made man" that helps explain Nixon's electoral triumphs also goes some way in accounting for the rapid coalescence of neoconservative thought during roughly the same period. However, although there were deeply troubled New Deal liberals who—anticipating the neoconservative turn in American political culture—would opt for Nixon over McGovern by 1972, there were many more for whom he and the Republican Party remained and would continue to remain anathema.[30] From the evidence of *American Pastoral* and *I Married a Communist*, it can be said that figures such as Lou Levov and Murray Ringold might safely be included in this category. For such types, Nixon stands for nothing less than the betrayal of the modern American promise—a tyrant, like all tyrants, disguised as a "patriot," whose crimes, like those of Aaron Burr, came close to destroying the republic.

Watergate, in particular, in both novels, serves as a defining moment in postwar political life—the juncture when liberalism itself stood on the verge of collapse. "These so-called patriots," Lou Levov exclaims during the hearings, "would take this country and make Nazi Germany out of it. ... These people have taken us to the edge of something terrible" (*AP*, 287). Such anti-Nixon, republican invective reaches its zenith, however, in the elderly Murray Ringold's remarks to Nathan Zuckerman concerning the collective amnesia surrounding Nixon's funeral in 1994. This is occasioned by his recollection of spotting his brother Ira's old McCarthyite antagonist, Katrina Van Tassel Grant, on television, among the mourners. In his description of Grant as "*the* Republican hostess of Washington" during the Eisenhower years, Murray draws a parallel with the decadent years of imperial Rome:

> In the hierarchical anxieties of the Washington dinner party, Katrina's capacity for rivalry, the sheer cannibal vigor of her taste for supremacy—for awarding and depriving the ruling class of their just desserts—found its ... imperium, I think the word would be. That woman drew up an invitation list with the autocratic sadism of Caligula ... [and] straddled Washington society like fear itself.
>
> (*IMAC*, 276)

As a congressman, moreover, Bryden Grant, we learn, had Richard Nixon for a "mentor." "Nixon had Alger Hiss, Grant had Iron Rinn," Murray recalls of their simultaneous rise to prominence. Indeed, the career of Bryden Grant stands alongside that of Richard Nixon as a metaphor for the *continuity* of those reactionary, illiberal elements as well as the corrupt moral ambition of American political culture between the 1950s and 1970s. Ultimately, "[Bryden] too was capsized by Watergate. Threw his lot in with Nixon and, in the face of all the evidence against his leader, defended him on the floor of the House right down to the morning of the resignation. That's what got him defeated in '74. But then he'd been emulating Nixon from the start" (*IMAC*, 276–277).

Nixon's funeral itself Murray finds "barely endurable." The ceremony's hollow patriotic rituals testify to a flattening of historical consciousness as "that most rousing of all those drugs that make everybody forget everything, the national narcotic, 'The Star Spangled Banner'" is joined to "the elevating remarks of Billy Graham, a flag-draped casket, and a team of interracial pallbearing servicemen." All this is designed "to induce catalepsy in the multitude." As if this is not enough, Murray finds that, for the eulogies, "the realists take command, the connoisseurs of deal-making and deal-breaking, masters of the most shameless ways of undoing an opponent, those for whom moral concerns must always come last, uttering all the well-known, unreal, sham-ridden cant about everything but the dead man's real passions" (*IMAC*, 278).

Surveying the audience listening to such speakers as "New Democrat" Bill Clinton ("under the spell of his own sincerity") and Henry Kissinger ("the court Jew ... high minded, profound, speaking in his most puffed-up unegoistical mode"), Murray locates a rogues' gallery of Watergate and post-Watergate corruption and ineptitude. As well as Katrina Van Tassel Grant there is Gerald Ford ("charged with intelligence"), Ronald Reagan ("his famous salute ... *always* half meshugeh"), the "Iran-Contra arms dealer" Adnan Khashoggi, the "burglar" G. Gordon Liddy, Spiro Agnew (that "most disgraced of vice-presidents"), and Dan Quayle ("lucid as a button") (*IMAC*, 279). Murray's final analysis, as one might expect, is scathing. The sense of despair registered both here and elsewhere by Murray in the novel would seem to intimate the terminal decline of the postwar liberal tradition, which, for the best part of three decades, effectively defined itself in opposition to Richard Nixon. The presence here of several of that tradition's other Watergate-era antagonists is merely an effort to perform "the Final Cover-Up":

All of them mourning platitudinously together in the California sunshine and the lovely breeze: the indicted and the unindicted, the convicted and the unconvicted, and, his towering intellect at last at rest in a star-spangled coffin, no longer grappling for no-holds-barred power, the man who turned a whole country's morale inside out, the generator of an enormous national disaster, the first and only president of the United States of America to have gained from a handpicked successor a full and unconditional pardon for all the breaking and entering he did while in office.

(IMAC, 279)

The final section of *American Pastoral,* entitled "Paradise Lost," takes the form of an extended account of a dinner party held by the Swede and his wife during the summer of the Watergate hearings. Among several topics of conversation are the candidacy of George McGovern in the 1972 presidential election and the recent movie *Deep Throat*—the first pornographic film to find mainstream commercial success. Roth here maps out both the major party political divisions as well as the origins of the "culture wars" that would help define the national conversation in the United States in the final quarter of the twentieth century.

George McGovern, as a result of embracing policies that appealed to many among New Left as well as more traditional Democratic party constituencies, remains the most left-wing candidate to win the party presidential nomination since World War II. Indeed, the particularly vituperative rhetoric McGovern directed at his incumbent opponent, Richard Nixon—comparing, for example, Nixon and his administration to Hitler and Nazi Germany respectively in the 1972 campaign—helped demonstrate McGovern's "radical" credentials. If Nixon, by this point—after events such as the Kent State killings and the bombing of Cambodia—had surpassed Johnson in the New Left pantheon of American "fascism," such analogies also resonated with older liberals such as Lou Levov, who recalled the accusations of anti-Semitism that attended the young Nixon's congressional and senatorial campaigns. Prominent too among liberals who came of age in the 1950s were images of Nixon as the respectable face of far-right conservatism or, in Irving Howe's memorable description, as "a well oiled drawbridge between McCarthyite barbarism and Eisenhower respectability."[31]

The early conversation at the dinner party begins with an effort to link the popularity of *Deep Throat* with the broader political climate. Guests are divided over the issue of whether the film's audience consists of Nixon/Agnew voters "hypocritically pretending to deep moral piety" or, by contrast, "McGovernites" such as themselves, most of whom have seen the film and are influenced to varying degrees by the values of the libertarian sexual politics of the counterculture. It is at this point that Lou Levov intervenes to point out that he is one McGovern supporter who finds the values of the film deeply objectionable. "What these two things have got to do with each other," he exclaims, "is a mystery to me" (*AP*, 344). Later, elaborating on this view, Lou combines a number of his prior political refrains in order to disavow any connection between the liberalism articulated by McGovern and the relaxation of broader cultural norms:

> What does McGovern have to do with that lousy movie? I voted for McGovern. I campaigned in the whole condominium for McGovern. You should hear what I put up with from Jewish people, how Nixon was this for Israel and that for Israel, and I reminded them, in case they forgot, that Harry Truman had him pegged for Tricky Dicky back in 1948, and now look, the reward they're reaping, my good friends who voted for Mr. Von Nixon and his storm troopers. Let me tell you who goes to those movies: riffraff, bums, and kids without adult supervision. Why my son takes his lovely wife to such a movie is something I'll go to my grave not understanding.
>
> (*AP*, 350)

It is here, in the final chapters of *American Pastoral*, that Roth begins to introduce issues of cultural politics first placed on the agenda by the New Left but cultivated and refined, mainly in the academy and sections of the media, by what later became designated the "cultural left." Important among these are the kind of questions pertaining to sexual politics, gender roles, and censorship raised by a phenomenon such as *Deep Throat*. For Lou Levov, the subversion of previously stable cultural values is yet another indicator of broader sociopolitical crisis. More specifically, the "lack of feeling for individuals that a person sees in that movie" as well as "the lack of feeling for places like what is going on in Newark" are both representative of social atomization on a massive scale. Without feeling some connection, however tenuous, to family, community, or country, he claims, "you are just out there on your own." The scale of historical rupture is immense for someone of Lou's background and values: "I sometimes think that more has changed since 1945 than in all the years of history there have been" (*AP*, 365).

Most prominent among Lou's interlocutors at the dinner table is Marcia Umanoff, a New York–based literature professor and the wife of an old school friend of the Swede's. She is described as a "militant nonconformist of staggering self-certainty much given to sarcasm and calculatedly apocalyptic pronouncements designed to bring discomfort to the lords of the earth" (*AP*, 339). Marcia stands, among other things, for the increasing relativism of the times, rejecting, via provocative analogy, Lou Levov's contempt for the new mainstream culture (she refuses to accept any distinction, for instance, between Linda Lovelace's appearance in *Deep Throat* and the young Dawn Dwyers's participation in the Miss America pageant).

For Marcia, moreover, the personal is not only political but the political itself must never be reined in by merely "personal" considerations. Nothing, for example, least of all conventional notions of "civility" and "sensitivity," can prevent her from repeatedly proclaiming the virtue of the North Vietnamese. "She never for a moment compromised her political convictions or her compassionate comprehension of international affairs," the Swede reflects, "not even when she saw from six inches away the misery that had befallen her husband's oldest friend" (*AP*, 342). It is clear that Marcia's self-righteous posturing here signposts the marginalization of the American Left by the mid-1970s—a process that would ultimately confine the type of left-liberal politics associated with George McGovern to universities and a few media outlets by the 1980s. Marcia Umanoff is, finally, characterized by the emptiness of her "talk ... senseless, ostentatious talk, words with the sole purpose of scandalously exhibiting themselves, uncompromising, quarrelsome words expressing little more than [her] intellectual vanity and the odd belief that all her posturing added up to an independent mind" (*AP*, 343). This, as we shall see, is a critique that will find expression in a later historical context in *The Human Stain*.

The notions of promiscuity and permissiveness that circulate within the group's discussion of *Deep Throat* and, by extension, the "mainstreaming" of the counterculture by the 1970s, however, also go no small way toward characterizing the relationships between the guests. We learn, for example, of an extramarital affair between the Swede and a friend's wife, Sheila Salzman. Notwithstanding this, Sheila, with her husband Shelly, has continued to conceal from the Swede the fact that it was the Salzmans who sheltered his daughter in the immediate aftermath of the bomb attack. Most dramatically, perhaps, the Swede discovers during the dinner party itself that his wife has been having a relationship with a neighbor, William Orcutt, a scion of the local WASP community, in order, he imagines, to "rid [herself] of the stain of our child, the stain on her credentials ... the stain of the destruction of the store." This, itself, he speculates, must be a desperate attempt to "resume the uncontaminated life" (*AP*, 385).

As narrator of the three novels, Nathan Zuckerman has come to represent the prominent yet politically problematic role of the pastoral in the United States, with its timeless, utopian promise of "uncontaminated life." Zuckerman the writer, enfolded away in pastoral isolation, is free from any obligations to "society" yet also at moments troubled by the wider implications of his own retreat. *The Human Stain*, of course, betrays such preoccupations with overtones of "contamination" and "purity" in its very title. Indeed, Zuckerman foregrounds a broader context for such themes at the very beginning of his narrative with a forthright piece of invective directed at those who, by the summer of 1998, viewed the presidency of Bill Clinton as irremediably "stained."

The Human Stain: Liberalism and the Cultural Left

The endless American quest for "purity" is, as we have seen in earlier chapters, an impulse that has been both promoted and policed within a copious liberal political tradition. At the close of the twentieth century, the failed attempt to impeach President Bill Clinton prompted yet another crisis in the relationship between liberalism and the moral impulse in American political culture. The specter of an earlier president threatened with impeachment, Richard Nixon, it might be recalled, loomed large in *I Married a Communist* and *American Pastoral*. The extent, however, to which the action in *The Human Stain* is more directly contextualized with reference to events unfolding simultaneously within national political institutions is especially significant. The frames of reference provided by the Clinton presidency in this way play an even greater, if distinctly more ambiguous, role here than those various contexts offered by Nixon's career did in the earlier works.

Somewhat more consciously, no doubt, *The Human Stain* is also a reflection upon the Clinton years; its action takes place over the latter half of 1998, Clinton's *annus horribilus*. It begins with a diatribe aimed at the president's opponents but closes, notably, with a scene that we are explicitly told occurs early the following year, "on the first February Sunday after the Senate's decision not to remove Bill Clinton from office" (*THS*, 344). This framework is augmented with a substantial number of allusions that invite an examination of the various forms of political allegiance and opposition—many of them novel—generated by America's forty-second president.

For Norman Podhoretz, reviewing *The Human Stain* alongside Saul Bellow's novel *Ravelstein* in *Commentary*, the function of Clinton in the novel is easily explained. The "peculiar choice … of the [Clinton] impeachment as a moment of historical impact to compare with McCarthyism and Vietnam" represents only another loss of political nerve on the author's part. "Here again," Podhoretz complains, "as in *I Married a Communist* [Roth] gives full play to the side of himself that has remained stuck in and intransigently uncritical of the liberal attitudes with which he grew up." The portrait of the Vietnam veteran Lester Farley, for example, it is claimed, is constructed from a repertoire of liberal cliché. "Has Roth forgotten," Podhoretz continues, "what he revealed about these very clichés in *An* [*sic*] *American Pastoral*? Or is he once more offering reassurance to those who worried after reading that book that he might be converting to neoconservatism?" It is difficult to detect any reservations of this specific type or indeed *any* negativity on political and/or aesthetic grounds amid the abundance of critical praise that met *American Pastoral.* As previously noted, Robert Boyers identified a feature of the novel that might be viewed in terms of cliché—its tendency to represent New Left politics predominantly as a species of psychopathology. This did not, however, prompt Boyers to entertain the notion that the author had undergone a "conversion" to neoconservatism. The robust articulation of liberal politics, evident elsewhere in the work and referred to earlier in this chapter, presumably satisfied most critics on that score.

Podhoretz is astute, nonetheless, in drawing attention to a dimension overlooked in most other reviews of *The Human Stain*. "Not a word, not a syllable, in the passages devoted by Roth to the Clinton scandals," he remarks, "so much as hints that the President (*unlike* Silk) committed and suborned perjury, and that this was the legal basis on which the attempt was made to remove him from office."[32] When one considers the extent to which *The Human Stain* is a novel chief among whose concerns is the politics of lying, the morality and consequences of systematic deceit, this is indeed a puzzling omission. As is the case, however, with *I Married a Communist* and *American Pastoral,* the overarching theme here is betrayal both in personal and in broader political and ideological contexts. *The Human Stain* is a novel not so much concerned with Bill Clinton but with the values of an age in which he could emerge as such a divisive figure. Like Richard Nixon, Clinton was a president whose character seemed to generate as much rancor as his policies, arousing among his supporters a strong sense that he was being unfairly maligned and persecuted while provoking powerful levels of animosity as well as feelings of "betrayal" within the ranks of his adversaries.

Moreover, the Nixon/Clinton analogy also extends to the realm of political strategy. As John J. Coleman and others have observed, Clinton, like Nixon, can be classified as a "preemptive" president, in so far as he sought to redefine the political center by "seek[ing] to occupy a middle ground largely defined by the priorities of his opponents." Similarly, both sought to do so as a means of detaching themselves from a "liberalism that was perceived as blaming society first and holding individuals accountable for their behaviour last."[33] Such motives might equally explain Coleman Silk's decision to "pass" as white in *The Human Stain*. Yet there are other reasons also, as I will argue, for reading Silk through the prism of the Clinton image as well as the Clinton years.

The subtle acts of "triangulation" required to sustain the "preemptive" strategy themselves require the acumen of the proverbial "political animal" (Clinton and Nixon certainly qualify on that count). Unsurprisingly then, perhaps, the strategies of such preemptive presidents inevitably return us to the "character" issue. The success of any "preemptive" president, as Coleman also notes, is frequently "offset by devastating attacks on his character and extraordinary political and personal distrust."[34] This too, it might also be said, has been as much in evidence in the U.S. public at large as well as within such presidents' own political constituencies. One only has to recall, for example, the defining popular soubriquets of "Tricky Dick" and "Slick Willie." This link between politics and "character" is indeed explicitly affirmed with regard to these two figures in *I Married a Communist*, via Murray Ringold's excoriating comments on Clinton's eulogy at Nixon's funeral: "Clinton exalting Nixon for his 'remarkable journey' and, under the spell of his own sincerity, expressing hushed gratitude for all the 'wise counsel' Nixon had given him" (*IMAC*, 278).

The connection between the two, however, as Roth here implies, has attributes relating to matters of political substance as well as those of style. Historians have already begun to reflect in some detail on the various facets of the relationship and the strength of the similarities between the Clinton and Nixon presidencies.[35] Nixon, they note, generated enormous suspicion—from the right as well as the left—as a consequence of embracing certain ideas originating from the first wave of neoconservative thought in the latter half of the 1960s. Probably the most important among these is evident in Nixon's commitment, early in his first term, to social policies that challenged both the shibboleths of New Deal orthodoxy and "paleoconservative" disdain for welfare per se. As one historian has commented, in his 1968 campaign "Nixon gave detailed speeches ... quoting 'new liberals,' who he said were rejecting bureaucracy and embracing private sector initiatives."[36]

Most notable was the retention by Nixon of Daniel Patrick Moynihan from previous Democratic administrations as a domestic policy advisor. Moynihan's authorship of a controversial 1965 report on urban unrest made him a revealing choice. The Moynihan Report went against the grain of the liberal consensus and, by extension, the social order in place since the New Deal, by associating urban blight and black poverty with a "tangle of pathology" within the black urban community. While being careful to explain this in terms of the terrible legacy of slavery as much as individual fecklessness, Moynihan nonetheless found himself accused of racism by black radicals, the New Left and, more importantly, many white establishment liberals who, in the charged atmosphere that followed the August 1965 race riots in Watts, Los Angeles, proved reluctant to defend him. The Moynihan Report subsequently went on to become an important ideological point of reference for the neoconservative movement. By the mid-1990s, moreover, its influence also mirrored that of neoconservative ideas on a much broader range of U.S. politicians than had been the case in the Nixon years. As Mark Gerson has observed, the speeches of such prominent political figures of the nineties as Newt Gingrich, Bill Bradley, and, most tellingly of course, Bill Clinton himself contained "more than an echo of old articles sitting in bound volumes of [the neoconservative journals] *Commentary* and *The Public Interest*."[37] As Gerson goes on to contend, the transition in American politics in large part facilitated by the neoconservative penetration of the public sphere has been remarkable. Not least, he adds, in the way it has altered what it means to be an "unrepentant left-liberal" at the end of the twentieth century:

> The tone of the ideas, rhetoric, and language used by both parties is drastically different to what it was only ten or fifteen years ago. Consider, for instance, Daniel Patrick Moynihan. His politics have not changed much in the last thirty years; in fact, his views on social policy have been remarkably consistent. ... Now the [Moynihan] report is regarded as conventional wisdom by the vast majority of the political spectrum and Moynihan is regarded as one of the last unrepentant left-liberal Democrats.[38]

The Human Stain negotiates many of the implications of this shift in U.S. political culture. Indeed, central to Roth's concerns in this novel are several of the issues that neoconservatism has helped to place on the political and cultural agenda: the relationships between rights and responsibility, sex and morality, community and individualism, and identity and difference, to name but a few. It is also, importantly, a novel dominated by a character who, in disavowing his black origins in order to "pass" as white, can be viewed in terms of an ideal crucial to any understanding of the tension between liberalism and neoconservatism over the last three decades. This is the notion first posited by John Rawls—the most important and influential liberal political philosopher of this period—of a self perceived through a "veil of ignorance."

For Rawls, a primary condition of social justice must be the assumption of the subject's "original position" prior to ties of class, race, gender, and so forth, an assumption that makes it possible to "nullify the effects of specific contingencies which put men at odds and tempt them to exploit social and natural circumstances to their own advantage."[39] One of Rawls's most trenchant critics, Michael Sandel, has redescribed this in terms of an "unencumbered self" or a self premised on "grounds of self-respect [that] are antecedent to any particular ties and attachments, and so beyond the reach of an insult to 'my people.'"[40] Thus, given the broad range of preoccupations associated with liberal thought at a particular historical moment, as with the other novels in the trilogy, *The Human Stain* can be read in the context of, to invoke Michael Sandel, "America's search for a public philosophy."

Coleman Silk, the central character in *The Human Stain*, is a Jewish neighbor of Zuckerman's and a former classics professor at nearby Athena College. After a distinguished academic career, including several successful years as dean, Silk resigns from his post after a classroom reference to two absent black students as "spooks" is construed as racist and made the subject of a formal complaint. Silk himself is unaware of the students' race (they are frequent absentees) but nonetheless refuses to offer the level of contrition demanded by the college authorities. A protracted legal battle ensues, which Silk blames, among other things, for the early death of his wife. Silk's success as dean, ironically, is built on the removal of a complacent WASP academic culture at the college and its replacement by more youthful and ambitious staff who now act as his persecutors. The sensitivity of this new generation of scholars to questions of "identity politics" first raised in the 1960s and 1970s represents both a generation gap and a transition in the meaning of liberal values. This irony is compounded, of course, when we learn fairly soon after that Silk is, in actual fact, black and has been "passing" for white for most of his adult life.

After his resignation and the death of his wife, the now seventy-one-year-old Silk becomes involved in a Viagra-assisted sexual relationship with a thirty-four-year-old cleaning woman named Faunia Farley. As a result, he is tormented, in contrasting ways, by both his partner's mentally unstable and abusive ex-husband, Lester, a veteran of the Vietnam war, and Delphine Roux, a languages and literature professor and former colleague of Silk's at Athena. Lester Farley's hostility is motivated not merely by sexual jealousy but also by anti-Semitism, revenge (he holds Faunia responsible for the tragic death of their two young children in a fire), and what might best be described as a sense of betrayal and alienation familiar from earlier cultural representations of the Vietnam-scarred sociopath. At the end of the novel, Lester is also revealed as the couple's probable murderer after their car is deliberately forced off the road. Delphine Roux's objections to Silk take a less directly menacing form but nonetheless, it would appear, also have important sociopolitical as well as psychological origins. Initially, Roux is responsible for an anonymous note informing Silk that "everyone knows you're sexually exploiting an abused, illiterate woman half your age" (*THS*, 38). While embracing a more or less feminist position, Roux's contempt for Silk mirrors the contempt of many (neo)conservatives for Bill Clinton insofar as both are *morally* oriented, that is, centered on notions of "propriety" and "appropriate behavior" (whether in the classroom or the Oval Office). Coleman reveals his experience to Zuckerman—including the details of his relationship with Faunia—"fittingly enough," the narrator claims, during the summer of 1998, when "Bill Clinton's secret emerged in every last mortifying detail." It is within this broader cultural and political climate of "persecution," then, that we are by several means invited to view Coleman Silk's life.

Zuckerman's description of Clinton's travails begins with an acknowledgment of both the transformation and persistence of American sexual mores. His first point of comparison, in this way, recalls both a more reproving past and, interestingly, that sense of great social change evident in the confidence with which Marcia Umanoff feels able to equate pornography with beauty contests in *American Pastoral*. "We hadn't," Zuckerman claims, "had a season like it since somebody stumbled upon the new Miss

America nude in an old issue of *Penthouse*, pictures of her elegantly posed on her knees and on her back that forced the shamed young woman to relinquish her crown and go on to become a huge pop star" (*THS*, 2).

Zuckerman's bilious attack on Clinton's antagonists, moreover, might not only aid an understanding of late twentieth-century questions of gender and sexual morality but also, more obliquely if no less consequentially, those of race too. Clinton himself was, of course, the first president young enough to have had his political development shaped, to any significant degree, by the events and ideas of the 1960s. He avoided (and in a letter to the authorities protested) the Vietnam draft; he also played the saxophone, enjoyed rock 'n' roll, and notoriously admitted to having smoked (though, crucially, it would seem, not inhaled) marijuana. Most importantly, perhaps, Clinton acquired the Democratic Party presidential nomination in 1992 by appealing to the "broadminded" sexual politics of the "baby-boomer" generation. Clinton's victory in the primaries and subsequent presidential election—notwithstanding his confession of a long-term adulterous relationship—was a signal that the sexual revolution of the 1960s had helped expand the boundaries of acceptable behavior for those wishing to assume even the most prominent position in American public life.

Yet Clinton's affair with White House intern Monica Lewinsky, Zuckerman remarks, "revived America's oldest communal passion, historically perhaps its most subversive and treacherous pleasure: the ecstasy of sanctimony" (*THS*, 2). In 1992, amid earlier allegations of infidelity, a number of journalists such as A. M. Rosenthal had praised the Clintons for "present[ing] to the American public a gift and a lasting opportunity" by insisting on their right to privacy following media inquiries about their marital history. This "gift," it was claimed, came in the form of "the presumption that Americans had achieved adulthood."[41] After citing Rosenthal's remarks, the novelist and political commentator Joan Didion noted in a *New York Review of Books* article first published in September 1998 at the height of the impeachment crisis that many Americans, by contrast, had a continuing appetite for reaffirmations of American "innocence" rather than such presumptions of a new "maturity." For critics such as William J. Bennett, author of *The Death of Outrage: Bill Clinton and the Assault on American Ideals* (which also appeared that year), Didion explained, the protracted investigation of Independent Counsel Kenneth Starr had, on this basis, assumed biblical significance. "American innocence itself," Didion concluded, "was now seen to hang on the revealed word of the *Referral*."[42]

In *The Human Stain*, the release of the type of intimate sexual detail evident in much of Starr's *Referral* is seen to represent an atavistic, Puritanical belief in provoking "calculated frenzy" designed primarily to shame individuals guilty of transgressing communal values. Only then, after a sufficient release of "outrage," can the lost, collective sense of virtue begin to be restored. The eagerness "to enact [such] astringent rituals of purification" as those overseen by the Office of Independent Counsel is thus itself evidence of the nation's refusal to "mature" and discard the myth of innocence. In this respect, Zuckerman laments, the summer of 1998 was

> when the moral obligation to explain to one's children about adult life was abrogated in favor of maintaining in them every illusion about adult life, when the smallness of people was simply crushing ... when—for the billionth time—the jumble, the mayhem, the mess proved itself more subtle than this one's ideology and that one's morality. It was the summer when a president's penis was on everyone's mind, and life, in all its shameless impurity, once again confounded America.
>
> (*THS*, 3)

Roth's work has elicited criticism as well as accolades on the basis of its own "shameless impurity," of course, since the days of *Portnoy's Complaint* (1969) and on through to *Sabbath's Theater* (1995), mostly for the candid accounts it offers of its protagonists' sexual and emotional embroilments. At the very beginning of his career, though, as previously noted, Roth's short fiction exploring Jewish American identity met with slightly different concerns connected with the "purity" of authorial intention. Interestingly, from the 1980s through the 1990s Roth's output becomes increasingly marked by an explicit effort to destabilize ideas of aesthetic as well as social and political notions of "purity."[43] Novels such as *The Counterlife* (1986), *Operation Shylock* (1988), and the Zuckerman works anthologized in *Zuckerman Unbound* (1989) as well as the unconventional autobiography *The Facts* (1992) all diverge from the "realistic" mode that the author himself, for the most part, had previously embraced. The desire to compound earlier "impurities" of content with those of form by radically experimenting with narrative structure is less pronounced in Roth's American trilogy, but the idea is perhaps more evident than ever in thematic terms.

The trope of "impurity" in *The Human Stain* manifests itself most obviously in the title of the novel, but elsewhere Roth returns to pursue the idea in ways previously encountered in the first two parts of the trilogy. In the first chapter of *The Human Stain*, for instance, Zuckerman notes the romanticized notions of country life propagated mainly by ex–city dwellers who have recently moved to the local community. Letters to the area weekly praising the "wholesomeness" of the local farm's organic milk seem to conceive of its consumption, Zuckerman remarks, "as if it were no less a religious rite than a nutritional blessing." Similarly, the overblown marketing material that accompanies the milk promotes its "nourishment" of the "soul" and the "spirit." As in *American Pastoral*, then, the idea of the pastoral as "pure" is subjected to critical pressure. The passage closes by linking such sentiment to the broader infantilization of American political culture that will sound a recurring note in *The Human Stain*. For Zuckerman, this discourse of pastoral hyperbole simply allows "otherwise sensible adults, liberated from whatever vexation had driven them from New York or Hartford or Boston [to] spend a pleasant few minutes ... pretending that they are seven years old" (*THS*, 46).

The most important spheres for Zuckerman's ruminations on this trope in *The Human Stain*, however, are those of sex and sexual morality. This extends to the narrator himself, whose position on these and other questions undergoes drastic revision as a result of his friendship with Silk. After curiously seeming to "disappear" as the speaking voice in *American Pastoral* about a third of the way through the narrative, Nathan Zuckerman once again, as he does in *I Married a Communist*, assumes a position in the final installation much closer to center stage.

At the beginning of the story, Zuckerman reveals details of a recent bout of cancer surgery that entailed the removal of his prostate gland. This results in impotence and episodes of incontinence. Living the same hermetical existence described in the final pages of *I Married a Communist*—removed from what he here describes as the "sexual caterwaul"—Zuckerman finds that his circumstances have helped reduce the effect of any "postoperative shock" that might normally be expected to attend such a condition. The fact is, he states, "the operation did no more than to enforce with finality a decision I'd come to on my own, under the pressure of a lifelong experience of entanglements but in a time of full, vigorous and restless potency, when the venturesome masculine mania to repeat the act—repeat it and repeat it and repeat it—remained undeterred by physiological problems" (*THS*, 37).

As his relationship with Coleman Silk develops, however, Zuckerman is prompted to radically reassess his initial decision to withdraw from the world. The intrusion of such a complex, sexual, and vigorously *human* presence as Silk at this late stage of his life, he admits, has resulted in a certain "loss [of] equilibrium." Overwhelmed as he has become by the power of Silk's "transgressive audacity," Zuckerman can only bemoan the bloodless, asocial, and emasculated existence he has imposed upon himself over the past few years. Hence, in reflecting on an earlier evening spent in part dancing sentimentally with Silk to some old swing records, Zuckerman claims that "having danced around like a harmless eunuch with this still vital, potent participant in the frenzy struck me now as anything but charming self-satire." The conclusion the narrator draws from this realization crucially informs the vision of sexual morality at the novel's heart: "How can one say, 'No, this isn't part of life,' since it always is? The contaminant of sex, the redeeming corruption that de-idealizes the species and keeps us everlastingly mindful of the matter we are" (*THS*, 37).

This inversion of Judeo-Christian configurations of "original sin"—corruption itself as a form of redemption—is extended later in the novel. In a remarkable passage, Zuckerman designates the paganism of ancient Greece as the source of a "great reality-reflecting religion" commensurate with the supercharged, chaotic, and complex realities embraced by Faunia and Coleman. This follows Faunia's invocation of the "human stain" trope in connection with a "hand-raised" crow harassed and bullied by other crows, alienated from the species, unable to find the "right voice" in which to communicate as a result of excessive contact with humans. Zuckerman goes on to substantiate Faunia's observation, stating that "we leave a stain, we leave a trail, we leave our imprint. Impurity, cruelty, abuse, error, excrement, semen—there's no other way to be here." Thus such "fantas[ies] of purity" as those implicit in both the Hebrew God ("infinitely alone, infinitely obscure, monomaniacally the only god there is, was, and always will be") and the "de-sexualized Christian man-god and his uncontaminated mother" (*THS*, 242) must be disavowed. Instead, Zuckerman wonders if the classics professor Silk has ever discussed with his lover, "Zeus, entangled in adventure, vividly expressive, capricious, sensual, exuberantly wedded to his own rich existence, anything but alone and anything but hidden. Instead the *divine* stain. ... As the hubristic fantasy has it, made in the image of God, all right, but not ours—*theirs*. God debauched. God corrupted. A God of life if ever there was one. God in the image of *man*" (*THS*, 243).

In another episode, Zuckerman, hearing music from Silk's house, imagines the couple alone inside: "There they dance, as likely as not unclothed, beyond the ordeal of the world, in an unearthly paradise of earthbound lust where their coupling is the drama into which they decant all the angry disappointment of their lives." The vision presented here is of an inverted Eden in which—as is the case in Melville's *Billy Budd*—notions of absolute guilt and innocence ultimately coalesce. The "incongruously allied" Silk and Faunia, irredeemably corrupted and "entrenched in disgust" with life, have nonetheless attained a purity of sorts in their Budd-like capacity to locate in each other "the simplest version possible of themselves" (*THS*, 203). It is this that leads Zuckerman to conjecture that Silk ultimately revealed the secret of his racial origins to Faunia.

In the American context, of course, nothing has "stained" the body politic as much as this idea of racial origins. The liberal tradition's affirmation of individualism, egalitarianism, and democracy has been perpetually undercut by the subordinate status of Native Americans, immigrant groups, and, perhaps most glaringly, African Americans. Very few Americans would now doubt that the single most implacable "stain" on the national historical record is that of the constitutionally protected slavery that existed until the Civil War. This, of course, after *Plessy v. Ferguson* (1896), was followed by over a half a century of legally protected segregation in the South. Race also continues to "contaminate" public discourse pertaining to a seemingly infinite variety of matter, from affirmative-action policy to the hugely disproportionate number of blacks executed by the state to the relative absence of black actors in mainstream Hollywood cinema.

It is hardly surprising then that racial dimensions also managed to emerge in a controversy that dominated the media for the best part of a year. Perhaps, because none of the main protagonists was black, the incredible degree of support President Clinton maintained among the black community was only intermittently remarked upon. When one now considers, however, the vehemence with which such support was expressed by a number of black writers and intellectuals, it does seem somewhat extraordinary, given the fact that this particular drama was performed by an all-white cast. Toni Morrison, for example, described Clinton as "our first black President" but then added a tellingly hardheaded qualifier: "Blacker than any actual black person who could ever be elected in our children's lifetime." Morrison then goes on to note, with dark irony: "After all, Clinton displays almost every trope of blackness: single-parent household, born poor, working-class, saxophone-playing, McDonald's-and-junk-food-loving boy from Arkansas." After noting the fact that "African-American men seemed to understand it right away," Morrison then reflects, "and when virtually all the African-American appointees began, one by one, to disappear, when the President's body, his privacy, his unpoliced sexuality became the focus of the persecution, when he was metaphorically seized and body-searched, who could gainsay these black men who knew whereof they spoke?"

Morrison was far from alone in her appraisal that Clinton's "blackness" in this figurative sense constituted an important subtext within Kenneth Starr's "sustained, bloody, arrogant coup d'état."44 The rhetoric of black commentators such as Ida E. Lewis ratcheted up the symbolism to an even greater degree. In the process, however, pieces such as Lewis's "Bill Clinton as Honorary Black" frequently deployed the racial essentialism without any of the covering irony that underwrote at least parts of Morrison's analysis: "Black people know that men's (and women's) lying about sex is ancient practice. They know that the Starr investigation is much less about sex than it is about overturning an election. . . . The right wing powers-that-be are working overtime to write the final chapter of The Niggerization of Bill Clinton." In remarks no doubt designed to play upon the notorious self-description of Supreme Court judge Clarence Thomas as the victim of a "high-tech lynching" during his 1991 nomination hearings, Lewis reappropriates both elements of Thomas's provocative metaphor for Clinton's "constituencies":

> The right wing has not rested in its shameless resolve to drag Clinton, his wife, and, unforgivably, their daughter, through the electronic gutters of America. In the process they are decapitating the office he holds, and the constituencies his will embodies, as surely as the good ole boys down in Jasper, Texas, last June reduced decency, humanity and compassion to bloody clumps of torn flesh littering a county road.45

Clinton can here be viewed not only as symbolically "black," as these writers contend, but also as someone whose predicament—privacy destroyed, sexuality policed, "metaphorically seized and body-searched," wife and children exposed to public scandal—is analogous to that undergone by Coleman Silk in *The Human Stain*. Still, what writers such as Morrison and Lewis elide in their focus on Clinton's "blackness" is what has been identified by others such as Steven E. Schier and Christopher Hitchens as the *variable* nature of Clinton's identity in all aspects, "race" most certainly included. For Schier, this allowed Clinton to appeal to what he characterizes as an increasingly "post-partisan" public, "evenly divided on major issues" and no longer motivated by traditional ethnic party political loyalties.[46] Hitchens takes up the more sinister dimension to this "variability" by focusing on Clinton's opportunist strategy of "triangulation" on racial matters.

Morrison fails to mention, for example, when she invokes the gradual disappearance of African American appointees, that some of the more prominent of these were very much at Clinton's own instigation. As Hitchens observes, the minor controversies that attended Lani Guinier's appointment as head of the Civil Rights Division of the Department of Justice and Jocelyn Elders's as surgeon general might have been ridden out had Clinton shown the merest hint of political courage. Guinier made the mistake of discussing the advantages of proportional representation in the South only to be labeled a "quota queen" by neoconservative critics; Elders committed the even more heinous crime of proposing an open discussion on masturbation (as well as protected intercourse and abstinence) at a forum on the topic of sex and American teenagers. Clinton did not hesitate to abandon both women at the first whiff of antiliberal "controversy." No black person's "disappearance" as a result of a Clinton decision, however, was more final than that of Ricky Ray Rector—the retarded Arkansas death-row inmate whose execution Clinton, then still governor of the state, authorized at the height of the 1992 Democratic primaries. Clinton, clearly, was not going to have his nomination chances scuppered by this potential "Willie Horton."[47]

Yet, Hitchens goes on to note, Clinton was always keen to advertise his credentials on the race issue—so long as he did not alienate conservative white voters in the process. Thus, relatively innocuous moves such as the promotion of black figures to non-senior administration posts, the offering of apologies for past wrongs such as slavery and the Tuskegee syphilis experiment, as well as regular visits to black churches could be undertaken with little political fallout. Similarly, during his darkest hour in 1998, Clinton rediscovered the benefits of being photographed with the Reverend Jesse Jackson and launched his famous "atonement" prayer at a fundraiser held in a black church. A classic instance of Clinton "triangulation" on a race issue was his promise to "mend not end" affirmative action, thereby indicating that such a policy had been unacceptable in the form it has largely taken since the Johnson civil-rights legislation (to appeal to neo-conservatives and the right) but could not be dispensed with completely (to maintain the support of the left). By such "last-minute improvisations" on these issues, Hitchens concludes, Clinton "had, without calling any undue attention to the fact, become the first president to play the race card both ways. . . . His opportunist defenders, having helped him with a chameleon-like change in the color of his skin, still found themselves stuck with the content of his character."[48]

It is for such reasons that Clinton was able to generate hostility from both the left and the right while also picking up votes from those across the center of the political spectrum who, largely for cultural reasons, took a less judgmental view of his actions. The left took issue with what they regarded as Clinton's "antiegalitarianism"—particularly in his approach to economic matters such as welfare—while the right was more angered by Clinton as a cultural figure. "At all times," Hitchens writes, "Clinton's retreat from egalitarian or even 'progressive' positions has been hedged by a bodyguard of political correctness."[49] While Podhoretz could share Hitchens's disdain for Clinton as a creature shaped by "political correctness," by 1999, he could also write in praise of Clinton's domestic economic and foreign policies on the basis that they concurred with the neoconservative agenda. Despite being "a scoundrel and a perjurer and a disgrace to the office he has held," Clinton has, nonetheless, in ideological terms, Podhoretz claims, successfully "de-McGovernized" the Democratic Party, pulling it "in a healthier direction than it had been heading in since its unconditional surrender to the Left thirty years ago."[50] Give us the policy without the personality, Podhoretz seemed to be saying; roll back the cultural effects of the 1960s: the sexual and moral turpitude, the political correctness, the ethical and cultural relativism.

It is these issues of character and culture exemplified in many ways by the Clinton presidency that recur in *The Human Stain*. As has been charted in differing contexts by critics such as Russell Jacoby, Richard Posner, and Todd Gitlin, the effects of 1960s cultural politics has waned in many areas of American public life since the 1980s but has, to a great extent, colonized the American academy, which now constitutes the main sphere of influence for the cultural left.[51] The acceptance of certain ideas of sexual freedom (particularly with regard to homosexuality) and the importance of "micropolitical" change in the realms of language and social attitudes (so-called political correctness) that originated with the new social movements of the 1960s are now features of most campuses in the United States. Jacoby, Posner, and Gitlin associate this development with a diminution in the standing of an earlier American left-liberal intellectual culture that spread beyond the university. Moreover, this confinement of many left-liberal intellectuals has led to a pernicious contraction of debate as their interests in "micropolitics" and esoteric "theory" serve only to alienate them from a broader public.

Roth, however, constructs Coleman Silk as a victim not only of a cultural left in the 1990s that views him as an establishment figure who abuses his position in order to exploit women and denigrate blacks, but also as a victim of an earlier pre–civil rights environment that closed off most avenues of opportunity on the basis of his skin color. Like Clinton, one could argue, Coleman Silk has, to paraphrase Hitchens, "played the race card both ways." He draws a good deal of moral and intellectual strength from the stock bestowed upon him by a proud black family in order to break his attachments to that family as a condition of "passing" as white. It is important to add, however—given the pressure placed on him as both a young "black" and an old "white" man to comply with social and cultural expectations—that Silk can also be said to have had the race card played *against him* both ways.

Notwithstanding this, as some of the most powerful passages in *The Human Stain* attest, the scale of Silk's "betrayal" cannot be underplayed. Roth draws out the full weight of Silk's predicament not only in the vivid portrayal of the elderly Silk but also in the intimate and astutely drawn picture of the Silk family's lives and history. As was the case with the earlier works in the trilogy, we see that one of the central formative relationships of the protagonist is between himself and his father. Silk's father was the owner of an optician's store that went bust during the Depression. A graduate then forced to work as a railcar steward, Coleman's father is a cultural conservative whose erudite lucidity, like Murray Ringold's, is wielded like a weapon. He is described, in this respect, as "the father who never lost his temper. The father who had another way of beating you down. With words. With speech. With what he called 'the language of Chaucer, Shakespeare and Dickens.'" Skill with language, once acquired, is seen by the senior Silk as a means of transcending many of the contingencies upon which "identity" depends in so far as, unlike a business or a job, "no one could ever take [language] away from you" (*THS*, 92).

The theme of "betrayal" is alluded to in this early depiction of Silk's family background. Each of the Silk children, we learn, have middle names taken from Shakespeare's *Julius Caesar*, which is described as "Mr. Silk's best-memorized play, in his view English literature's high point and the most educational study of treason ever written" (*THS*, 92). Walter Antony, Silk's elder brother, is named, of course, after Caesar's successor, who distanced himself from the assassination plot; Ernestine Calpurnia, Silk's younger sister, is named after Caesar's loyal wife; and Coleman Brutus is named after Caesar's former ally, the most treacherous of his assassins but also, interestingly, the most suspicious of his power and the most republican in his politics. Brutus, it was rumored, was also Caesar's son from an affair in his early life.

The epiphanic moment that first triggers Silk's betrayal comes with his arrival as a student at the all-black Howard University in Washington (an option heavily pressed on him by his family) and his father's death shortly after. The motivating impulse is, however, not initially at least, one of rebellion against his father's influence but rather one of sympathy as to the lengths his father went to in order to shield him from realities he is as yet unacquainted with. Racially abused and refused a hot dog at a Woolworth's store in the nation's capital, Silk ruminates upon this previously unconsidered aspect of his father's experience as a black American in the early twentieth century:

> Never before, for all his precocious cleverness, had Coleman realized how protected his life had been, nor had he gauged his father's fortitude or realized the powerful force that man was—powerful not merely by virtue of being his father. At last he saw all that his father had been condemned to accept. He saw all his father's defenselessness, too, where before he had been a naïve enough youngster to imagine, from the lordly, austere, sometimes insufferable way Mr. Silk conducted himself, that there was nothing vulnerable there. But because someone had called him a nigger to his face, he finally realized the enormous barrier against the great American menace his father had been for him.
>
> (*THS*, 105–106)

It is, symbolically, at his father's funeral that Coleman begins to formulate the philosophy—that is, I will argue, the inherently American, *liberal* philosophy—that will underpin his decision to renounce his racial origins. This is the subject as construed in classical liberalism—what is described in the novel as the "raw I"—against which, for John Locke, as we saw in chapter 1, the American context can be viewed as a primary site. "Overnight," Silk reflects on his brief spell at Howard, "the raw I was part of a we with all the we's overbearing solidity, and he didn't want anything to do with it or with the next oppressive we that came along either" (*THS*, 108). Yet, in its resistance to such co-option, this predilection equally cuts against the assimilationist grain within American culture. Coleman Silk's quandary can here be viewed as a dramatic project of self-fashioning that works through the tensions between liberalism and republican, individualist and communitarian imperatives also examined in earlier chapters. In a key passage, the first intimation of how Coleman will ultimately seek to resolve these issues is made apparent. Should he settle for always being a "nigger" to the "they" of Woolworth's and a "negro" to the "we" of Howard?

> No. No. He saw the fate awaiting him, and he wasn't having it. Grasped it intuitively and recoiled spontaneously. You can't let the big they impose its bigotry on you anymore than you can let the little they become a we and impose its ethics on you. Not the tyranny of its we and its we-talk and everything that the we wants to pile on your head. Never for him the tyranny of the we that is dying to suck you in, the coercive, inclusive, historical, inescapable moral *we* with its insidious *E pluribus unum*. Neither the they of the Woolworth's nor the we of Howard. Instead the raw I with all its agility. *Self*-discovery—*that* was the punch to the labonz. Singularity. The passionate struggle for singularity. The singular animal. The sliding relationship with everything. Not static but sliding. Self-knowledge but *concealed*. What is as powerful as that?
>
> (*THS*, 108)

The overwhelming Emersonian tenor of this passage also recalls the distinctly modernist consciousness of Owen Brown in *Cloudsplitter*, sandwiched between past and future, rejecting both the "theys" of the Southern "slaveocracy" and nonviolent abolitionist politics but also the "we" of his father's apocalyptic route to racial concord. The self envisioned here is, largely, that of a self "unencumbered" by those values connected with tradition and society that in some way constrain this Emersonian project of self-discovery and "self-reliance." For Silk, living in midcentury America, the greatest of these encumbrances happened to be his skin color. Despite having passed as a "white" boxer in his teenage years (Silk and his coach operating under a Clintonesque "don't ask, don't tell" compromise policy), it is only on joining the navy soon after his father's death that he finally decides to deliberately conceal his racial identity. Silk disavows the idea that such a move represents an abrogation or betrayal of any kind. After dating a girl in New York City, Steena Palsson, a Dakotan of Scandinavian forebears who believes Silk to be white, he decides to introduce her to his family without forewarning her of his racial origins:

> He would get her to see that far from there being anything wrong with his decision to identify himself as white, it was the most natural thing for someone with his outlook and temperament and skin color to have done. All he'd ever wanted, from his early childhood on, was to be free: not black, not even white—just on his own and free. He meant to insult no one by his choice, nor was he trying to imitate anyone who he took to be his superior, nor was he staging some sort of protest against his race or hers.
>
> (*THS*, 120)

The dinner with the Silks goes well, but Steena then breaks down in tears on the way home, claiming that she is unable to continue with the relationship. When Silk meets the woman who will become his future wife some years later, Iris Gittelman, he claims that he, like her, is Jewish. In his review of *The Human Stain*, Norman Podhoretz claims to be mystified by what he regards as the author's failure to elaborate on the provenance of this particular decision of Silk's. After having introduced, in this way, a Jewish dimension to the novel, he would "have expected [Roth] to do more than he does with the changes in American society which have persuaded Silk that pretending to be Jewish has in some quarters become a greater advantage than passing as a WASP."[52] Podhoretz's view indeed appears to be substantiated by an interview Roth himself gave to Charles McGrath, editor of the *New York Times Book Review*, shortly after the novel's publication, in which he states that Coleman's choice is "strictly utilitarian" and has "nothing to do with the ethical, spiritual, theological, or historical aspects of Judaism."

Yet this is in response to McGrath's view that *The Human Stain* is "a book . . . about issues of race and *Judaism* and where the two intersect," and

Roth here appears to be responding to questions that might have some bearing on Judaism or the Jewish faith rather than Jewish or Jewish American culture in a wider sense.[53] The idea that the choice is "strictly utilitarian," as the author claims, also seems at least partially at odds with certain passages of the book. Early on, for instance, a strong note is struck regarding the way in which Jews were viewed by the Silks as blazing something of an assimilationist trail in midcentury America. "For Coleman's father," we learn, "the Jews . . . were like Indian scouts, shrewd people showing the outsider his way in, showing the social possibility, showing an intelligent colored family how it might be done" (*THS*, 97). Podhoretz's assessment—that the novel "ignores the Jewish issue almost entirely"—is, furthermore, belied by the careful sketches of Iris's family. It is even more surprising in the light of Coleman's own summary of the historical, intellectual, and cultural context that informed his decision to "pass" as a Jew. Those years in New York City, he believes, represented

> a moment when Jewish self-infatuation was at a postwar pinnacle among the Washington Square intellectual avant-garde, when the aggrandizing appetite riving their Jewish mental audacity was beginning to look uncontrollable and an aura of significance emanated as much from their jokes and their family anecdotes, from their laughter and their clowning and their wisecracks and their arguments—even from their insults—as from *Commentary*, *Midstream*, and the *Partisan Review*, who was he not to go along for the ride . . .
>
> (*THS*, 131)

Notwithstanding the author's own disavowals of the novel's connections with *Judaism*, then, Podhoretz's failure to acknowledge such passages as pertinent to Coleman's story appears a little remiss. It is particularly puzzling given that this "self-infatuated" milieu's representative figures are seen by many to include Podhoretz himself, who began his career and subsequently became editor at *Commentary* in the 1950s and 1960s. Indeed, Podhoretz and, more tangentially, Philip Roth himself were part of a Jewish American intellectual generation that succeeded prominent immediate postwar figures such as Lionel Trilling and Irving Howe, coming of age, so to speak, in the 1960s, when the issue of race was, it seemed, never more than a few months away from being the subject of a *Commentary* "roundtable" discussion. As historians such as Seth Forman have shown, the relationship, both intellectual and political, between blacks and Jews was one of the most controversial and explosive subjects on the cultural agenda of these years.

Such relationships were, inevitably, shaped by the imperatives of the dominant political tradition, a tradition that the type of upwardly mobile Jews celebrated in *American Pastoral* (and unlike an increasingly vocal number of blacks as the 1960s took their course) maintained a considerable degree of faith in. This belief in the capacity of American political culture to neutralize cultural and ethnic differences previously viewed as a barrier to achievement, Forman argues, is rooted in a particular Jewish American historical experience. "Knowing that the United States bore no responsibility for Jewish history and so offered the Jews no special quarter," he writes, "Jews set about adjusting their Jewishness to American life, and the connecting link for Americanization was liberalism."[54] The specifics of the Jewish past, in particular the long history of persecution, furthermore, "bound Jews to the American ideals of equality and freedom much more intensely than even the 'real Americans' and thus made it possible for Jews to carve out a place for themselves in American life by helping Blacks."

This Jewish sense of solidarity with oppressed African Americans finds several outlets in the trilogy's other works, particularly *American Pastoral.* The continuing loyalty of both the Swede and Lou Levov to the black employees at their glove factory, for example, is a common refrain in that novel's treatment of race relations in postwar Newark. Likewise, Murray's refusal to abandon inner-city black schoolchildren forms the basis of the tragic coda to *I Married a Communist.* Forman goes on to speculate that such commitment underwrites the Jewish American understanding of modern liberalism and represented a further stage for Jews on the path to assimilation. Looking back on this period, he believes that "liberalism and involvement in Black affairs was, in large measure, an accommodation of Judaism and the Jewish past to American life." Roth's decision to have Coleman Silk "pass" as an American Jew then, at least at some level, would appear to be a further recognition of this cultural dynamic.

Looking more closely at the ideas of ethnicity and "Americanization" emerging from the Jewish New York intellectual circles that the novel invokes, we find that many anticipate that sense of a "raw I" identity that Coleman Silk seeks to fashion for himself in *The Human Stain.* Writing in *Commentary* in 1950, for instance, Harold Rosenberg speculates that "being an American means being free precisely in that the American possesses that room, and can keep multiplying and transforming himself without regarding . . . his nationality."[55] This, Rosenberg also claims, is related to modernity more generally and, in particular, to what he defines as "the modern condition of freedom to make ourselves according to an image we choose."[56] Over twenty years later, Robert Alter, responding in a cultural climate more hostile to this idea as a result, no doubt, of the entrenchment of new forms of "identity" politics, asserted that "people *preoccupied* with their own identity are not wholly free."[57]

It is fair to say that the "culture wars" that have dominated American intellectual debate since the 1980s are premised, in large part, on a rejection of the type of assimilation projects embraced in both theory and practice by successive postwar generations of Jewish Americans. Instead, the identity politics of the 1960s has fashioned a new discourse of multiculturalism that promotes the retention of ethnic and racial identities. This finds widespread institutional expression in everything from affirmative-action employment policy to reappraisals of the process of literary canonization in the American academy. Although such changes have been the subject of continual critique from neoconservative and more entrenched liberal quarters,[58] by the mid-1990s the post–civil rights era sensitivity to issues of race and gender also began to be reappraised by some younger left-liberal critics who came of age during this time.

This critique of "multiculturalism" and identity politics among a new generation of scholars has led to some tentative proposals along the lines of what David A. Hollinger has described as a "postethnic" understanding of American identity. Indeed, one of the strategies deployed by Hollinger in his important study *Postethnic America: Beyond Multiculturalism* (1995) involves pointing to the degree to which various scientific and cultural histories have effectively established the category of "race" itself as an "invention" or "fiction." This fact, however, as the author freely admits, has no bearing on the reality of "racism" in America. "Racism is real," he writes, "races are not"[59]—a distinction that somewhat serves to separate Hollinger from "color-blind" neoconservatives who, with an often similar level of conviction, view racism itself as something of a "fiction."[60] The "deracialization" of Jews in America during the twentieth century is instructive in this context. As Hollinger notes, it stands in contrast to the process of "racialization" that might be said to have occurred with regard to other ethnic groups such as Latinos:

Jews were once widely thought of as a race, but are no longer. This transformation did not result primarily from scientific advances in biology and physical anthropology. Rather, the prejudice against Jewish Americans within American historical experience is judged to be less severe and damaging than the prejudice against Latinos, who, because of that greater perceived victimization, are now said to constitute a race.⁶¹

Here, too, we might find clues as to the appeal of Jewish American identity as a basis for Coleman Silk's reinvention of himself. In the postwar context of mass Jewish assimilation, Coleman's decision to assume the "ersatz prestige of an aggressively thinking, self-analytic, irreverent American Jew reveling in the ironies of the marginal Manhattan existence" is both a renunciation of race and a recognition of the fallibility of any notionally "pure" ethnic identity. By coming to see himself as a Jew, Coleman finally attains a form of "singularity . . . his inmost ego-driven ambition all along." It is precisely the gap that emerged between Jewish and African American experience, between altered ideas concerning race and ethnicity in postwar America, that explains the particular form Coleman's "passing" takes: "As a heretofore unknown amalgam of the most unalike of America's historic undesirables, he now made sense" (*THS*, 132).

One contemporary black critic who picks up on the idea of the renunciation of race as an indispensable feature to any twenty-first-century notion of progressive politics is Paul Gilroy. In *Between Camps: Nations, Cultures, and the Allure of Race* (2000), Gilroy laments the damage done to black political thought by a preoccupation with "race" and "racial identity." This is achieved, at one point, by retrieving an episode from recent history wherein blacks played a significant role in the fight against "race thinking" in its most extreme historical form. Recalling the testimonies of black Allied soldiers involved in the liberation of Nazi death camps at the end of World War II, Gilroy concludes that such "encounters are powerful reminders of the arbitrariness of racial divisions, the absurdity and pettiness of racial typologies, and the mortal dangers that have always attended their institutionalisation."⁶² *Between Camps*—which was, interestingly, retitled *Against Race: Imagining Political Culture Beyond the Color Line* for American publication—closes with a call for a new "planetary humanism" and "strategic universalism" that "re-connect[s] . . . with democratic and cosmopolitan traditions that have been all but expunged from today's black political imaginary."⁶³

Race "passing," as one recent literary critic has identified, is itself a part of such democratic and cosmopolitan traditions, albeit a controversial and, until fairly recently, relatively hidden one. While many scholars of "passing" have tended to focus on its more problematic aspects—regarding it at best as a misguided form of "resistance" to racial categories, at worst, a form of race betrayal—Kathleen Pfeiffer's *Race Passing and American Individualism* (2003) has resituated the phenomenon in a broader cultural context. In this schema, "passing" is understood with reference to the emphasis placed on individualism within the pantheon of American democratic values. Passing narratives, for Pfeiffer, in this way primarily represent a "celebration of achievement and independence, the sense of unlimited possibility that characterizes the 'rags to riches' mythology—the consent-based structure of value."[64] This latter notion is drawn from the work of Werner Sollors, who in his work *Beyond Ethnicity* (1986) distinguishes between a "language of consent" (which stresses "our abilities as mature free agents and 'architects of our fate' to choose our spouses, our destinies and our political systems") and a "language of descent" (which stresses "our position as heirs, our hereditary qualities, liabilities and entitlements").[65] "America," Sollors adds, "is a country which, from the times of Cotton Mather to the present, has placed great emphasis on consent at the expense of descent definitions. The widely shared public bias against hereditary privilege ... has strongly favored *achieved* rather than *ascribed* identity, and supported 'self-determination' and 'independence' from ancestral, parental and external definitions."[66]

Race Passing and American Individualism highlights this powerful tradition in U.S. political thought—perhaps best exemplified by Abraham Lincoln—that understands American democracy as contingent, a work in progress, an unconsummated idea, or, in Lincoln's own words from the Gettysburg Address, a "proposition" (to be realized). This is fused, moreover, with what might be described as an Emersonian political ontology that foregrounds the "power of the individual, as opposed to the group, to effect change." "Passing" is, in such Emersonian terms, principally a metaphor for all subjectivity, and Pfeiffer's study, accordingly, concludes with a stray but, in this context, telling remark from "Self Reliance": "We pass for what we are."[67]

The final chapter of *Race Passing and American Individualism* deploys a few elements from *The Human Stain* in support of its thesis (noting, for instance, Silk's funeral eulogy, in which he is described as "an American individualist *par excellence*" [*THS*, 311] by a former black colleague in the faculty), but the conception of subjectivity Pfeiffer works with in her study is also given profound expression in Roth's novel. This is evident not only in the "sliding" notion of self that underwrites Silk's own subjectivity but also in the resigned voice of the narrator, Nathan Zuckerman. In each novel in Roth's trilogy, characters driven by such ideals have met tragic ends as a result of what we might call a crisis of expectation. Chastened, perhaps, by his encounters with "Swede" Levov, the Ringold brothers, and now Coleman Silk, Zuckerman reflects at Silk's funeral that "the expectation of completion, let alone of a just and perfect consummation, is a foolish illusion for an adult to hold" (*THS*, 315).

This sense of illusion is made manifest in *The Human Stain* from the point in which Silk begins to feel himself entangled in forms of intimacy and relation he has previously held at a distance. Silk's liberal-individualist project of self-sovereignty runs aground, of course, in the face of pressures within the academy that question the intellectual and political tenability of such a project. More telling, perhaps, is his relationship with Farley, within which context the abandonment of self-sovereignty can only be seen as a *voluntary* act—a recognition of the limits of liberal individualism. It is Zuckerman, of course, as the narrator, who records this gradual process of Silk giving himself up to a world of intersubjectivity. As a result, however, it must be said that it would be a mistake to interpret the portrayal of Silk in the novel as an uncomplicated endorsement of the ideology of liberal individualism. Roth here assumes his mantle within a tradition of American writers, Melville perhaps chief among them, that subject such "classic" American ideology to unswerving scrutiny.

It is perhaps nonetheless wholly understandable that radical forms of cultural politics in the United States since the 1960s have embraced the channels of "procedural liberalism" defined by John Rawls. The courts, in particular, over the past few decades, have certainly been the most productive branch of government for those pursuing the "minoritarian" aims of contemporary liberalism. Constitutional legal procedures originally designed around classical liberal notions of individual rights have been reconceived in the light of more modern concerns about group rights. At a more fundamental level, it is this very idea of a "stable" and "complete" self that grounds theories of liberal individualism which has underwritten the identity politics of the cultural left since the 1960s and given rise to popular notions of racial "pride," "kinship," and "loyalty" among minority groups. Thus what Werner Sollors categorized as "the language of descent" has been privileged over the "language of consent," "achieved" identity has given way to "ascribed" identity, and a "dissensus" has replaced a "consensus."

Black legal scholar Randall Kennedy, however, is another commentator who has taken issue with the idea that "descent" matters more than "consent" or, to invoke his own phraseology, "loyalties of blood" outweigh "loyalties of will." In the 1997 article "My Race Problem—and Ours" (a provocative allusion, of course, to Podhoretz's essay), Kennedy eschews the notion of "racial pride" in favor of what he believes "should properly be the object of pride for an individual: something that he or she has accomplished."[68] As well as citing such prominent black figures from American history as Frederick Douglass in support of this distinction, he also asks why, given the contribution of numerous *white* abolitionists and civil-rights advocates in the struggle toward racial equality, gratitude felt for achievements in this sphere should be "racially bounded"? In this context, Kennedy invokes a number of figures such as Elijah Lovejoy, Viola Liuzzo, and James Reeb—but one might also, of course, add John Brown to this pantheon.

"My Race Problem—and Ours" also carries an implicit debt to Rawlsian liberalism. Kennedy's rejection of the idea of racial kinship is motivated by a desire to "avoid its burdens and . . . be free to claim what the distinguished theorist Michael Sandel labels 'the unencumbered self.' " Sandel, of course, believes that such a conception of self "fails to capture those loyalties and responsibilities whose moral force consists partly in the fact that living by them is inseparable from understanding ourselves as the particular persons we are—as members of this family, or city or people or nation, as bearers of that history, as citizens of this republic."[69] In other words, Rawls and by extension Kennedy fail to recognize that any "self" is always a *situated* self; subjectivity is always, in effect, intersubjectivity.

Kennedy, however, questions the inherent political conservatism that underpins Sandel's communitarian critique of Rawls. The "deference to tradition" presupposed by an unquestioning adherence to such preexisting "loyalties" and "responsibilities," he claims, frequently serves to stifle social change and inhibit progressive political projects. Furthermore, not only do such "feelings of primordial attachment" posit an unduly static (rather than, to use Zuckerman's term, "sliding") model of subjectivity, but they "often represent mere prejudice or superstition, a hangover from childhood socialization from which many people never recover."[70] This too is how Coleman Silk frames himself philosophically in *The Human Stain*: in the voluntarist discourse of the Rawlsian liberal center ground:

> [Silk] was not a firebrand or an agitator in any way. Nor was he a mad-man. Nor was he a radical or revolutionary, not even intellectually or philo-sophically speaking, unless it is revolutionary to believe that disregarding prescriptive society's most restrictive demarcations and asserting indepen-dently a free personal choice which is well within the law was something other than a basic human right.
>
> (*THS*, 155)

Kennedy also stresses the importance of the "unencumbered self" to critical thinking and includes himself among those "animated by a liberal, individualistic and universalistic ethos that is skeptical of, if not hostile to, the particularisms—national, ethnic, religious and racial—that seem to have grown so strong recently, even in arenas, such as major cosmopolitan universities, where one might have expected their demise."[71]

Such liberal voluntarism, the preference for "achieved" over "ascribed" understandings of identity, can be viewed as a reaction not only to con-servative and communitarian efforts to discredit the Rawlsian idea of an "original" or "unencumbered" self but also to the "identity" politics of the "cultural" left. Since the 1960s, the American left has ceased to designate economics as the primary sphere within which to address injustice and, instead, has turned to the cultural realm. Thus the "identity" of both indi-viduals and social groups is no longer seen as contingent or malleable—a product, primarily, of unequal economic relations that has in the past and can continue to be in the future reshaped by egalitarian political move-ments. Identity becomes, rather, a more or less fixed category requiring carefully calibrated acts of contrition or unreflective celebration depend-ing upon the levels of humiliation one's particular "group" has either experienced or inflicted on others' historically.

The American philosopher and social commentator Richard Rorty also laments the shift from "achieved" to "ascribed" forms of American iden-tity and the concomitant rise of a cultural left. A consequence of this is what he describes in his 1997 William E. Massey lectures as the "eclipse of [a] reformist left" that embraced a more inclusive, radical, and, ultimately, patriotic agenda. Like Kennedy, Rorty sees the U.S. academy—the arena where the cultural left has made its influence most conspicuously felt—as indicative of this trend. If 1968 might be said to be the moment when left-liberal intellectuals first became suspicious of those patriotic values that sustained Wallace supporters in 1948, then the humanities faculties of American universities had by 1998 institutionalized such suspicion. The fact that culture has superseded class as the organizing category for the American Left is evident in the myriad forms of cultural and ethnic studies courses and degrees available (in gender, queer, and African American studies). "Nobody," however, as Rorty caustically notes, "is setting up a program in unemployed studies, homeless studies or trailerpark studies."

For Rorty, the cultural left and the conservative "punditocracy" have combined to keep issues of culture rather than economics at the top of the U.S. political agenda. The prime motivation for the cultural left, in this respect, he claims, appears to be "to do something for people who have been humiliated—to help victims of socially acceptable forms of sadism by making such sadism no longer acceptable."[72] It is within this context of a response to a historically sited sense of "humiliation" that we might situate Delphine Roux's relationship with Silk in *The Human Stain* and, in particular, her reaction to his affair with Faunia Farley.

The pair initially clash after a female student approaches Roux complaining that the plays of Euripides taught in Silk's class are "degrading to women" (*THS*, 184). Silk responds with disdain to such "narrow, parochial ideological concerns," or what he regards as a symptom of the politicization of culture since the 1960s. For Silk, the only way to respond to the plays is as an individual, rather than from a perspective selected from the arsenal of identity politics. As someone who has been "reading and thinking about these plays all [his] life," he resents the attempt to undermine a pedagogical hierarchy based on achievement. Roux responds that this may be so, but he has never confronted such texts "from Elena's feminist perspective." Silk emphatically rejects the idea that the meaning of a text can be generated from such "narrow, parochial ideological" cultural (or theoretical) sources. "Never even," he thus replies, "from Moses's Jewish perspective. Never even from the fashionable Nietzschean perspective about perspective" (*THS*, 191).

Coleman Silk's cultural concerns, of course, invariably have a political dimension too. Earlier in the same chapter, Silk overhears on campus "three young guys, new to the faculty since his day . . . relaxing together, talking over the day's Clinton news before heading home to their wives and children." Their conversation is described as a "chorus"—an obvious indication that, as in a Greek tragedy, what is being said can be interpreted as a "detached" reflection on the main action (*THS*, 151). It is perhaps unsurprising that much of what is said in the following passage about Monica Lewinsky has significant bearing on the novel's broader themes and motifs. "She was talking to everybody," one of the young men begins,

> She's part of that dopey culture. Yap, yap, yap. Part of this generation that is proud of its shallowness. The sincere performance is everything. Sincere and empty, totally empty. The sincerity that goes in all directions. The sincerity that is worse than falseness, and the innocence that is worse than corruption. . . . Their whole language is a summation of the stupidity of the last forty years. Closure. *There's* one. My students cannot stay in the place where thinking must occur. Closure! They fix on the conventionalized narrative, with its beginning, middle and end—every experience, no matter how ambiguous, no matter how knotty or mysterious, must lend itself to this normalizing, conventionalizing, anchorman cliché.
>
> (*THS*, 147)

We find here, then, an example of what was described in chapter 3 in connection with Lionel Trilling as a certain "allergy to closure." Silk picks up this theme, as well as that of an increasingly moribund post-1960s intellectual culture, in his response to the student complaint of misogyny in Euripides. "They know, like, nothing. After nearly forty years of teaching such students," he claims, "I can tell you that a feminist perspective on Euripides is what they *least* need. Providing the most naive of readers with a feminist perspective on Euripides is one of the best ways you could devise to close down their thinking before it's even had a chance to begin to demolish one of their brainless 'likes'" (*THS*, 192).

Shortly after the Euripides episode, Delphine Roux receives the "spooks" complaint from a black female student, and Silk's fate is ultimately sealed. It is only when, however, Roux later learns of Silk's relationship with Faunia that the themes of "humiliation" and "sadism" Rorty draws attention to in relation to the cultural left come fully to the fore. Roux is clearly frustrated by the fact that Silk is unimpressed by her impeccable academic credentials (École Normale Supérieure, Yale) and her rise to department chair while still in her twenties. She believes that Silk uses the notion of "intellectual independence" as a screen for the maintenance of unequal power relations, particularly those pertaining to race and gender. Thus his relationship with Farley is cast as an act of revenge on those women, such as herself, who questioned and eventually overturned the intellectual and institutional authority that has been acquired on the basis of such unequal power relations:

> With no more female students who dared question his bias for him to intimidate, with no more black girls needing nurturing for him to ridicule, with no more young women professors like herself threatening his hegemony for him to browbeat and insult, he had managed to dredge up, from the college's nethermost reaches, a candidate for subjugation who was the prototype of female helplessness: a full-fledged battered wife.
>
> (*THS*, 194)

Roux, moreover, perceives the Silk-Farley relationship as a projection of her own relationship with the ex-dean. She perceives Farley as a "mirror-image" of or "substitute for herself, a woman, like Roux, who is half his age and employed by the college yet a woman otherwise [her] opposite in every way" (*THS*, 195). The Silk-Roux psychodrama is given much currency in the novel, yet, as with Greek dramas such as *Medea*, it would be a mistake to read this in reductive terms as a misogynist tale of a neurotic woman unable to secure the attention of the man she desires. The character of Delphine Roux is very carefully drawn, her resistance to male power sympathetically described, but, more interestingly, the crisis of identity she undergoes is analogous to that experienced by Silk himself. This explains why Roux is so unnerved by the fact of her own transparency in Silk's eyes. As a once intellectually gifted child himself, Silk alone is able to identify and thus expose the nature of her internal struggle: "To this day, she continued to be disquieted by Coleman Silk's presence just to the degree that she wished for him now to be unsettled by her. Something about him always led her back to her childhood and the precocious child's fear that she is being seen through; also to the precocious child's fear that she is not being seen enough" (*THS*, 185).

Delphine Roux is depicted in the novel as a highly intelligent individual "encumbered" by the social and professional disguises she is forced to assume. Like Silk, she chooses to "pass" for what people take her to be: a beautiful, precocious, but intellectually aloof French feminist professor. Yet the type of ersatz solidarities and identifications this imposes are an encumbrance to Roux. This finds expression in her alienation from her immediate American surroundings—the students absorbed in popular culture, uninterested in her prestigious French intellectual pedigree—but it is also evident in the deeply ambivalent attitude she has toward her up-bringing. This manifests itself in her earlier decision to reject the French higher education system for a place at Yale—the first step in what is characterized as an "imperfect revolt against her Frenchness" (*THS*, 272). Like Silk, she is also forced to define herself against the image of an overbearing parent who stands for much that she wishes to escape: "family ideals as they were *set* in the thirteenth century . . . the pure and ancient aristocracy of the provinces, all of them thinking the same, looking the same, sharing the same stifling values and the same stifling religious obedience." Roux's mother, we learn, "embodied those values"(*THS*, 275).

It is her status as a woman within the context of her own specific academic métier, however, that constitutes the major aspect of Roux's crisis of identity. She struggles to establish good relationships with a "cabal" of women tutors on the campus, preferring the company of the male tutors and visitors who are less dismissive of her cashmere and leather clothing and less disapproving of her more open sexuality. She is, in this way, caught not only between two cultures but also between contrasting ideas as to the significance of gender relations in these cultures more generally: "All they see is Delphine using what she understands they sarcastically call 'her little French aura' on all the tenured men. Yet she is strongly tempted to court the cabal, to tell them in so many words that she doesn't *like* the French aura—if she did she'd be living in France" (*THS*, 271–272). Likewise, in intellectual terms, Roux feels caught between the traditional humanism exemplified by a writer such as Milan Kundera—whose lectures in Paris helped ignite her love of literature—and the expertise in literary theory she must continue to embrace in order to succeed as a foreign female scholar of literature in the United States in the 1990s.

It is within such contexts that we once again return to both this novel's and the trilogy's single most powerful theme: betrayal. To the cabal of women tutors, for example, "everything is an issue, everything is an ideological stance, everything is a betrayal—everything's a selling out. Beauvoir sold out, Delphine sold out, et cetera, et cetera" (*THS*, 269). For Delphine Roux, the theme of betrayal also extends to the philosophical-aesthetic sphere. "The humanist," for example, we learn, "is the very part of her own self that she sometimes feels herself betraying." Milan Kundera himself functions as a conduit for such feelings of betrayal. The shame imposed by a professional life that willfully disregards those humanist aesthetic principles espoused by a writer such as Kundera that once enchanted her has now "become at times like the shame of betraying a kindly, trusting, absent lover" (*THS*, 266–267). Delphine Roux, at the end of the novel, is as besieged by social forces as Coleman Silk. This is a consequence, it might be said, of their unrelenting pursuit of an "unencumbered self." If Roux's ultimate fate is to be "isolated in America," then the same conditions of such isolation attend the fate of Silk:

> De-countried, isolated, estranged . . . in a desperate state of bewildered longing and surrounded on all sides by admonishing forces defining her as the enemy. And all because she'd gone eagerly in search of an existence of her own. All because she'd been courageous and refused to take the prescribed view of herself. She seemed to herself to have subverted herself in the altogether admirable effort to *make* herself.
>
> (*THS*, 272)

This brings us back to the accusations of treachery, betrayal, and deception leveled at presidents such as Bill Clinton and Richard Nixon discussed earlier. Truth and politics, however, as Hannah Arendt warned, have always been wary partners. In an essay responding to one of the defining moments of the Vietnam War (and a high-profile instance of Nixon administration mendacity), "Lying in Politics: Reflections on the Pentagon Papers" (1971), Arendt perceives a more intimate relationship between lying and political action:

> In order to make room for one's own action, something that was there before must be removed or destroyed, and things as they were before are changed. Such change would be impossible if we could not mentally remove ourselves from where we physically are located and imagine that things might as well be different from what they actually are. In other words, the deliberate denial of factual truth—the ability to lie—and the capacity to change facts—the ability to act—are interconnected; they owe their existence to the same source: imagination.[73]

The pertinence of this observation to the decision made by Coleman Silk to "pass" is clear. Silk, in pursuing the logic of the American goal of self-creation to the point that he does, is a man of action par excellence. Lest this escape us, Arendt goes on to state that those "who act, to the extent that they feel themselves to be the masters of their own futures, will forever be tempted to make themselves masters of the past, too."[74] The formidable extent of such "mastery" on Silk's part, of course, is evident in the awful finality of the break he makes with his "black" past. To be "unencumbered" of one's past in this way then—to be *free* in a Rawlsian sense—obviously involves a degree of denial, a capacity to imagine the world otherwise that can only be enacted by "living a lie" on some level. This voluntarism, premised on a willful "ignorance" of present social and historical realities is, of course, apparent in the deep ambiguity that underwrites Rawls's "veil of ignorance" formulation. Nonetheless, Arendt's claim in an earlier essay, "Truth and Politics"(1967), that "our ability to lie . . . belongs among the few obvious, demonstrable data that confirm human freedom," strikes the same complex note.[75]

Indeed Martin Jay, in a review of former Clinton aide George Stephanopoulos's memoir *All Too Human: A Political Education* and Christopher Hitchens's *No One Left to Lie to*, invokes Arendt to defend Bill Clinton from the various charges of "betrayal." For Hitchens, Clinton's slippery weaving or "triangulation" between populist democratic rhetoric ("it's the economy, stupid"), corporate conservatism, and the politics of personal ambition and power-lust (what Hitchens sees as his "ruthless vanity") constitutes a betrayal of (New Deal) liberalism. Stephanopoulos's understanding of Clinton's treachery has, obviously, a more personal dimension, but the same ideological aspect is never far from the surface. As Jay notes: "For [Stephanopoulos], as for Hitchens, 'triangulation' is just a fancy word for betrayal."[76]

Jay here usefully distinguishes between "the Big Lie, the Orwellian reversal of the truth typical of totalitarian societies" and what he describes as "democratic fabulation." The former, he claims, "seeks to still the conflict of disparate opinions and install a monolithic belief system to which no alternative is possible . . . [and] . . . the imaginative potential of lying is squashed in the name of a perfectly realized myth, which can brook no critical resistance." The latter, however, is characterized by a public realm premised on the free exchange of "opinion" that, by its very existence, downgrades the idea of "truth" in the political sphere. Jay then goes to explain both the process and outcome of the Clinton-Lewinsky crisis as products of such "democratic fabulation" that "allow a thousand mendacious flowers to bloom."

The problem with critics of such self-created, "sliding" subjects as Clinton, Jay suggests, is that they ignore this context of "democratic fabulation"—the only political context that makes room for such subjectivity. As Jay says: "Not only does Hitchens discern a consistent pattern of duplicitous triangulation in everything Clinton has done, he is also confident of knowing all the motives underlying the President's actions. No action is overdetermined or indeterminate; they all serve the same triangulating function: maintaining political viability at the cost of betraying a liberal agenda."[77]

It is precisely the idea of "overdetermination"—that is, of an effect produced by more than one cause—that heavily informs Roth's novelistic constructions of "character." This is the case not only in *The Human Stain*, where Coleman's act of "passing" and his affair with Faunia Farley are obviously overdetermined in this sense, but also in the other novels. It underwrites too the theme of "betrayal" as it is articulated through the construction of character. If figures such as the Swede, Ira Ringold, and Coleman Silk are "representative," they are so in complex, "overdetermined" ways—as both the agents and the victims of the various social, cultural, and ideological forces of their times. They are not only accused of "betrayal" on the basis of reductive interpretations of their character but, as we have seen, also "betrayed" themselves by the promise of a specific midcentury expression of American liberalism. This might best be described as a "paleoliberalism" squeezed to the margins of American life by the end of the century as a result of the rise of neoconservatism and the cultural left.[78] This is the "majoritarian" liberalism of the midcentury "proud decades" of American life that was both anti-McCarthy *and* unambiguously anticommunist. The emphasis here is on the relationship of the individual to the republic or broader national collective rather than any ethnic subgroup.

If a political position can be consistently traced in these late novels of Philip Roth, then this is surely it. Such "paleoliberalism" is perhaps best characterized by its unapologetic commitment to the *idea* of America and, in this way, is deeply rooted in the aspirational, optimistic, yet pragmatic politics of the founding fathers discussed in chapter 1. It is also this specific form of patriotic ardor that connects this politics to the republican origins of the United States. The postwar political developments most hostile to this "paleoliberalism" of what Arthur Schlesinger Jr. famously described as the "vital center," are those that come under the strongest fire in these novels. They include the un-American "Americanism" of McCarthyist demagoguery, the totalitarian terminus point of communist politics, the infantile "popular democratic" political theater of the New Left during the Vietnam years, the conservative and neoconservative assault on the private sphere that produced such hysteria over Clinton's sexual behavior in the nineties, and the antiélitist, anti-Americanism of the late twentieth-century cultural left. It is this notion of the American political novelist as, in some sense, "republican," that I believe unites the fictions examined thus far and that will now be explored in greater detail.

WRITING THE REPUBLIC

Moby Dick and the Form of American Political Fiction

> Artistic form, correctly understood, does not formulate content that has already been prepared and discovered, but rather allows it to be found and seen for the first time.
>
> —MIKHAIL BAKHTIN

> The choice of one narrative voice over another is not a technical problem, but a moral one.
>
> —RUSSELL BANKS

I n the latter half of the 1960s, Irving Howe developed and refined some of the themes he had discussed in the previous decade connected with the relationship between politics and the American novel. In *Politics and the Novel* (1957), Howe, taking his cue from the myth critics, had been more or less content to dismiss the American novel as hopelessly imprisoned by a "politics of isolation." His 1967 essay "Anarchy and Authority in American Literature," however, signaled a retreat of sorts from this view by tracing a latent political strain in classic American fiction. This turned out to be a politics of foundations rather than a politics of the structures built upon them, that is, "a politics concerned with the *idea* of society itself, a politics that dares consider—wonderful question—whether society is good and—still more wonderful—whether society is necessary." From this, Howe remarks on a "paradox" that would seem to completely reconceptualize the status of politics in American literature as it is understood in his earlier study: "The paradox of it all is that a literature which on any manifest level is not really political at all should nevertheless be precisely the literature to raise the most fundamental question in political theory: What is the rationale for society, the justification for the state?"

Accordingly, what we find in this "fundamental" form of political questioning, he avows, is "a strong if subterranean current of anarchism." Howe is then careful—perhaps too careful—to distinguish this "anarchist" strain from its nineteenth-century European variants, which he associates, by implication, with urbanism, industrialization, and "a spectrum of emphases from Populism to terrorism." What he wishes to convey, rather, is that sense of "anarchism as a social vision arising spontaneously from the conditions of preindustrial American culture, anarchism as a bias of the American imagination releasing its deepest, which is to say its most frustrated, yearnings."[1] This is something akin, we might say, to the almost visceral, emotion-invested idea of "persuasion" discussed in chapter 1. Here then, as in the conclusion to his excursion on the American novel in *Politics and the Novel*, Howe wishes to draw a distinction between America and Europe.

One of the political novels Howe refers to as representative of the type American culture seems incapable of producing is Dostoevsky's *The Possessed* (1871). Anarchism of the "European" cast, as understood by Howe in his 1967 piece, is, of course, one of this novel's chief concerns. Yet, as Howe himself notes in his chapter on Dostoevsky (which focuses largely on *The Possessed*), the cultural context for this exploration of anarchism stands in sharp contradistinction to those of Western Europe, familiar from the novels of a writer such as Joseph Conrad. It is one of a continental landmass that is neither wholly Asiatic or European, characterized by an intellectual culture in which, in Howe's phrase, a "mania for totality" looms ever large as the twentieth century approaches. Modern Russian literature, as it begins to find expression in the novels of Dostoevsky, is an outlet for an understanding, in Howe's words, of "religion as a branch of politics and politics as a form of religion," informed by ideas such as myth, prophecy, and salvation—ideas conspicuously remote from the concerns of European realism. "The school of criticism which treats the novel mainly in terms of social manners will," in this respect, Howe continues, "consequently face great difficulties when confronted with a writer like Dostoevsky."[2]

It is clear that this cultural context ensures that, at least in some respects, Dostoevsky's novels would appear to resemble more closely the loose, prophetic, theologically informed romances of Herman Melville or Nathaniel Hawthorne as opposed to the sober and secular political fictions of a Stendhal or Conrad. As with so much else though, Alexis de Tocqueville had already alerted the mid-nineteenth-century reading public to the shared sense of providential design underwriting American and Russian national identity. His fascinating comparative analysis of the two nations at the close of the first volume of *Democracy in America* (1835) also serves to illuminate the differing cultural contexts that give shape to the respective expressions of "anarchism" in Dostoevsky and classic American literature. "The American," he notes,

> fights against natural obstacles; the Russian is at grips with men. The former combats the wilderness and barbarism; the latter, civilization with all its arms. America's conquests are made with the plowshare, Russia's with the sword.
>
> To attain their aims, the former relies on personal interest and gives free scope to the unguided strength and common sense of individuals.
>
> The latter in a sense concentrates the whole power of society in one man.
>
> One has freedom as the principal means of action; the other has servitude.[3]

Though the former can, in quite straightforward fashion, be associated with "democratic" characters such as Natty Bumppo and Huck Finn, the latter might equally be seen in the "autocratic" light of Aaron Burr, Captain Ahab, or John Brown as well as a figure such as Peter Verkhovensky, the charismatic anarchist revolutionary in *The Possessed*. These are all, to embrace the apposite metaphor, "tsarist" figures seeking to annihilate the agency or autonomous capacities of their followers; their aim is to operate as "concentrations" of "the whole power of society in one man." The nineteenth-century American context, nonetheless, is democratic rather than autocratic. Accordingly, the "tsarist" usurper figure is reconstituted in American culture as the ambivalent classical dictator who seeks to wrest control of republican institutions from the people but also claims to act in their name. What connects Russia and the United States in their shared cultural compulsion to explore such figures is an awareness of their respective cultures' powerful self-conceptions of the nation-state in terms of "manifest destiny." Both, after all, turned out to be the most significant imperial powers of the twentieth century, the respective architects, as Tocqueville so curiously anticipated, of a "bipolar" world for close to five decades: "their point of departure is different and their paths diverse; nevertheless, each seems called by some secret design of Providence one day to hold in its hands the destinies of half the world."[4]

Equally, in pursuing this connection, we might take note of what Mikhail Bakhtin identifies as the stress on "simultaneity" evident in Dostoevsky's work—a stress that would appear to resonate with notions more familiar from the repertoire of myths uncovered by the postwar group of American literary critics. Just as Howe, like these earlier critics, reads much classic American literature "spatially," Bakhtin views Dostoevsky's work as expressive of a "persistent urge to see all things as being coexistent and to perceive and depict all things side by side and simultaneously, as if in space rather than time."[5] This leads, Bakhtin continues, to a very specific conception of novelistic character:

> [Dostoevsky's] characters recall nothing, they have no biography, in the sense of something in the past or of something fully experienced and endured. They remember from their past only those things which have not ceased to be current for them and which continue to be experienced in the present: an unexpiated sin or crime, an unforgiven insult. ... Therefore there is no causality in the Dostoevskian novel, no origination, no explanations based on the past, on the influence of the environment or of upbringing, etc. The hero's every act is in the present, and in this sense is unpredetermined; it is conceived of and depicted by the author as being free.[6]

Dostoevsky, we might conclude, is a purveyor of nineteenth-century Russian "Adams"—or representations of "anarchy" that stand in extreme tension to tsarist and Orthodox Christian "authority." Not only do the above examples of a perspectiveless, ahistorical view of "an unexpiated sin or crime, an unforgiven insult" obviously bring to mind Captain Ahab or John Brown, they also recall the predicaments of those "Adamic" figures associated with the idea of destructive "innocence" explored in earlier chapters. These would include Owen Brown, Seymour Levov, or Coleman Silk, but this Bakhtinian understanding of character equally returns us to the invocations of Melville's *Billy Budd* and Dostoevsky's Grand Inquisitor in Lionel Trilling's *The Middle of the Journey* covered in chapter 3. The chief concern that connects these fictions is the meaning of such Adamic "innocence" in the domain of the political—a sense of innocence, many contend today, that finds in the American literary tradition more expression than it merits historically.

Irving Howe, nonetheless, is surely right to suggest that among Dostoevsky's major achievements as a novelist of politics is his capacity to problematize this will to innocence. As he writes of Dostoevsky's characters: "None escapes humiliation and shame, none is left free from attack. In the world of Dostoevsky, no one is spared, but there is a supreme consolation: no one is excluded." This "will to innocence" is connected with an aversion to politics and the "dirty hands" and shabby compromises, the potential for "humiliation and shame" it entails, an aversion that the American liberal tradition—especially in its privileging of the economy over the polity as the realm of "freedom"—has done much to engender. It is precisely this perception of the political that the republican impulse in American political fiction seeks to confront, counter, and, ultimately, correct.

In *Political Fiction and the American Self,* John Whalen-Bridge puts forward a negative definition of "republican criticism" as a repudiation of the notion that "politics is 'Other' to the concerns of literature."7 However, this important if tentative attempt to articulate an American literary tradition of "radical republicanism"—in the absence of an account of what might differentiate a "radical" form of republicanism from any other in Whalen-Bridge's study—requires further substantiation. The "republican" proposal appears briefly at the close of a chapter in the middle of *Political Fiction and the American Self* before quickly fading from view. Whalen-Bridge's concluding chapter, while usefully suggesting, among other things, that "novels that combine politics with literary purpose" should not be sidelined in favor of "novels *about* politics," nonetheless leaves the republican impulse, which might enable us to discriminate between the two, undefined.

It is my view that there is a clearly discernible tradition of American political fiction whose formal narrative qualities locate it within a nexus of republican values that serve to distinguish it from other fictional works or genres. Like many others before me, I am here indebted to Hayden White's work on the relationship between narrative and meaning within historiographical contexts. In particular, I am interested in the relationship between ideology and form, that is, the type of questions White has posed pertaining to the "content of the form." My approach rests, finally, on White's supposition that "narrative is not merely a neutral discursive form that may or may not be used to represent real events in their aspect as developmental processes but rather entails ontological and epistemic choices with distinct ideological and even specifically political implications."[8]

This is not to say that such political fictions are unrelated to what John Carlos Rowe has described as the "liberal tradition [of] *aesthetic dissent*"[9] grounded in an "Emersonian . . . assumption that rigorous reflection on the processes of thought and representation constitutes in itself a critique of social reality and effects a transformation of the naive realism that confuses truth with social convention."[10] For Rowe, this "Emersonian aura" has marginalized a literature rooted in political action rather than contemplation but, once more, the political design of his analysis appears to be no more than to extend the range of both the historical and contemporary literary canons. We are asked, yet again, to "purify" an American past and create some new American Adams (with a few prelapsarian Eves thrown in for good measure), only this time from the raw materials provided by politically "innocent" victims of the by now familiar catalogue of American oppression (slavery, racism, sexism, genocide). The novels that I examined in earlier chapters, however, were not selected on the basis that they fail to discuss the various stains on the American historical record, but that they do so while problematizing—rather than seeking to sustain at all costs—the idea of innocence in these or any other highly charged political contexts. Moreover, in their adherence to a set of recognizable formal qualities, they remain within the philosophical contours of what I take to be a *usable* Emersonian tradition of "aesthetic dissent."

The particular narrative feature that connects a broad range of American political novels can be characterized by the tension between what we might describe as a "conflicted narrator" and an ambivalently viewed central character who is the prime focus of the narrative. The novelistic template for this form, as I will demonstrate, is inaugurated with Herman Melville's *Moby Dick* but goes on to provide the architecture for numerous American political novels from Henry Adams's *Democracy* (1880) through to Robert Penn Warren's *All The King's Men* (1946) and on to the bestselling *roman á clef* of the Clinton era *Primary Colors* (1996). The form, too, is evident in the novels examined in the previous chapters of this study, where the requisite "republican" tension is apparent between (the narrator) Schuyler and (the "narrated" character) Burr in Gore Vidal's *Burr*, Owen and John Brown in Banks's *Cloudsplitter*, John Laskell and Gifford Maxim in Trilling's *The Middle of the Journey*, and Zuckerman and, respectively, "Swede" Levov,

Ira Ringold, and Coleman Silk in the various installments of Philip Roth's trilogy.

The "republican" aspect of this tension between a narrating and a narrated character in this tradition of American political fiction, however, only slides into view once the nature of the oppositions they usually establish—to varying though always ascertainable degrees—are fully understood. The most important among these is the idea of the narrated character as the embodiment of a "totalizing"—and in novels such as *Moby Dick, Cloudsplitter*, and *The Middle of the Journey*, even "totalitarian" logic—that the narrating subject finds both deeply unnerving but also undeniably compelling. In only slightly more schematic philosophical terms, the former is usually associated with action, the latter with thought. From a cultural perspective, the former is seen in terms of "corruption," the latter "innocence." Finally, in a more circumscribed literary sense, the former might be associated with the "monological" imagination of nineteenth-century realist fiction, the latter with the "dialogical" imagination evident in the fiction of Dostoevsky lionized by Bakhtin.

John Whalen-Bridge understandably takes issue with the way in which Bakhtinian literary theory implicitly disqualifies politics from its system via a relativist celebration of "heteroglossia" and "polyphony." Despite the significant influence of this idea of the post-Dostoevskian novel as a "democratic" vehicle in its expression and affirmation of a multiplicity of voices, the overall effect is undoubtedly to devalue the idea that some voices might be more persuasive than others. Perhaps inevitably, as a result the reader becomes immobilized by the effect of what Whalen-Bridge labels "interpretive wonder." So although political action may originate from the type of complex and numerous interpretive judgments presupposed in the Bakhtinian schema, it also ultimately demands "an end or at least a suspension of interpretive wonder." As Whalen-Bridge concludes:

> The political act itself requires the suspension of interpretation. One of the things literature often resents about politics is just this delimitation of a horizon of possibilities, an exclusion of *some* possibilities—which will frequently strike some literary observers as "unimaginative." Politics, from a strictly literary point of view, opens the door to a flawed dimension of human existence. Literary study favours open-ended interpretation (the celebration of Bakhtin's heteroglossia), whereas politics tends towards a finality of meaning that is called monologic.[11]

It is, accordingly, an act of *discrimination* (with all the connotations that term signifies) that results in a final choice between competing interpretive judgments that is the *sine qua non* of political action. In politics, "dialogue" must always eventually give way to "monologue" insofar as one option "discriminates" against others that are either compromised via absorption or excluded altogether. Whalen-Bridge's point here constitutes another breakthrough in our understanding of political fiction, but, if we go on to pursue the idea of a republican-oriented literature (as well as criticism), we can perceive the degree to which, in the American political novel at least, the dynamic between those *literary* inclinations that favor the dialogical and those *political* inclinations that lean toward the monological provide a fruitful basis for both comprehending a political tradition and thinking about politics more generally.

In order to do this, we must first take account of the opinion William R. Everdell puts forward in his magisterial history of republicanism *The End of Kings* (1983). "The essential republican principle," he posits, "is that no one person shall rule the community, that everyone shall have a part in the public's business."[12] This most basic of prohibitions against autocracy is at the very heart of the tension between the narrators and the central narrated characters in the American political novel. The central moral problem that arises in this situation presents itself as one primarily of *character*—what is it about the "character" of the figures under description that makes them a threat to the republic? However, as Everdell astutely recognizes, this is merely symptomatic of a political culture that has degenerated to the point that questions of character tend to arise only in a very limited context:

> American history itself has resolved, at the elementary level, into a chronicle of presidential character, conveniently divided into thirty-nine presidential administrations. ... The most trivial events of a presidential election get more attention than the passage and publication of laws. Children are taught virtue through the contemplation of Washington, Jefferson, Jackson, Lincoln and Roosevelt (first names unnecessary except for the Roosevelts) and are not even taught the last names of John Milton, Roger Sherman, Thaddeus Stevens, or George Norris. Ben Franklin hangs on grimly, despite the fact that no-one celebrates his birthday, and despite being dropped off the half-dollar in favor of a president whose most lasting accomplishment was to fall before an assassin's bullet in the age of television.[13]

Republican political fiction serves to counter this impulse by bringing to bear on the "monological" outlook of the dictator the consciousness of a conflicted, ambivalent narrator. This narrator is generally critical but also, importantly, conditioned by a "presiding" authority in the text or, alternatively, the "presidential" qualities of the character whose story he narrates. In this respect, in republican political terms, the narrator most resembles the figure of the senator whose "rank" depends on the characteristics Everdell denotes as "intelligence, judgment and preparation."[14] It is through our own assessments of these particular "senatorial" qualities of the narrator that we, in turn, pass judgment on their "reliability." Such novels, furthermore, insofar as they seek to distribute or "balance" narrative power, deploy their narrators in a way that recalls the upper chamber's most important responsibility in a republic—to provide the final barrier against dictatorship. This might go some way to explaining why, though the narrated character usually dies by the close of the narrative, the narrator almost always survives, invariably as a chastened *isolato* and/or Ishmaelian exile.

The resolution of such fictions, nonetheless, invariably involves articulations of pastoral, sometimes even "Adamic" renewal. We might here recall Ishmael, adrift "on a soft and dirge-like main" amid "unharming sharks ... and savage sea-hawks ... with sheathed beaks,"[15] Owen Brown making his way westward under a "sky [that] had cleared" over "fields covered with a skin of powdery snow" (*Cloudsplitter*, 758), Charles Schuyler in *Burr* representing the United States government in Europe at a Feast of the Immaculate Conception, the final image here being that of the "crowned figure of the Virgin" (*Burr*, 574). We should consider, finally, Zuckerman's description of the stars above the New England countryside at the end of *I Married a Communist* as a "colossal spectacle of no antagonism" (*IMAC*, 323) or his "pure and peaceful" vision at the close of *The Human Stain* of a "solitary man on a bucket, fishing through eighteen inches of ice in a lake that's constantly turning over its water atop an arcadian mountain in America" (*THS*, 361). The central point is that while subordination to the "monological" will of the "dictator" invariably generates tragedy, nevertheless an American sense of freedom that reasserts the importance of judgment and intelligence always allows for the possibility of a republican return to first principles. Such novels are Janus-faced insofar as they reflect a society that, at once, reveres a political act of founding yet produces a literature, as Philip Fisher has written, premised on "creative destruction."[16]

The republic is couched in literal terms in the novels I have examined, but it can also be presented through metaphor or allegory—an attribute John Whalen-Bridge construes in terms of "submerged" politics in relation to *Moby Dick*. For Whalen-Bridge, *Moby Dick* represents a loss of political nerve on Melville's part, a recognition that art in mid-nineteenth-century America was obliged to conform to the bourgeois imperatives of a relatively narrow reading public. Notwithstanding this though, he believes, the novel's digression into a tale that foregrounds the "politics of storytelling" confronts readers with the residue of a "censored chapter" that provides some intimation of an "honorific treatment of class revolt" that was, finally, aborted.[17] "The novel as it is written, mainly as Ahab's story," it is claimed in this way, "only comes into being by displacing a different story. Any novel is the displacement of innumerable possible novels, but *Moby Dick* is different since it suggests so strongly what that other novel would have been: the story of a democratic hero's repudiation of tyranny."[18]

Whalen-Bridge offers a close reading of the "The *Town-Ho*'s Story" chapter, in which Ishmael recalls the occasion he relayed the tale of a ship rebellion to a group of aristocratic Peruvian Dons in Lima. This metafictional frame, it is argued, allows Melville to present the chapter as a parabolic commentary on the politics of storytelling. Ishmael's self-censorship and carefully choreographed evasions in this narrative are the result of a sensitivity to his audience, who—despite being fascinated by the specter of mutiny—are equally constrained by aristocratic values that reject any questioning of the existing social order. This neo-Marxist reading of *Moby Dick* is supported by various "two book" theories recruited from earlier Melville scholarship. These theories, based on interpretation of Melville's correspondence and other documentary evidence, account for the novel's discontinuities and structural puzzles in a number of ways, but more than one proposes that both "The *Town-Ho*'s Story" and Steelkilt (the "democratic hero" character who features in Ishmael's tale) once provided the basis for the novel as originally conceived by Melville.

Whalen-Bridge offers some persuasive close readings of "The *Town-Ho*'s Story" chapter as well as of other episodes in *Moby Dick* but leans too heavily, as many earlier political readings of the novel perhaps have, on interpretation that must reduce the level of ambiguity in the text (and its subtexts). By reading the novel primarily through the prism of "The *Town-Ho*'s Story," he betrays a predilection to unearth and celebrate a "democratic hero" without exploring—as Melville does—the political (as well as aesthetic) merits of such an unambiguous enterprise. For Whalen-Bridge, further-more, the political novel must, by definition, not only be *activist* in this sense but, judging by both the works he chooses and his readings of them, it must be activism of a left-leaning, feminist, and pro-choice stripe. At one point the need to avoid "preaching to the choir" is asserted, but it remains difficult to see in his study of works by Jack London, Norman Mailer, Toni Morrison, and Margaret Atwood how any space is made available in these texts for the possibility of *persuasion* rather than mere affirmation.

Twentieth-century "republican" notions of the public sphere as formu-lated by thinkers such as Hannah Arendt, by contrast, conceive the con-cept of persuasion as absolutely crucial to a healthy democratic polity. This can be viewed in Nietzschean terms, as an "agonistic" process, or as a more benign instantiation of what Jürgen Habermas has described as "commu-nicative action," but, either way, it posits an open-ended relation between speaker and listener.[19] This is a relation, ultimately, that allows for a much greater degree of cognitive dissonance than that evident between the author of *Political Fiction and the American Self* and the novelists under con-sideration in that work. One of the central ideas too of modern Rawlsian liberalism, it might be added, is that a self "unencumbered" by those pre-existing structural or ideological constraints that distort judgment must be the first condition of social justice.

When Whalen-Bridge disavows the "either/or formulation in which a book *either* sends us to the barricades *or* enlarges our experience," the dis-avowal involves more than the suggestion that it can do both; the infer-ence is that it *must*. The "barricades" here, of course, are no more than a metaphor for the more general notion of activism championed elsewhere in the study. We might, however, respond by asking whether an effective political novel should not only be capable of "send[ing] us to the barri-cades" but, alternatively, by asking why might it not also be possible for it to prompt us to question some of the assumptions that helped assemble those barricades in the first place. In other words, why does there appear to be an implicit prohibition against the idea of an effective *conservative* political novel? Or, for that matter, a novel with powerful conservative strands? Why is it hard to imagine grappling, under these conditions, with the relative complexity of the political vision in, to take just one example considered earlier, Philip Roth's *American Pastoral*? This is not to say that the studies of novels such as London's *The Iron Heel* or Mailer's *Harlot's Ghost* presented in *Political Fiction and the American Self* are reductive in any critical sense (or the novels themselves flawed in any aesthetic sense), merely that it seems curious that the only identifiable politics in either the criticism or the fiction itself continually falls within certain recognizably left-liberal parameters.

Such a limited political ambit perhaps explains why Whalen-Bridge views the fact that *Moby Dick* cannot be read as a "democratic hero's repudiation of tyranny" as effectively undermining any claims it might have as a political novel. Despite his own earlier acknowledgement that "aesthetic language and political language are not mutually exclusive,"[20] he then goes on to state the following:

> Melville's novel, then, was certainly connected with politics, and its political representations are not merely background scenery. It alluded to explosive controversies that would, in a few years, sunder the nation, yet these allusions are buried beneath teeming references to the Bible, literature of the more secular sort, general history, American and world geography, as well as subjects cetological. My claim is that the political portion is not merely outweighed by these other matters; it is masked by them. The political content dives beneath an ocean of literariness.[21]

For a critical study that leans to the left in the way Whalen-Bridge's does, the slippage between thought and action in his conception of the political novel is strange. "Action," reductively reframed as "activism," is privileged over the "act" of judging or, in Melville's case, dramatizing those conditions marked by the absence of requisite judgment. My point in relation to *Moby Dick* would be that, though Ishmael may not have "repudiated" the dictatorship of Ahab, he has *survived* it and, it would seem, imparted an invaluable amount of political wisdom in his account of the travails of the *Pequod*. It might be seen, in any case, as a very shallow "submersion" of politics that—a century and a half after its original appearance—allows a number of cultural critics to plunge into *Moby Dick* as a way of understanding American foreign policy since September 11, 2001.[22]

The political point of Melville's novel, nevertheless, is undoubtedly more ambiguous than such appropriations ultimately permit. As with Hannah Arendt's famous account of the trial of the Nazi functionary Adolf Eichmann, the meanings of *Moby Dick* may not be apparent so much in its dramatization of a "failure to repudiate" but, rather, in its depiction of the repercussions of a certain kind of "thoughtlessness" or "inability to think."[23] In the context of the American political novel, this often takes the form of an examination of the *bien pensant* or "thoughtless" liberal.[24] It is a similar "thoughtlessness" to that exhibited by Owen Brown in *Cloudsplitter*, Gifford Maxim (and Arthur and Nancy Croom) in *The Middle of the Journey*, Ira Ringold in *I Married a Communist*, and Seymour Levov in *American Pastoral*.

Nonetheless, the motivation behind American fictional explorations of such phenomena has its roots in more than just the residual or attenuated republican persuasion referred to above. It is also a deeply entrenched component of a more recognizably modern liberal tradition within the intellectual and artistic culture of the United States—a tradition of immanent critique that often seeks to reintroduce moral issues bracketed from public philosophy in the name of "procedural" efficiency. One of the most notable contributions to this intellectual tradition in the last decade or so is Michael Sandel's *Democracy's Discontent* (1996), which attempts to excavate a broadly republican tradition before presenting a comprehensive critique of "procedural" liberalism in its contemporary Rawlsian guise. But as other intellectual historians have been increasingly keen to stress (some in direct response to Sandel's work),[25] it makes little sense to speak of a politics informed by republicanism, liberalism, Protestant Christianity or, returning to Howe's more fluid designation, "anarchism," in terms of autonomous spheres. Americans, as James Kloppenberg has remarked, have been uniquely positioned to ensure that they yielded to no single vision: "In the absence of rigid traditions requiring differentiation by bloodlines, classes, or creeds, it was possible in nineteenth-century America . . . for diverse interpretations of these ideas to coexist and for loose and fluid coalitions to form and dissolve as different issues appeared and vanished."[26]

The contrapuntal structure of the American political novel I have outlined represents an attempt to negotiate some of the difficulties in maintaining the forms of "coexistence" and "coalition" Kloppenberg cites. The counterpoint drawn in these works between the "presiding" authority of the central narrated character and a countervailing "senatorial" authority, of course, is not the only source of political tension in these works. It does, however, in its choice of a certain culturally informed type of narrative voice, signal an attempt to return a *moral* component to the debate about the evolution of liberalism in the United States as well as its relationship to the development of an American literary tradition.

In *Democracy's Discontent*, Sandel notes the "drift to storylessness" that attends a modern civic virtue stretched to breaking point by the complex identities of "multiply encumbered selves."[27] As Russell Banks hints in the epigraph to this chapter, storytelling is never simply a question of writerly technique resolved by strictly literary practice or innovation. Each political culture generates its own specific moral and ideological conflicts at any one time. The conflicted narrator of the American political novel thus must be viewed as a symptom of the "republican" crisis of artistic and political representation brought to our attention by Sandel in a broader context. As with the prototypical *Moby Dick*, there are invariably a good deal of alternative compensatory voices which endeavor to mediate such conflict, giving these works much of the dialogical and "democratic" flavor Bakhtin uncovered in Dostoevsky. Nevertheless, what makes American political novels primarily "republican" rather than democratic in character is their foregrounding of this central tension between the two narrating and narrated personages: the man of action and the man of thought, the novel's "executive" power and its (unacknowledged) legislator.

The difficulty in disentangling the republican and democratic facets of political fiction in the United States is testimony to the complexity of the American political tradition more generally. While the identification of this tradition with "liberalism"remains the unavoidable starting point in the study of U.S. intellectual history, literary critics concerned with understanding the dynamics of the American political novel must begin to share the more complex understanding of that liberal tradition advanced by postconsensus intellectual historians. In short, they could do worse than to reconsider, in fresh contemporary contexts, the understanding of the "liberal imagination" articulated by Lionel Trilling in the years immediately following World War II. For Trilling, liberalism itself is uniquely imbued with the resources to interrogate its own premises. Confronted by the coercive rationalizations of an institutionalized liberalism at midcentury, Trilling called for an intellectual culture once again energized by a liberalism of self-reflexivity. This would constitute a liberalism, he added, once more embedded in "its first essential imagination of variousness and possibility, which implies the awareness of complexity and difficulty."[28]

In his famous preface to *The Liberal Imagination*, Trilling goes on to assert the "unique relevance" of literature to such a project. As well as the fact that so much modern literature has taken politics for its subject, he notes, "more importantly ... literature is the human activity that takes the fullest and most precise account of variousness, possibility, complexity, and difficulty."[29] This emphasis on critical attributes such as "variousness" and "complexity" has been taken up by cultural critic Stefan Collini, who appreciatively invokes Trilling's supple methodology in order to reaffirm the importance of "persuasion" in political and cultural debate. Cultural criticism of this type, Collini claims, distances itself from the "tidier intellectual worlds" typical of post-1960s theory and ideology critique along with the zero-sum closure of debate they implicitly engender.

Although Whalen-Bridge's *Political Fiction and the American Self* is keen to undermine the quest for purity and the reinscribed Adamicism of the New Americanists, the overriding impression is still of a related quest to preserve intellectual and political purity on the author's own part. There is no sense, for instance, of any of the novels Whalen-Bridge examines having *persuaded* him of an alternative political view, only perhaps of giving a more sophisticated expression to those he already held. For all its stress on "activism" and "conflict," the result, ultimately, is a relatively innocuous encounter between writer and critic in which both emerge politically unscathed.

By contrast, the process of persuasion, Collini states, is "more like coming to enjoy someone's company than like losing at chess."[30] It is in this spirit that I have approached the novels under consideration here, the political positions within which, as it were, I am not always fully comfortable with but whose "company" has undoubtedly prompted me to think (and rethink) through, sometimes to the point of *persuasion*, a number of the issues they raise. It is in this sense that the novelists who embrace the "republican" narrative form can be regarded, more pointedly, as political thinkers. Caught between the standpoints of Ishmael and Ahab, the conflicted narrator and the unconflicted narrative object, such novelists embrace the understanding of thinking advanced by Hannah Arendt: "the two in one of the soundless dialogue."[31] Stranded in the often larger gap than is customary between the politics *of* a novel and the politics *in* a novel, the reader of "republican fiction" undergoes the destabilizing effects of political thinking proper, which, as Arendt claims, "inevitably has a destructive and undermining effect on all established criteria, values, measurements for good and evil."[32]

The concept of persuasion, of course, returns us to that term's earlier application as an abstract noun, a loose-limbed ideology or "half-formulated moral perspective involving emotional commitment."[33] It is the idea of a "persuasion"—a republican persuasion—that is identified here in the genre of American political fiction, given that such fiction is hardly airtight in ideological terms (indeed, as I have just argued, this represents its political strength). These novels, of course, do not demonstrate anything so intellectually "tidy" as a coherent republican ethos committed to civic virtue, an autonomous public sphere of politically active citizens, a suspicion of centralized power, and so on. Nonetheless such commitments are implicitly and, on occasions, explicitly evident in the works in the form of a republican persuasion that serves to distinguish them from *less* political forms of American fiction.

Moreover, in taking account of the importance of "variousness," "complexity," and "persuasion," these works reflect the ways in which such values have historically coalesced and clashed with those others forged by Lockean liberalism, nonconformist Protestant Christianity, Marxism, and neoconservatism. The result is that these values generally appear in complex, hybridized forms that, since Melville's *Moby Dick*, have underwritten a clearly discernible novelistic structure. This structure has enabled American novelists to convey complex crystallizations of ideas at a number of historical junctures. American ideals, whether republican, liberal, Protestant, radical, or neoconservative, are filtered through this novelistic form as a means of digesting the meaning of social and cultural change for the health of the polity. It is this essential concern for the *republic*, that is, with the political foundations that sustain and support the idea of the American polity, that gives these novels their political vitality and often encourages critics to classify them with reference to that chimerical but seemingly irrepressible beast: the Great American Novel.

In *Blood of the Liberals* (2000), George Packer presents a genealogy of American liberalism since the Civil War in the form of a family memoir. He sees no contradiction in recording the beliefs, careers, and fates of three generations of liberals using the vehicle of a literary form traditionally marked by "sentiment." "Goethe said that there are no liberal ideas, only liberal sentiments," Packer writes, "but sentiments and ideas are more closely related than we usually think. Few people reach a political opinion by deduction from some abstract system of philosophy; most feel their way into the opinions they hold, often contradictory ones, and are hardly aware of the forces within and without that drive them."[34]

Packer's exquisite fusion of memoir and intellectual history, of "sentiment" and ideas, has a corollary in the American political novels considered in this study. Each is concerned with the meaning of intellectual "inheritance" in the context of a liberal tradition, each exhibits grave political tensions between fathers and sons (literal or metaphorical), each is aware that to write the republic is always to write a tale of generational conflict, to write the story of, in Packer's words, "an inherited idea crashing up against the hard rock of new circumstance."[35] This, of course, underlies the idea of republican "declension" or what J. G. A. Pocock described as the "Machiavellian moment" when the republic's finitude or its perceived detachment from a pristine moment of origin serves to generate a sense of political and cultural crisis. American republicanism, like earlier incarnations, has a celebrated historical birth, its own rich gallery of personalities, myths, motifs, and revelatory moments. The novelists here give voice to the solicitude with which the republican persuasion inevitably confronts historical change.

"A republic, if you can keep it!" announced Benjamin Franklin to the throng outside the Philadelphia Constitutional Convention in 1787. In order to keep it, however, as Franklin no doubt meant to imply, one must first be aware of how precious it is: how it was acquired via conflict and sacrifice, how it was "consummated"' (to use Lincoln's term) only after a four-year orgy of fratricidal slaughter, and how, finally, it negotiated the internal and external pressures brought on by neoimperial imperatives in a nuclear age. It is the tradition that has unfolded in response to developments such as these that has here been subject to several novel understandings. In this way, the American political novelist's task is to make sense of the republic in time, to shed light on the evolution of its political tradition, to chart the process of punctuated equilibrium evident in those moments where idea can no longer be reconciled with circumstance. As such, the American political novelist, like the republican, has less interest in wielding power via, say, "activism" than he has in examining its (always) theoretically informed basis. "Given the choice," William Everdell has remarked, "a republican would prefer to tinker not with nuclear command but with symbolism and mythology. He believes, as someone once wrote, if one can but tell the stories of a people, one cares not who makes its laws."[36]

NOTES

Introduction.
Liberalism and the Problem of Tradition in American Literature

1. Tocqueville, *Democracy in America*, 473–474.

2. Lawrence, *Studies in Classic American Literature*, 7.

3. Ibid., 10.

4. Howe, *Politics and the Novel*, 161.

5. Smith, "Symbol and Idea in *Virgin Land*," in Bercovitch and Jehlen, *Ideology and Classic American Literature*, 28.

6. Pease, "Melville and Cultural Persuasion," in Bercovitch and Jehlen, *Ideology and Classic American Literature*, 412.

7. Ibid., 415.

8. Whalen-Bridge, *Political Fiction and the American Self*, 29.

9. Pease, "New Americanists: Revisionist Interventions into the Canon," 19.

10. Ibid., 31. Emphasis in the original.

11. Jameson, *The Political Unconscious*, 20.

12. Whalen-Bridge, *Political Fiction and the American Self*, 29.

13. Ibid., 31.

14. Ibid., 32.

15. We would do well here also to recall Louis Althusser's own famously melancholy reflection that "the lonely hour of the 'last instance' never comes." See "Contradiction and Overdetermination" (1962), in Althusser, *For Marx*, 113.

16. Whether this is the case with non-Western literary traditions is an interesting question but not one, unfortunately, that can be negotiated within the confines of this study.

17. One thinks here of the nearly unbearable "intimacy" of Alexander Solzhenitsyn's fiction or George Orwell's 1984.

18. Horton and Baumeister, *Literature and the Political Imagination*, 13.

19. Zuckert, *Natural Right and the American Imagination*, 247–248.

20. Spanos, "American Studies in the 'Age of the World Picture,'" in Pease, *The Futures of American Studies*, 401.

21. Ibid., 402.

22. Lenz, "Towards a Dialogics of International American Culture Studies: Transnationality, Border Discourses, and Public Cultures," in Pease, *The Futures of American Studies*, 473.

23. Castronovo, *Fathering the Nation: American Genealogies of Slavery and Freedom*, 227–228.

24. Ross, "Liberalism," in Kloppenberg and Wightman Fox, *A Companion to American Thought*, 398.

1. Elusive Republicanism

1. For the former view see Boorstin, *The Genius of American Politics*; for the latter, see Hartz, *The Liberal Tradition in America*.

2. Appleby, *Liberalism and Republicanism in the Historical Imagination*, 279.

3. Shalhope's "Toward a Republican Synthesis" was the best outline of the new thinking.

4. See Banning, *The Jeffersonian Persuasion*; and McCoy, *The Elusive Republic*.

5. John Adams' *Defence of the Constitution of Government of the United States of America*, the first volume of which reached the delegates at Philadelphia in 1787, is greatly indebted to the "aristocratic republicanism" of Montesquieu. Although Adams' work was admired by several delegates, it was criticized by James Madison, who was troubled by the proximity of its principles to those of England's constitutional monarchy.

6. Pocock, "Virtue and Commerce in the Eighteenth Century," 120.

7. See Rodgers, "Republicanism: The Career of a Concept," for a fine bibliographical essay tracing this process.

8. For an important excavation of this "lost" concept of Enlightenment political thought, see Arendt, *On Revolution*, 126–135.

9. The influence of *Cato's Letters* in particular has been accepted by most historians of the revolutionary period, although whether this automatically endorses the "republican synthesis" has been disputed. For an alternative reading of Trenchard and Gordon stressing their Lockean roots, see Hamowy, "*Cato's Letters*, John Locke, and the Republican Paradigm."

10. Pocock, *The Machiavellian Moment*, viii.

11. Paine, *Rights of Man, Common Sense, and Other Political Writings*, 19.

12. Ibid., 42.

13. Pocock, *The Machiavellian Moment*, 38. For Pocock, as opposed to "fortuna," commerce "represented a principle more universal, and of another order, than that of the finite polis" (493).

14. Quoted in Pocock, *The Machiavellian Moment*, 492.

15. Appleby, *Liberalism and Republicanism in the Historical Imagination*, 136.

16. Ibid., 289.

17. Ibid., 288.

18. Ibid., 31.

19. See Hofstadter, *The Age of Reform from Bryan to FDR*, 23–24.

20. Appleby, *Liberalism and Republicanism in the Historical Imagination*, 258.

21. See Onuf, *Jeffersonian Legacies*; and Ellis, *American Sphinx*.

22. See Peterson, *The Jefferson Image in the American Mind*. For a more recent overview of Jefferson scholarship, see Onuf, "The Scholars' Jefferson." The turn toward Jefferson's private life began in earnest with the publication of Fawn Brodie's *Thomas Jefferson: An Intimate History*, although historians had begun to seriously interrogate Jefferson's record on slavery since the mid-1960s. More recently, Joseph Ellis's *American Sphinx* explicitly focuses on Jefferson's "character." Douglas L. Wilson also discusses the character question within the context of a defense of Jefferson's record on slavery in "Thomas Jefferson and the Character Issue." Important among recent studies of slavery and Jefferson's alleged relationship with his slave-servant Sally Hemings (with whom he is alleged to have fathered as many as four children) are, respectively, Finkelman "Jefferson and Slavery: 'Treason Against the Hopes of the World,'" in *Jeffersonian Legacies*, 181–221; and Gordon-Reed, *Thomas Jefferson and Sally Hemings: An American Controversy*.

23. For a more sympathetic treatment of Burr, which stresses the values he might be said to have *shared* with his contemporaries, see Daniels, *Ordeal of Ambition*.

24. Vidal, *Burr*, 500. Hereafter, references to the novel will be in the text.

25. Because of their assault on the National Bank and commitment to *economic* decentralization, the Jackson and Van Buren administrations' record of

political centralization in the form of bureaucracy and the "spoils system" is often unacknowledged. Gordon Wood focuses on these aspects of Jacksonian democracy in his *The Radicalism of the American Revolution*, 298–305.

26. "This cumbersome phrase," Burr explains in the novel, "was of Jefferson's coinage."

27. Jackson himself wrote in 1835: "I have long believed, that it was only by preserving the identity of the Republican party as embodied and characterized by the principles introduced by Mr Jefferson that the rights of the states and the people could be maintained as contemplated by the constitution. I have labored to reconstruct this great party and bring the popular power to bear with full influence upon the Government, by securing its permanent ascendancy." Quoted in Peterson, *The Jefferson Image in the American Mind*, 72–73.

28. Hofstadter, *The American Political Tradition and the Men Who Made It*, 55.

29. Wood, "Hellfire Politics," 30.

30. Speaking of the political culture of 1800, Elkins and McKitrick write: "A trustworthy man was not even supposed to desire power, but when he was seen to reach for it, other men needed at the very least some idea of what he thought about its acceptable uses and limits. Aaron Burr was the only man of prominence in his time who disdained to provide, through either word or example, any such information or even misinformation." Elkins and McKitrick, *The Age of Federalism*, 746. This seems to me the most persuasive explanation of why Burr is not seen to be a *representative* figure in the manner of his contemporaries. It does, however, overlook certain instances, such as his widely admired speech on leaving the Senate (which is referred to in Vidal's novel) and his sponsorship of a bill in the New York State legislature in 1786 to abolish slavery in New York (which is not). The latter would hardly have endeared him to his fellow Republicans in the Virginia junto who controlled the party. Most were, of course, slaveowners. The rejection of Burr's bill by the state legislature is mentioned in Gronowicz, *Race and Class Politics in New York City Before the Civil War*, 21.

31. John R. Howe has written of how political life during this period was "gross and distorted, characterised by heated exaggeration and haunted by conspiratorial fantasy," and of how "individuals who had not so long ago co-operated closely in the struggle against England and even in the creation of a firmer continental government now found themselves mortal enemies, the basis of their earlier trust somehow worn away," in "Republican Thought and the Political Violence of the 1790s," 150–151. For an intriguing examination of the politically motivated duel, see Freeman, "Duelling as Politics: Re-interpreting the Burr-Hamilton Duel."

32. Banning, "Jeffersonian Ideology Revisited: Liberal and Classical Ideas in the New American Republic," 12.

33. This is the thesis of Wood's *The Radicalism of the American Revolution*.

34. Daniel T. Rodgers traces the deployment of "the people" as a term within American political discourse in *Contested Truths: Keywords in American Politics Since Independence*. "By the 1840s," he writes of this transitional period, "when the Democratic party's opponents, sensing the dangers and the possibilities in the slogan, tried to co-opt and nationalize it, talk of the people's sovereign will had risen to earsplitting volume" (83–84).

35. Peterson, *The Jefferson Image in the American Mind*, 28.

36. Ibid., 72.

37. Quoted in Peterson, *The Jefferson Image in the American Mind*, 144.

38. Quoted in Peterson, *The Jefferson Image in the American Mind*, 29.

39. References to the Roman republic abound in *Burr*. The image of Burr as an American Cataline (the infamous Roman conspirator who plotted to have Cicero and other prominent noblemen killed) is at least implicit in Vidal's novel. The idea of Burr as a Cataline figure is discussed in Nolan, *Aaron Burr and the American Literary Imagination*, 157–161.

40. Meyers, *The Jacksonian Persuasion*, 12.

41. For an elaboration of this "privatization" or "domestication" of virtue, see Wood, *The Radicalism of the American Revolution*, 217–218. For discussions of how this development additionally served to "feminize" virtue, see Kerber, *Women of the Republic*; and Diggins, *The Lost Soul of American Politics*.

42. It is worth recalling here that the Mexican War was opposed by the young Abraham Lincoln, among others, and was also the catalyst for Henry David Thoreau's *On the Duty of Civil Disobedience*.

43. Vidal, *Inventing a Nation*, 176.

44. Lazare, "Skeletons in the Closet."

45. See Vidal, *Imperial America: Reflections on the United States of Amnesia* (2004).

46. See "Homage to Daniel Shays," (1972) in Vidal, *United States*, 906–918; and, for Vidal's morally obtuse defense of McVeigh (including excerpts from their correspondence), "The Meaning of Timothy McVeigh," (2001) in Vidal, *The Last Empire*, 270–302.

47. Vidal, *Lincoln*, 859.

48. Vidal, *Inventing a Nation*, 166.

49. Despite their many sharp observations and deft characterizations, the subsequent installments in Vidal's sequence of historical novels are marked by this political vision, which appears more and more incongruous as a more explicitly

liberal and modern ideology begins to take hold. If the "corruption" of the Jackson administration documented in *Burr* marks the decline of the Jeffersonian republic, then the Bismarckian machinations of the chief executive in *Lincoln* serve to restore the preceding years to certain republican heights—years of course, dominated by the influence of Jacksonian democracy. Likewise, the disputed election depicted in *1876* (1976) marks a later fall from innocence. The same "original" sin is attributed to the McKinley-Roosevelt administrations in the years following the Spanish-American War in *Empire* (1987) and then to the onset of a pernicious Wilsonian and FDR-mandated internationalism in *Hollywood* (1989) and *Washington D.C.* (1967), respectively. It comes as no major surprise then that the final installment, which charts American empire building during the cold war era and beyond, is entitled (what else?) *The Golden Age* (2000).

50. Lazare, "Skeletons in the Closet."

2. "Our Divine Equality"

1. Emerson, *Selected Essays*, 88.

2. Ibid., 101. Emphasis mine.

3. Ibid., 103. Emphasis mine.

4. Gougeon, *Virtue's Hero*; and Teichgraeber, *Sublime Thoughts and Penny Wisdom* contain more radical readings of Emerson's politics that stress the strength and consistency of his opposition to slavery.

5. Lincoln, "On the Perpetuation of Our Political Institutions: Address Before the Young Men's Lyceum of Springfield, Illinois, January 27, 1838," in Cuomo and Holzer, *Lincoln on Democracy*, 19–20.

6. See, for instance, White, *Lincoln's Greatest Speech*; and "Lincoln's Sermon on the Mount: *The Second Inaugural*," in Miller et al., *Religion and the American Civil War*, 208–225.

7. Cuomo and Holzer, *Lincoln on Democracy*, 21.

8. Wilson, *Patriotic Gore*, 108.

9. See, for examples, Forgie, *Patricide in the House Divided*; and Strozier, *Lincoln's Quest for Union*.

10. Wilson, *Patriotic Gore*, 129.

11. Burt, "Lincoln's Address to the Young Men's Lyceum," 304–305.

12. Cuomo and Holzer, *Lincoln on Democracy*, 155.

13. Wills, *Inventing America*, xii–xiii.

14. Maier, *American Scripture: Making the Declaration of Independence*, 186.

15. Quoted in Maier, *American Scripture: Making the Declaration of Independence*, 186.

16. Jaffa, *Crisis of the House Divided*, 243. Jaffa is presumably thinking here of, among other statements, Jefferson's notorious admission with regard to American slavery: "I tremble for my country when I recall that God is just."

17. See Foner, *Free Soil, Free Labor, Free Men*.

18. Cuomo and Holzer, *Lincoln on Democracy*, 117.

19. Quoted in Angle, *Created Equal: The Complete Lincoln-Douglas Debates*, 294.

20. Zarefsky, *Lincoln, Douglas, and Slavery*, 140.

21. Greenstone, *The Lincoln Persuasion*, 6; Diggins, *The Lost Soul of American Politics*, 7; Sandel, *Democracy's Discontent*, 6.

22. Greenstone, *The Lincoln Persuasion*, 282.

23. For Berlin's famous distinction between "positive" and "negative" liberty, see his "Two Concepts of Liberty."

24. *Democracy's Discontent*, 319. The "lost soul" invoked in the title of Diggins's 1984 work also advances the idea of a fundamentally positive relationship between religion and the American political tradition. Indeed, as Diggins's latest work makes clear, Lincoln is a crucial figure in this respect and is at the center of the vision of American political life Diggins seeks to affirm. See Diggins, *On Hallowed Ground*.

25. Banks, *Cloudsplitter*, 9. Hereafter references will be in the text.

26. The epigraph to *Cloudsplitter* from Job 1:16—"and I only am escaped alone to tell thee"—is also cited by Melville in the epilogue to *Moby Dick*. A line from Coleridge's poem, it is worth noting, serves as the epigraph to one of the twentieth century's most notable examples of this genre, Primo Levi's *The Drowned and the Saved*: "and till my ghastly tale is told/this heart within me burns."

27. Melville, *Moby Dick*, 104.

28. See "Speech on Kansas-Nebraska Act, Peoria, Illinois, 16th October 1854," in Cuomo and Holzer, *Lincoln on Democracy*, 65–78.

29. See the "Manufactures" chapter from *Notes on the State of Virginia* (1787), reprinted in Koch and Peden, *The Life and Selected Writings of Thomas Jefferson*, 258–260.

30. The parallels between these figures of the *Risorgimento* and Brown (and, for that matter, Lincoln and Emerson) are interesting. All embraced a republican vision of national union premised on the rejection of the twin *ancien régime* authorities of monarchy and institutionalized religion. For Mazzini and Garibaldi, attempting to unify Italy, this authority came in the forms of the Hapsburg dynasty and the Vatican respectively.

31. Emerson, *Selected Essays*, 338.

32. See Jaffa, *A New Birth of Freedom*; and Guelzo, *Abraham Lincoln: Redeemer President*.

33. See Quarles, *Allies for Freedom: Blacks and John Brown*; and Quarles, *Blacks on John Brown*.

34. Emerson, *Selected Essays*, 340.

35. Ibid., 343–344.

36. Ibid., 351.

37. Oakes's key point in this respect is that slaveholders were *economic* liberals who shared the possessive individualism and acquisitive instincts of Northern capitalists but rejected the democracy this had hitherto entailed.

38. Emerson, *Selected Essays*, 175.

39. Tocqueville, *Democracy in America*, 254.

40. Thoreau, *Walden and "On the Duty of Civil Disobedience,"* 230.

41. Richard Hofstadter famously described Calhoun as the "Marx of the Master Class" for his critique of industrial capitalism and ability to justify slavery in similarly materialist, social-scientific terms. See Hofstadter, *The American Political Tradition*, 67–91.

42. See DuBois, *John Brown*. Robert Penn Warren's *John Brown: The Making of a Martyr* was the first revisionist work to subsequently obscure this aspect of Brown, influencing later Southern historians such as C. Vann Woodward.

43. Bruce Olds's depiction of Brown, *Raising Holy Hell* (1995), is a more formally daring though less intimate and philosophically penetrating treatment of its subject.

44. See Greenblatt, *Hamlet in Purgatory*, for a fascinating and erudite New Historicist analysis of the strange spectral presence of the Catholic concept of "purgatory" in *Hamlet* and within early Protestant England more generally.

3. Ideas in Modulation

1. Diggins, *The Rise and Fall of the American Left*, 232.

2. Although this chapter will focus on the ideological tensions between leftist credos and liberalism, it is important to point out that homegrown *right-wing* populist movements with fascist undercurrents, spearheaded by demagogues such as Huey Long and Father Coughlin, represented another important dynamic in the political climate of the Roosevelt era. See Lipsett and Raab, *The Politics of Unreason*, 167–203; and Brinkley, *Voices of Protest*, for treatments of this phenomenon. It is also worth noting that the New Deal itself was seen by the CPUSA before 1935 as

"social fascism"—a contemptible epithet premised on the idea that such new forms of "big government," in their authoritarianism and rearguard efforts to salvage capitalist economies, were indistinguishable from fascist states.

3. Sandel, *Democracy's Discontent*, 262.

4. Ibid, 259–260.

5. Trilling, *The Middle of the Journey*, xx. Hereafter references will be to *TMOTJ* and will be in the text.

6. The pair had met at Columbia University in the 1920s, where, as a young communist, Chambers had been involved at one point in an "underground assignment" for the party. By the late forties, Chambers, repudiating the radicalism of his youth, had become a born-again Christian and was working for *Time* magazine. He came to public prominence as the chief witness in the high-profile espionage trial in 1949 of Alger Hiss, a prominent establishment left-liberal accused of passing secrets to the Soviet Union in the 1930s. Trilling's 1975 introduction provides a brief biographical portrait of Chambers and an account of his bearing on the novel.

7. Warren, *Liberals and Communists*, 65.

8. Some examples of treatises that testify to the importance of planning as an organizing principle in the economic sphere during this period are Charles A. Beard's essays "The Rationality of Planned Economy" and "A Five Year Plan for America," from *America Faces the Future* (1932), Stuart Chase's *Government in Business* (1935), and George Soule's *The Planned Society* (1932). For a discussion of attitudes to the Five-Year Plan in the United States during the early 1930s, see Filene, *Americans and the Soviet Experiment, 1917–1933*.

9. See Brinkley, *Liberalism and Its Discontents*, 24–27, for an appraisal of the link between the earlier Progressive and later New Deal emphasis on planning.

10. Pells, *Radical Visions and American Dreams: Culture and Social Thought in the Depression Years*, 64.

11. Ibid.

12. Quoted in Warren, *Liberals and Communists*, 72.

13. For a study comparing the "progressive" impulse in the two respective Roosevelt eras, see Hofstadter, *The Age of Reform*.

14. Kutulas, *The Long War*, 88.

15. Rahv, quoted in Kutulas, *The Long War*, 125.

16. Conquest's *The Great Purge Trials* remains the most powerful study of Stalin's show trials.

17. See Deutscher, *The Prophet Outcast: Trotsky, 1929–1940*.

18. For a discussion of Trotsky's sometimes clandestinely exerted influence on left-wing American politics in the 1930s, see M. S. Venkataraman, "Leon Trotsky's

Adventure in American Radical Politics." For Trotsky's important intellectual affinity with the influential cultural critics and artists associated with the *Partisan Review*, see Hitchens, "The New York Intellectuals and the Prophet Outcast," in *For the Sake of Argument*, 199–207; and Wald, *The New York Intellectuals*.

19. See Wald, *The New York Intellectuals*, 128–132.

20. This was only after some deliberation. Writing after Dewey's death, Hook testified to the physical and intellectual courage of Dewey, who was then seventy-eight years old, in eventually agreeing to embark upon such an undertaking. "Scarcely anyone knows the variety and intensity of pressure he had to withstand," Hook claimed, "not least of all from members of his immediate family, some of whom feared he might be killed in the excitable political milieu of Mexico City. . . . The simple truth is that Dewey made up his mind irrevocably [to go] only after he became aware of the efforts and far-flung stratagems of the Communist Party to *prevent* him from going." Quoted in Wald, *The New York Intellectuals*, 132.

21. The most famous of these was the "Open Letter to American Liberals" signed by CPUSA members and "fellow travelers," which included such luminaries as Malcolm Cowley, Henry Roth, Theodore Dreiser, Dorothy Parker, and Nathanael West. See Wald, *The New York Intellectuals*, 132.

22. Quoted in Wald, *The New York Intellectuals*, 132.

23. Warren, *Liberals and Communists*, 188.

24. Merleau-Ponty, *Humanism and Terror*, 44.

25. Quoted in Spitzer, "John Dewey, the 'Trial' of Leon Trotsky and the Search for Historical Truth," 29.

26. Albert Glotzer, the reporter for the commission, recalled one occasion when "a great laughter broke out in one corner of the large room where Dewey and Trotsky were conversing. They were surrounded by several people listening to their conversations. I asked Frankel what happened in the corner. He smiled, 'Dewey said to Trotsky, "if all Communists were like you I would be a Communist." And Trotsky replied "if all liberals were like you, I would be a liberal."'" See Glotzer, *Trotsky: Memoir and Critique*, 271.

27. Quoted in Wald, *The New York Intellectuals*, 131.

28. Quoted in Diggins, *The Rise and Fall of the American Left*, 181–182.

29. Trotsky, "Their Morals and Ours," reprinted in Novack, *Their Morals and Ours*, 16.

30. Ibid, 32. Italics in original.

31. Ibid, 38.

32. Dewey, "Means and Ends," reprinted in Novack, *Their Morals and Ours*, 71.

33. Ibid., 72.

34. Trilling, *Prefaces to the Experience of Literature*, i.

35. Ibid., 79.

36. Dostoevsky, *The Brothers Karamazov*, 291.

37. Ibid., 296.

38. The overlap between the issues I discuss in relation to Trilling in this essay and Levinas's broader theoretical focus on the theme of the "messianic" in theology and philosophy also offer a point of entry for understanding Trilling as a Jewish thinker. This is often overlooked by commentators preoccupied with the "Arnoldian" tendencies of Trilling's criticism or his Anglophilia more generally. One of the central tensions of *The Middle of the Journey*—between responsibility and necessity—is echoed, for instance, in the following passage from Levinas's essay "A Religion for Adults" (1957): "Why does your God, who is the God of the poor, not feed the poor? a Roman asks Rabbi Akiba. So we can escape damnation, replies Rabbi Akiba. One could not find a stronger statement of the impossible situation in which God finds himself, that of accepting the duties and responsibilities of man." From Levinas, *Difficult Freedom*, 20.

39. Trilling, *Prefaces to the Experience of Literature*, 83.

40. Interestingly, Whittaker Chambers, while working on the editorial staff of *Time*, published a parable in which Satan appears in New York. In terms obviously imitating the rhetoric of Stalin, he announces his plans to counter the "infantile leftism" of revisionists by launching a "Five Hundred Year Plan" of world domination!

41. Trotsky, "Their Morals and Ours," 16.

42. Dewey, "Means and Ends," 73.

43. Kubal, "Trilling's *The Middle of the Journey*: An American Dialectic," 64.

44. Dostoevsky's profound religious convictions underwrote his reactionary vision of a state dominated by the twin pillars of tsarism and the Russian Orthodox Church. Such religious "fundamentalism," as it would now be understood, is likewise responsible for the image of a grossly corrupted Catholic Church in "The Grand Inquisitor."

45. Arendt, *On Revolution*, 82.

46. Indeed the very terms "freedom," "necessity," "spirit," "law," and so forth in this context derive from Hegel and Kant, the philosophical titans of German Idealism—a body of theory, according to Herbert Marcuse, itself composed "largely as a response to the challenge from [the French Revolution] to reorganize the state and society on a rational basis, so that social and political institutions might accord with the freedom and interest of the individual." Marcuse, *Reason and Revolution*, 3.

47. Arendt, *On Revolution*, 75.

48. Ibid., 81.

49. Ibid., 85.

50. Ibid.

51. Trilling, *Prefaces to the Experience of Literature*, 82.

52. Melville's novel *White-Jacket* (1850), for instance, explicitly foregrounds this synecdoche in its subtitle, "The World in a Man-of-War."

53. "The tragedy [of *Billy Budd*]," writes Arendt, "is that the law is made for men, and neither for angels nor for devils. Law and all 'lasting institutions' break down not only under the onslaught of elemental evil but under the impact of absolute innocence as well. The law, moving between crime and virtue, cannot recognize what is beyond it." Arendt, *On Revolution*, 84.

54. Melville, *Billy Budd, Sailor and Other Stories*, 330.

55. Ibid., 378.

56. Ibid., 390.

57. For an outline of this difference of critical opinion see Johnson, "Melville's Fist: The Execution of *Billy Budd*," 567–568.

58. Melville, *Billy Budd, Sailor and Other Stories*, 331. Emphasis mine.

59. Ibid., 400–401.

60. Diggins, *The Lost Soul of American Politics*, 295.

61. Ibid.

62. Ibid., 291.

63. This understanding is reflected in John Stuart Mill's belief in the "necessity" that there be "in the constitution of the State *something* which is settled, something permanent and not to be called into question; something which, by general agreement, has a right to be where it is, and to be secure against disturbance, whatever else may change." Such permanence can only be assured by an "absolute" commitment to this "something," which, for Arendt, like Captain Vere, would presumably take the form of "lasting institutions." Mill is quoted in Rahe, *Republics Ancient and Modern: Classical Republicanism and the American Revolution*, 22.

64. The "uncertain movement" of protest exhibited by the crew when Billy's body is dispatched overboard intimates that Melville's view of Vere's decision is ambiguous. At the end of the story, after Vere is wounded, it is the petty officers who wished to save Budd who go on to defeat the vessel *Atheiste* (again, a clue as to the importance of Christianity in Melville's politics). As Diggins writes: "It may be true that the preservation of discipline on British warships was essential to the preservation of England's freedom, but it is hard to see how Billy's execution contributed to that end." Diggins, *The Lost Soul of American Politics*, 293.

65. Ruttenburg, "Melville's Handsome Sailor: The Anxiety of Innocence," 98.

66. Krupnick, *Lionel Trilling and the Fate of Cultural Criticism*, 188.

67. Trilling touches on this when he cites, elsewhere, F. Scott Fitzgerald's oft-quoted remark that "the test of a first-rate intelligence is the ability to hold two opposed ideas in the mind, at the same time, and still function." Quoted in Trilling, *The Liberal Imagination*, 246.

68. Trilling, *The Liberal Imagination*, 14.

69. Ibid.

70. See Diggins' discussion of the inquiry and its bearing on their subsequent debate in *The Promise of Pragmatism*, 266–270.

71. Arendt, however, took her inspiration from the work of Martin Heidegger as opposed to strictly theological sources, seeking to reconcile a classical notion of politics with his revival of pre-Socratic ontology. For a first-rate explication of this influence, see Villa, *Arendt and Heidegger*.

72. Reprinted as "Dostoevsky in *The Possessed*" in Rahv, *Essays on Literature and Politics, 1932–1972*, 107–128.

73. Trilling, *The Liberal Imagination*, 13.

74. For cultural left critiques of Trilling, see West, "Lionel Trilling: Godfather of Neo-Conservatism" and Reising, "Lionel Trilling, *The Liberal Imagination*, and the Emergence of the Cultural Discourse of Anti-Stalinism."

75. Hilton Kramer and Trilling's old pupil Norman Podhoretz are the most prominent among these.

76. Teres, *Renewing the Left*, 260.

77. Trilling, *E. M. Forster*, 23.

4. Liberalism Betrayed

1. Tallack, *Twentieth-Century America*, 201.

2. Trilling, *The Middle of the Journey*, 300.

3. Pells, *The Liberal Mind in a Conservative Age*, 63.

4. See Culver and Hyde, *American Dreamer*, 464–467.

5. Ibid., 112.

6. Hereafter, these novels will be referred to as *IMAC*, *AP*, and *THS* respectively. All references will be in the text.

7. McGrath, " 'Zuckerman's Alter Brain': An Interview with Philip Roth."

8. See, for example, Kakutani, "Manly Giant Versus Zealots and Scheming Women"; and Grant, "The Wrath of Roth."

9. Quoted in Gerson, *The Neo-Conservative Vision,* 73. Despite Kristol's acknowledgment that he made the remark some time in the 1970s, its precise origins remain uncertain.

10. Gerson, *The Neo-Conservative Vision,* 93.

11. Matthew Berke's entry under "neo-conservatism," in Kloppenberg and Wightman Fox, *A Companion to American Thought,* 484.

12. This description is invoked in Ellis, *The Dark Side of the Left: Illiberal Egalitarianism in America.*

13. See the editors' introduction in Kramer and Kimball, *The Betrayal of Liberalism,* 3–18, for a delineation of this latter position. It is also important to distinguish between the mainly domestic provenance of the thought of this generation of neoconservatives and the foreign-policy orientation of a later group, including officials and intellectuals such as Paul Wolfowitz and William Kristol, the extent of whose influence on the Bush administration since the events of September 2001 has been a subject of some dispute.

14. Steinfels, *The Neo-Conservatives,* 179.

15. Podhoretz, "The Adventures of Philip Roth," 28.

16. Ibid., 32.

17. Ibid., 34.

18. Ibid., 35.

19. Podhoretz, "The Adventures of Philip Roth," 36.

20. Tomes, *Apocalypse Then,* 171–174.

21. Podhoretz, "My Negro Problem—and Ours," 98.

22. See Jackson, "'Days of Rage': The Life and Death of Newark," for a succinct and compelling account of the riots.

23. Boyers, "The Indigenous Berserk," 41.

24. Diggins, *The Lost Soul of American Politics,* 118–119.

25. Although works such as Leslie Fiedler's *Love and Death in the American Novel* (1960) and D. H. Lawrence's *Studies in Classic American Literature* (1923) were using the idea of the "pastoral" as a way of reaching an understanding of American literary culture, it is only with William Empson's *Some Versions of the Pastoral* (1935) that the ideological function of the concept is critically assessed. Leo Marx's *The Machine in the Garden: Technology and the Pastoral Ideal in America* (1964) applies a similar approach to the American cultural context. Lawrence Buell's "American Pastoral Ideology Reappraised" (1989), meanwhile, is an excellent later analysis of the pastoral mode in American literary culture.

26. Most famous among these, perhaps, was the notorious (and successful) Senate campaign Nixon fought in 1950 against Helen Gahagan Douglas, whom he

labeled as a communist sympathizer ("the Pink Lady" who was "pink right down to her underpants"). Nixon also, more circumspectly, resorted to sexual and ethnic slurs during the campaign by insinuating that Douglas had slept with President Truman and "unintentionally" referring to his opponent as "Helen Hessenberg" (Douglas was married to Mervyn Douglas, a Jewish film director whose original name was Hessenberg). The Nixon team was also responsible for an anonymous phone-call campaign that informed voters of Douglas's Jewish association. See Summers, *The Arrogance of Power*, 83–87.

27. Responding to a number of revisionist accounts of the Nixon presidency that emphasize its "liberal" features, this historian remarks: "[Reagan] ratcheted up the anti-government oratory and cemented the negative associations with liberalism, successfully transforming the word 'liberal' into an epithet. In the flamboyantly conservative Reagan era, Nixon appeared progressive." See Greenberg, *Nixon's Shadow*, 322.

28. Wills, *Nixon Agonistes*, xiv.

29. Ibid., 598.

30. In voting for Nixon in 1972, Irving Kristol and Gertrude Himmelfarb became the first of those who were later characterized as neoconservatives to embrace the Republican Party. The process of "breaking ranks," in party political terms, would be complete by Ronald Reagan's 1980 electoral victory. Reagan not only garnered the votes of most of the neoconservative intellectuals but went on to give several of them important posts in his administrations. See Gerson, *The Neo-Conservative Vision*, 135, 189, 249–250.

31. McGovern cited the bombing of Cambodia as "the most barbaric thing . . . since the Nazis were in power" and, reacting to the Watergate break-in, described it as "the kind of thing you expect under a person like Hitler." McGovern and Howe are both quoted in Greenberg, *Nixon's Shadow*, 59, 99.

32. Podhoretz, "Bellow at 85, Roth at 67," 40.

33. Coleman, "Clinton and the Party System in Historical Perspective," 153.

34. Ibid., 154.

35. Presidential funeral pieties aside, the personal relationship between Clinton and Nixon was surprisingly warm given the two men's respective party political affiliations. Moreover, as David Greenberg documents, unlike every succeeding president, Republican or Democrat, who saw *any* association with their disgraced predecessor as highly undesirable, Clinton went so far as to invite Nixon to the White House for a private meeting in 1993. See Greenberg, *Nixon's Shadow*, 300–301.

36. Pitney, "Clinton and the Republican Party," 174.

37. Gerson, *The Neo-Conservative Vision*, 349.

38. Ibid., 349–350.

39. Rawls, *A Theory of Justice*, 136.

40. Sandel, *Liberalism and the Limits of Justice*, xiv.

41. Rosenthal is quoted in Didion, *Political Fictions*, 218.

42. Didion, *Political Fictions*, 236.

43. I am indebted to Professor Hayden White for this observation, which was made in some remarks on an earlier truncated version of the first third of this chapter covering Roth's *I Married a Communist*. See White, "Introduction: Historical Fiction, Fictional History, and Historical Reality," 153.

44. Morrison, *The New Yorker*, October 5, 1998.

45. Lewis, "Bill Clinton as Honorary Black," 5. Jasper, Texas, was the setting for the brutal racist murder of African American James Byrd Jr. in June 1998. Byrd, who was born and raised in the town, was dragged by a pickup truck for three miles by a group of men well-known locally as white supremacists.

46. Schier, "American Politics After Clinton," in Schier, *The Postmodern Presidency*, 259.

47. Horton was the black prisoner released by Massachusetts governor Michael Dukakis in the 1980s who went on to commit further crimes including rape. The Republican Party's advertising that drew attention to Horton during Dukakis's 1988 presidential election campaign has been widely viewed as a significant contributory factor in his failure at the polls.

48. Hitchens, *No One Left to Lie to*, 48.

49. Ibid., 28.

50. Podhoretz, "Life of His Party: How Bill Clinton Saved His Party," 3.

51. See Jacoby, *The Last Intellectuals* (1987) and *The End of Utopia* (1999); Gitlin, *The Twilight of Common Dreams* (1995); and Posner, *Public Intellectuals* (2002).

52. Podhoretz, "Bellow at 85, Roth at 67," 37.

53. McGrath, "'Zuckerman's Alter Brain': An Interview with Philip Roth." Emphasis mine.

54. Forman, *Blacks in the Jewish Mind*, 17.

55. Rosenberg, "Jewish Identity in a Free Society," 510.

56. Ibid., 509.

57. Alter, "A Fever of Ethnicity," 70.

58. See Bloom, *The Closing of the American Mind*, for an example of the former, and Schlesinger, *The Disuniting of America*, for one of the latter.

59. Hollinger, *Postethnic America*, 39.

60. This would explain, for example, Hollinger's support for affirmative-action programs—a frequent target of neoconservative criticism—which he takes the opportunity to reassert in a postscript to the 2000 edition of *Postethnic America*.

61. Hollinger, *Postethnic America*, 38.

62. Gilroy, *Between Camps*, 305.

63. Ibid., 356.

64. Pfeiffer, *Race Passing and American Individualism*, 5.

65. Sollors, *Beyond Ethnicity*, 6.

66. Ibid., 37.

67. Pfeiffer, *Race Passing and American Individualism*, 151.

68. Kennedy, "My Race Problem—and Ours," 55.

69. Sandel, *Democracy's Discontent*, 14.

70. Kennedy, "My Race Problem—and Ours," 57.

71. Ibid., 58.

72. Rorty, *Achieving Our Country*, 80.

73. Arendt, *Crises of the Republic*, 5.

74. Ibid., 11–12.

75. Arendt, *Between Past and Future*, 250.

76. Jay, "Mendacious Flowers," 21.

77. Ibid., 22.

78. I wish to distinguish this understanding of "paleoliberal" from that now occasionally propounded by contemporary conservatives and neoconservatives who deploy the term pejoratively to dismiss those who "stubbornly" cling to a "minoritarian" liberalism rooted in the identity politics of the 1960s. It is this "McGovernite" wing of the Democratic Party that Norman Podhoretz praises Bill Clinton for marginalizing in the 1990s.

Conclusion. Writing the Republic

1. Howe, *Selected Writings*, 107.

2. Howe, *Politics and the Novel*, 52.

3. Alexis de Tocqueville, *Democracy in America*, 412.

4. Ibid.

5. Bakhtin, *Problems in Dostoevsky's Poetics*, 23.

6. Ibid., 24.

7. Whalen-Bridge, *Political Fiction and the American Self*, 95.

8. White, *The Content of the Form*, ix.

9. Rowe, *At Emerson's Tomb*, ix.

10. Ibid., 1.

11. Whalen-Bridge, *Political Fiction and the American Self*, 172.

12. Everdell, *The End of Kings*, 297.

13. Ibid., 313.

14. Ibid., 270.

15. Melville, *Moby Dick*, 470.

16. See Fisher, *Still the New World: American Literature in a Culture of Creative Destruction.*

17. Whalen-Bridge, *Political Fiction and the American Self,* 47.

18. Ibid., 57.

19. This division, in fact, is represented in later scholarship on Arendt. For an example of the "agonistic" approach to the concept of a public sphere in Arendt, see Villa, *Arendt and Heidegger: The Fate of the Political* (1996); for an expression of the "Habermasian" interpretation of Arendt, see Benhabib, *The Reluctant Modernism of Hannah Arendt* (1996).

20. Whalen-Bridge, *Political Fiction and the American Self,* 4.

21. Ibid., 46.

22. See Epstein, "Leviathan"; and Patrick McGrath, "Deep Waters," for readings of Melville's novel as "prophetic" in the wake of the post–September 11 U.S. military interventions in Afghanistan and Iraq.

23. Arendt, *Eichmann in Jerusalem,* 49.

24. The term translates as "right thinking" from the French, but it is normally invoked with the derogatory implication of "mindless" or "thoughtless" compliance with fashionable intellectual and moral positions.

25. See, for example, Kymlicka, "Liberal Egalitarianism and Civic Republicanism: Friends or Enemies?" and Frohnen, "Sandel's Liberal Politics."

26. Kloppenberg, *The Virtues of Liberalism,* 62.

27. Sandel, *Democracy's Discontent,* 350–351.

28. Trilling, *The Liberal Imagination,* 14.

29. Ibid.

30. Collini, "On Variousness; and on Persuasion," 96.

31. Arendt, "Thinking and Moral Considerations," 37.

32. Ibid., 24.

33. Meyers, *The Jacksonian Persuasion,* 12.

34. Packer, *Blood of the Liberals,* 7.

35. Ibid., 8.

36. Everdell, *The End of Kings*, 313.

BIBLIOGRAPHY

Adams, Henry. *Democracy: An American Novel.* 1880. New York: Random House, 2003.

Alter, Robert. "A Fever of Ethnicity." *Commentary* 53, no. 6 (June 1972): 68–73.

Althusser, Louis. *For Marx.* 1969. Translated by Ben Brewster. London: Verso, 1986.

Angle, Paul M., ed. *Created Equal: The Complete Lincoln-Douglas Debates.* Chicago: University of Chicago Press, 1958.

Appleby, Joyce. *Liberalism and Republicanism in the Historical Imagination.* Cambridge, Mass.: Harvard University Press, 1992.

Arendt, Hannah. *The Origins of Totalitarianism.* 1951. Orlando, Fla.: Harcourt, Brace & Co., 1973.

——. *The Human Condition.* 1958. Chicago: University of Chicago Press, 1989.

——. *Between Past and Future: Eight Exercises in Political Thought.* 1961. New York: Penguin, 1993.

——. *On Revolution.* 1963. Harmondsworth: Penguin, 1990.

——. *Eichmann in Jerusalem: A Report on the Banality of Evil.* 1963. New York: Penguin, 1994.

——. *Crises of the Republic.* New York: Harcourt, Brace & Co., 1973.

——. "Thinking and Moral Considerations: A Lecture." *Social Research* 51, no. 1 (Spring 1984): 7–37.

Bailyn, Bernard. *The Ideological Origins of the American Revolution.* Cambridge, Mass.: Harvard University Press, 1967.

Bakhtin, Mikhail. *Problems of Dostoevsky's Poetics.* 1929. Translated by R.W. Rotsel. New York: Ardis, 1973.

——. *The Dialogic Imagination: Four Essays.* 1975. Edited by Michael Holquist. Translated by Caryl Emerson and Michael Holquist. Austin: University of Texas Press, 1981.

Banks, Russell. *The Book of Jamaica.* 1980. New York: HarperCollins, 1996.

——. *Continental Drift.* 1985. New York: HarperCollins, 2000.

——. *Affliction.* 1989. London: Picador, 1999.

——. *The Sweet Hereafter.* 1991. New York: HarperCollins, 1996.

——. *Rule of the Bone.* 1995. New York: HarperCollins, 1996.

——. *Cloudsplitter.* London: Secker & Warburg, 1998.

——. *The Darling.* London: Secker & Warburg, 2004.

Banning, Lance. *The Jeffersonian Persuasion: Evolution of a Party Ideology.* Ithaca, N.Y.: Cornell University Press, 1978.

——. "Jeffersonian Ideology Revisited: Liberal and Classical Ideas in the New American Republic." *The William and Mary Quarterly* 43, no. 1 (Jan 1986): 3–19.

Bell, Daniel. *The End of Ideology: On the Exhaustion of Political Ideas in the Fifties.* 1960. Cambridge, Mass.: Harvard University Press, 2000.

Bellow, Saul. *Ravelstein.* New York: Viking Penguin, 2000.

Benhabib, Seyla. *The Reluctant Modernism of Hannah Arendt.* London: Sage Publications, 1996.

Bennett, William J. *The Death of Outrage: Bill Clinton and the Assault on American Ideals.* New York: Free Press, 1998.

Berlin, Isaiah. "Two Concepts of Liberty." In *Four Essays On Liberty,* 118–172. Oxford: Oxford University Press, 1969.

Berman, Paul. *A Tale of Two Utopias: The Political Journey of the Generation of 1968.* New York: W. W. Norton, 1996.

Bloom, Allan. *The Closing of the American Mind.* New York: Simon & Schuster, 1987.

Boorstin, Daniel. *The Genius of American Politics.* Chicago: University of Chicago Press, 1953.

Boyers, Robert. "*The Middle of the Journey* and Beyond: Observations on Modernity and Commitment." *Salmagundi* 1, no. 4 (Spring 1967): 8–18.

——. *Atrocity and Amnesia: The Political Novel Since 1945.* New York: Oxford University Press, 1985.

——. "The Indigenous Berserk." Review of *American Pastoral,* by Philip Roth. *The New Republic,* July 7, 1997.

➤ Brinkley, Alan. *Voices of Protest: Huey Long, Father Coughlan, and the Great Depression.* New York: Random House, 1982.

———. *Liberalism and its Discontents.* Cambridge, Mass.: Harvard University Press, 1998.

➤ Brodie, Fawn. *Thomas Jefferson: An Intimate History.* New York: W. W. Norton, 1974.

Budick, Emily Miller. *Blacks and Jews in Literary Conversation.* New York: Cambridge University Press, 1998.

Buell, Lawrence. "American Pastoral Ideology Reappraised." *New Literary History* 20, no. 2 (Spring 1989): 1–29.

Burt, John. "Lincoln's Address to the Young Men's Lyceum: A Speculative Essay." *Western Humanities Review* 51, no. 3 (Fall 1997): 304–320.

➤ Camus, Albert. *The Rebel.* 1951. Translated by Anthony Bower. Harmondsworth: Penguin, 1982.

➤ Carnes, Mark C., ed. *Novel History: Historians and Novelists Confront America's Past (and Each Other).* New York: Simon & Schuster, 2001.

Castronovo, Russ. *Fathering the Nation: American Genealogies of Slavery and Freedom.* Berkeley: University of California Press, 1995.

Chambers, Whittaker. *Witness.* New York: Random House, 1952.

Clinton, Bill. *My Life.* New York: Alfred A. Knopf, 2004.

Coleman, John J. "Clinton and the Party System in Historical Perspective." In *The Postmodern Presidency: Bill Clinton's Legacy in U.S. Politics,* edited by Steven E. Schier, 145–166. Pittsburgh, Pa.: University of Pittsburgh Press, 2000.

Collini, Stefan. "On Variousness; and on Persuasion." *New Left Review* 27 (May/June 2004): 65–97.

Conquest, Robert. *The Great Purge Trials.* New York: Oxford University Press, 1978.

Culver, John C., and John Hyde. *American Dreamer: A Life of Henry A. Wallace.* New York: W. W. Norton, 2001.

Cuomo, Mario M., and Harold Holzer, eds. *Lincoln on Democracy: His Own Words, with Essays by America's Foremost Historians.* New York: HarperCollins, 1990.

Daniels, Jonathan. *Ordeal of Ambition: Jefferson, Hamilton, Burr.* Garden City, N.Y.: Doubleday & Co., 1970.

Davis, David Brion. *The Problem of Slavery in an Age of Revolution, 1770–1823.* 1973. New York: Oxford University Press, 1999.

Denning, Michael. *The Cultural Front: The Laboring of American Culture in the Twentieth Century.* London: Verso, 1997.

Deutscher, Isaac. *The Prophet Outcast: Trotsky 1929–1940.* London: Oxford University Press, 1963.

Didion, Joan. *Political Fictions.* New York: Alfred A. Knopf, 2001.

Diggins, John Patrick. *The Lost Soul of American Politics: Virtue, Self-Interest, and the Foundations of Liberalism.* 1984. Chicago: University of Chicago Press, 1986.

———. *The Rise and Fall of the American Left.* New York: W. W. Norton, 1992.

———. *The Promise of Pragmatism: Modernism and the Crisis of Knowledge and Authority.* Chicago: University of Chicago Press, 1994.

———. *On Hallowed Ground: Abraham Lincoln and the Foundations of American History.* New Haven, Conn.: Yale University Press, 2000.

Doctorow, E. L. *The Book of Daniel.* 1971. New York: Vintage, 1991.

Dostoevsky, Fyodor. *The Possessed* (or *The Devils*). 1871. Translated by David Magarshack. Harmondsworth: Penguin, 1981.

———. *The Brothers Karamazov.* 1880. Translated by David Magarshack. Harmondsworth: Penguin, 1982.

DuBois, W. E. B. *John Brown.* 1909. New York: International Publishers, 1962.

Elkins, Stanley, and Eric McKitrick. *The Age of Federalism.* New York: Oxford University Press, 1993.

Ellis, Joseph J. *American Sphinx: The Character of Thomas Jefferson.* New York: Alfred A. Knopf, 1997.

Ellis, Richard J. *The Dark Side of the Left: Illiberal Egalitarianism in America.* Lawrence: University Press of Kansas, 1998.

Emerson, Ralph Waldo. *Selected Essays.* Edited by Larzer Ziff. London: Penguin, 1982.

Empson, William. *Some Versions of the Pastoral: A Study of the Pastoral Form in Literature.* London: Chatto & Windus, 1935.

Epstein, Jason. "Leviathan." *New York Review of Books* 50, no. 7 (May 1, 2003): 13–14.

Everdell, William R. *The End of Kings: A History of Republics and Republicans.* 1983. Chicago: University of Chicago Press, 2000.

Fast, Howard. *Citizen Tom Paine.* 1943. New York: Grove Press, 1983.

Fehrenbacher, Don E. *Lincoln in Text and Context: Collected Essays.* Stanford, Calif.: Stanford University Press, 1987.

Fiedler, Leslie. *Love and Death in the American Novel.* 1960. London: Penguin, 1984.

Filene, Peter G. *Americans and the Soviet Experiment, 1917–1933.* Cambridge, Mass.: Harvard University Press, 1967.

Finkelman, Paul, ed. *His Soul Goes Marching on: Responses to John Brown and the Harpers Ferry Raid.* Charlottesville: University Press of Virginia, 1995.

Fisher, Philip. *The New American Studies: Essays from* Representations. Berkeley: University of California Press, 1991.

———. *Still the New World: American Literature in a Culture of Creative Destruction.* Cambridge, Mass.: Harvard University Press, 1999.

Foner, Eric. *Free Soil, Free Labor, Free Men: The Ideology of the Republican Party Before the Civil War.* New York: Oxford University Press, 1970.

———. *The Story of American Freedom.* New York: W. W. Norton, 1998.

Forgie, George B. *Patricide in the House Divided.* New York: W. W. Norton, 1979.

Forman, Seth. *Blacks in the Jewish Mind: A Crisis of Liberalism.* New York: New York University Press, 1998.

Freeman, Joanne B. "Duelling as Politics: Re-interpreting the Burr-Hamilton Duel." *The William and Mary Quarterly* 53, no. 2 (April 1996): 289–318.

Frohnen, Bruce. "Sandel's Liberal Politics." In *Debating Democracy's Discontent: Essays on American Politics, Law, and Public Philosophy,* edited by Anita L. Allen and Milton C. Regan, Jr., 159–171. New York: Oxford University Press, 1998.

Gerson, Mark. *The Neo-Conservative Vision: From the Cold War to the Culture Wars.* Lanham, Md.: Madison Books, 1996.

Gerstle, Gary. *American Crucible: Race and Nation in the Twentieth Century.* Princeton, N.J.: Princeton University Press, 2001.

Gilroy, Paul. *Between Camps: Nations, Cultures, and the Allure of Race.* London: Penguin, 2000.

Gitlin, Todd. *The Twilight of Common Dreams: Why America Is Wracked by Culture Wars.* New York: Henry Holt & Company, 1995.

Glotzer, Albert. *Trotsky: Memoir and Critique.* New York: Prometheus Books, 1989.

Gordon-Reed, Annette. *Thomas Jefferson and Sally Hemings: An American Controversy.* Charlottesville: The University Press of Virginia, 1997.

Gougeon, Len. *Virtue's Hero: Emerson, Antislavery, and Reform.* Athens: University of Georgia Press, 1990.

Grant, Linda. "The Wrath of Roth." Review of *I Married a Communist,* by Philip Roth. *The Guardian,* October 3, 1998. Available online at http://books.guardian.co.uk/reviews/generalfiction/0,,98984,00.html.

Greenberg, David. *Nixon's Shadow: The History of an Image.* New York: W. W. Norton, 2003.

Greenblatt, Stephen. *Renaissance Self-Fashioning: From More to Shakespeare.* Chicago: University of Chicago Press, 1980.

——. *Hamlet in Purgatory*. Princeton, N.J.: Princeton University Press, 2001.

Greenstone, J. David. *The Lincoln Persuasion: Remaking American Liberalism*. Princeton, N.J.: Princeton University Press, 1993.

Gronowicz, Anthony. *Race and Class Politics in New York City Before the Civil War*. Boston: Northeastern University Press, 1998.

Guelzo, Allen C. *Abraham Lincoln: Redeemer President*. Grand Rapids, Mich.: William B. Eerdmans, 1999.

Habermas, Jürgen. *The Theory of Communicative Action*. Vol. 1, *Reason and the Rationalization of Society*. London: Heinemann, 1984.

Hamowy, Ronald. "*Cato's Letters*, John Locke, and the Republican Paradigm." In *John Locke's* Two Treatises of Government*: New Interpretations*, edited by Edward J. Harpham, 148–172. Lawrence: University Press of Kansas, 1992.

Hartz, Louis. *The Liberal Tradition in America: An Interpretation of American Political Thought Since the Revolution*. New York: Harcourt, Brace & Co., 1955.

Hitchens, Christopher. *For the Sake of Argument: Essays and Minority Reports*. London: Verso, 1993.

——. *No One Left to Lie to: The Triangulations of William Jefferson Clinton*. London: Verso, 1999.

——. *Unacknowledged Legislation :Writers in the Public Sphere*. London: Verso, 2000.

Hofstadter, Richard. *The Age of Reform from Bryan to FDR*. New York: Vintage, 1955.

——. *The American Political Tradition and the Men Who Made It*. 1949. London: Jonathan Cape, 1967.

Hollinger, David A. *Postethnic America: Beyond Multiculturalism*. 1995. New York: Basic Books, 2000.

Horton, John, and Andrea T. Baumeister, eds. *Literature and the Political Imagination*. London: Routledge, 1996.

Howe, Irving. *Politics and the Novel*. Cleveland: Meridien Books, 1957.

——. *Selected Writings: 1950–1990*. New York: Harcourt Brace Jovanovich, 1990.

Howe Jr., John R. "Republican Thought and the Political Violence of the 1790s." *American Quarterly* 19, no. 2 (Summer 1967): 147–165.

Hutchison, Anthony. "'Purity Is Petrifaction': Liberalism and Betrayal in Philip Roth's *I Married a Communist*." *Rethinking History* 9, no. 2/3 (June/September 2005): 315–327.

Jackson, Kenneth T. "'Days Of Rage': The Life and Death of Newark." In *Days of Destiny: Crossroads in American History*, edited by James M. McPherson and Alan Brinkley, 418–439. New York: Dorling Kindersley Publishing, 2001.

Jacoby, Russell. *The Last Intellectuals: American Culture in the Age of Academe.* 1987. New York: Basic Books, 2000.

——. *The End of Utopia: Politics and Culture in an Age of Apathy.* New York: Basic Books, 1999.

Jaffa, Harry V. *Crisis of the House Divided: An Interpretation of the Issues in the Lincoln-Douglas Debates.* Chicago: University of Chicago Press, 1959.

——. *A New Birth of Freedom: Abraham Lincoln and the Coming of the Civil War.* Lanham, Md.: Rowman and Littlefield, 2000.

James, C. L. R. *Mariners, Renegades, and Castaways: The Story of Herman Melville and the World We Live in.* 1953. Hanover, N.H.: University Press of New England, 2001.

Jameson, Fredric. *The Political Unconscious: Narrative as Socially Symbolic Act.* 1981. London: Routledge, 1989.

Jay, Martin. "Mendacious Flowers." Review of *No-One Left to Lie to: The Triangulations of William Jefferson Clinton,* by Christopher Hitchens, and *All Too Human: A Political Education,* by George Stephanopoulos. *London Review of Books* 21, no. 15 (July 29, 1999): 20–23.

Johnson, Barbara. "Melville's Fist: The Execution of *Billy Budd.*" *Studies in Romanticism* 18, no. 4 (Winter 1979): 567–599.

Johnson, Peter. *Politics, Innocence, and the Limits of Goodness.* London: Routledge, 1988.

Kakutani, Michiko. "Manly Giant Versus Zealots and Scheming Women." Review of *I Married a Communist,* by Philip Roth. *New York Times,* October 6, 1998. Available online at http.//www.nytimes.com/books/98/10/04/daily/roth-book-review.html.

Kaplan, Fred. *Gore Vidal: A Biography.* New York: Doubleday, 1999.

Kazin, Alfred. *God and the American Writer.* New York: Alfred A. Knopf, 1997.

Kennedy, Randall. "My Race Problem—and Ours." *Atlantic Monthly* 279, no. 5 (May 1997): 55–62.

Kerber, Linda K. *Women of the Republic: Intellect and Ideology in Revolutionary America.* Chapel Hill: University of North Carolina Press, 1980.

Klein, Joe [Anonymous]. *Primary Colors.* London: Chatto & Windus, 1996.

Kloppenberg, James T., and Richard Wightman Fox, eds. *A Companion to American Thought.* Oxford: Blackwell, 1995.

——. *The Virtues of Liberalism.* New York: Oxford University Press, 1998.

Koch, Adrienne, and William Peden, eds. *The Life and Selected Writings of Thomas Jefferson.* New York: Random House, 1993.

Kramer, Hilton, and Roger Kimball, eds. *The Betrayal of Liberalism.* Chicago: Ivan R. Dee, 1999.

Kristol, Irving. *Neoconservatism: The Autobiography of an Idea.* New York: Free Press, 1995.

Krupnick, Mark. *Lionel Trilling and the Fate of Cultural Criticism.* Evanston, Ill.: Northwestern University Press, 1986.

Kubal, David L. "Trilling's *The Middle of the Journey*: An American Dialectic." *Bucknell Review: A Scholarly Journal of Letters, Art, and Science* 14, no. 1 (Winter 1966): 60–73.

Kutulas, Judy. *The Long War: The Intellectual People's Front and Anti-Stalinism, 1930–1940.* Durham, N.C.: Duke University Press, 1995.

Kymlicka, Will. "Liberal Egalitarianism and Civic Republicanism: Friends or Enemies?" In *Debating Democracy's Discontent: Essays on American Politics, Law, and Public Philosophy,* edited by Anita L. Allen and Milton C. Regan Jr., 131–148. New York: Oxford University Press, 1998.

Lawrence, D. H. *Studies in Classic American Literature.* 1923. Harmondsworth: Penguin, 1977.

Lazare, Daniel. "Skeletons in the Closet." Review of *Inventing a Nation: Washington, Adams, Jefferson,* by Gore Vidal. *The Nation,* January 5, 2004. Available online at http://www.thenation.com/doc/20040105/lazare.

Lenz, Günther. "Toward a Dialogics of International American Culture Studies: Transnationality, Border Discourses, and Public Culture(s)." In *The Futures of American Studies,* edited by Donald E. Pease and Robyn Wiegman, 461–485. Durham, N.C.: Duke University Press, 2002.

Levi, Primo. *The Drowned and the Saved.* 1986. London: Abacus, 2000.

Levinas, Emmanuel. *Difficult Freedom: Essays on Judaism.* Translated by Seán Hand. London: The Athlone Press, 1990.

Levine, Bruce. *Half Slave and Half Free: The Roots of Civil War.* New York: Hill & Wang, 1992.

Lewis, Ida E. "Bill Clinton as Honorary Black: To Those Who Fail to Understand Why the Majority of African-Americans Do Not Support the Removal of President Clinton." *Crisis* (September–October 1998): 5.

Lewis, R. W. B. *The American Adam: Innocence, Tragedy, and Tradition in the Nineteenth Century.* Chicago: University of Chicago Press, 1955.

Lipset, Seymour Martin, and Earl Raab. *The Politics of Unreason.* New York: Harper & Row, 1970.

Maier, Pauline. *American Scripture: Making the Declaration of Independence.* New York: Alfred A. Knopf, 1997.

Mailer, Norman. *Barbary Shore.* London: Jonathan Cape, 1952.

Marcuse, Herbert. *Reason and Revolution: Hegel and the Rise of Social Theory.* London: Oxford University Press, 1941.

Martin, Terence. *Parables of Possibility: The American Need for Beginnings.* New York: Columbia University Press, 1995.

Marx, Leo. *The Machine in the Garden: Technology and the Pastoral Ideal in America.* 1964. New York: Oxford University Press, 1967.

Mattson, Kevin. *Intellectuals in Action: The Origins of the New Left and Radical Liberalism, 1945–1970.* University Park: Pennsylvania State University Press, 2002.

McCoy, Drew. R. *The Elusive Republic: Political Economy in Jeffersonian America.* Chapel Hill: University of North Carolina Press, 1980.

McGrath, Charles. "'Zuckerman's Alter Brain': An Interview with Philip Roth." *New York Times*, December 7, 2000.

McGrath, Patrick. "Deep Waters." *The Guardian,* July 12, 2003. Available online at http://books.guardian.co.uk/news/articles/0,,996274,00.html.

McPherson, James M. *Battle Cry of Freedom: The American Civil War.* New York: Oxford University Press, 1988.

Melville, Herman. *Moby Dick; or, The Whale.* 1851. New York: W. W. Norton, 1967.

———. *Billy Budd, Sailor, and Other Stories.* 1929. Harmondsworth: Penguin, 1967.

Menand, Louis. *The Metaphysical Club.* London: HarperCollins, 2001.

Merleau-Ponty, Maurice. *Humanism and Terror: An Essay on the Communist Problem.* 1947. Translated by John O' Neill. Boston: Beacon Press, 1969.

Meyers, Marvin. *The Jacksonian Persuasion: Politics and Belief.* Stanford, Calif.: Stanford University Press, 1957.

Michaels, Walter Benn. *The Gold Standard and the Logic of Naturalism.* Berkeley: University of California Press, 1988.

Montesquieu, Charles Louis de Secondat. *Considerations on the Causes of the Greatness of the Romans and Their Decline.* 1734. Indianapolis, Ind.: Hackett Publishing Co., 1999.

———. *The Spirit of the Laws.* 1748. New York: Hafner Publishing, 1966.

Morone, James. *Hellfire Nation: The Politics of Sin in American History.* New Haven, Conn.: Yale University Press, 2003.

Morrison, Toni. The Talk of the Town. *New Yorker,* October 5, 1998.

Nolan Jr., Charles J. *Aaron Burr and the American Literary Imagination.* Westport, Conn.: Greenwood Press, 1980.

Novack, George, ed. *Their Morals and Ours: Marxist Versus Liberal Views on Morality.* New York: Pathfinder Press, 1969.

Oakes, James. *The Ruling Race: A History of American Slaveholders.* New York: Alfred A. Knopf, 1982.

——. *Slavery and Freedom: An Interpretation of the Old South.* New York: Alfred A. Knopf, 1990.

Oates, Stephen B. *To Purge This Land with Blood: A Biography of John Brown.* New York: Harper and Row, 1970.

Olds, Bruce. *Raising Holy Hell.* New York: Henry Holt, 1995.

Onuf, Peter S., ed. *Jeffersonian Legacies.* Charlottesville: University Press of Virginia, 1993.

——. "The Scholars' Jefferson." *The William and Mary Quarterly* 50, no. 4 (October 1993): 671–699.

Packer, George. *Blood of the Liberals.* New York: Farrar, Straus & Giroux, 2000.

Paine, Thomas. *Rights of Man, Common Sense, and Other Political Writings.* London: Oxford University Press, 1995.

Pease, Donald E., ed. *Revisionary Interventions Into the Americanist Canon.* Durham, N.C.: Duke University Press, 1994.

Pells, Richard H. *Radical Visions and American Dreams: Culture and Social Thought in the Depression Years.* Middletown, Conn.: Wesleyan University Press, 1973.

——. *The Liberal Mind in a Conservative Age: American Intellectuals in the 1940s and 1950s.* 1985. Middletown, Conn.: Wesleyan University Press, 1989.

Perlstein, Rick. *Before the Storm: Barry Goldwater and the Unmaking of the American Consensus.* New York: Hill and Wang, 2001.

Peterson, Merrill D. *Lincoln in American Memory.* New York: Oxford University Press, 1994.

Pettit, Philip. *Republicanism: A Theory of Freedom and Government.* Oxford: Oxford University Press, 1997.

Pfeiffer, Kathleen. *Race Passing and American Individualism.* Amherst: University of Massachusetts Press, 2003.

Pitney Jr., John J. "Clinton and the Republican Party." In *The Postmodern Presidency: Bill Clinton's Legacy in U.S. Politics,* edited by Steven E. Schier, 167–182. Pittsburgh, Pa.: University of Pittsburgh Press, 2000.

Pocock, J. G. A. "Virtue and Commerce in the Eighteenth Century." *Journal of Interdisciplinary History* 3, no. 1 (1972): 119–134.

——. *The Machiavellian Moment: Florentine Political Thought and the Atlantic Republican Tradition.* Princeton, N.J.: Princeton University Press, 1975.

Podhoretz, Norman. "My Negro Problem—and Ours." *Commentary* 35, no. 2 (February 1963): 93–101.

——. *Breaking Ranks: A Political Memoir.* New York: Harper and Row, 1979.

——. "The Adventures of Philip Roth." Review of *American Pastoral* and *I Married a Communist,* by Philip Roth. *Commentary* 106, no. 4 (October 1998): 25–36.

———. "Life of His Party: How Bill Clinton Saved His Party." *National Review* 13 (September 1999): 2–6.

———. "Bellow at 85, Roth at 67." Review of *Ravelstein*, by Saul Bellow, and *The Human Stain*, by Philip Roth. *Commentary* 110, no. 1 (July–August 2000): 35–43.

Posner, Richard. *Public Intellectuals: A Study in Decline.* Cambridge, Mass.: Harvard University Press, 2002.

Quarles, Benjamin. *Allies for Freedom: Blacks and John Brown.* Champaign: University of Illinois Press, 1972.

———, ed. *Blacks on John Brown.* New York: Oxford University Press, 1974.

Rahe, Paul A. *Republics Ancient and Modern.* Vol. 3, *Inventions of Prudence: Constituting the American Regime.* Chapel Hill: University of North Carolina Press, 1994.

Rahv, Philip. *Essays on Literature and Politics, 1932–1972*, edited by Arabel J. Porter and Andrew J. Dvosin. New York: Houghton Mifflin Co., 1978.

Rakove, Jack N. *Original Meanings: Politics and Ideas in the Making of the Constitution.* New York: Alfred A. Knopf, 1996.

Rawls, John. *A Theory of Justice.* Cambridge, Mass.: Harvard University Press, 1971.

Reising, Russell. *The Unusable Past: Theory and the Study of American Literature.* New York: Methuen, 1986.

———. "Lionel Trilling, *The Liberal Imagination*, and the Emergence of the Cultural Discourse of Anti-Stalinism." *boundary 2* 20 (Spring 1993): 94–124.

Renehan Jr., Edward J. *The Secret Six: The True Tale of the Men Who Conspired with John Brown.* Columbia: University of South Carolina Press, 1997.

Rodgers, Daniel T. "Republicanism: The Career of a Concept." *The Journal of American History* 79, no. 1 (June 1992): 11–38.

———. *Contested Truths: Keywords in American Politics Since Independence.* New York: Basic Books, 1987.

Rogin, Michael Paul. *Subversive Genealogy: The Politics and Art of Herman Melville.* New York: Alfred A. Knopf, 1983.

Rorty, Richard. *Philosophy and Social Hope.* London: Penguin, 1999.

———. *Achieving Our Country: Leftist Thought in Twentieth-Century America.* Cambridge, Mass.: Harvard University Press, 1999.

Rosenberg, Harold. "Jewish Identity in a Free Society." *Commentary* 9, no. 6 (June 1950): 508–512.

Roth, Philip. *Portnoy's Complaint.* New York: Random House, 1969.

———. *Our Gang.* London: Jonathan Cape, 1971.

———. *Zuckerman Bound: A Trilogy and Epilogue.* London: Penguin, 1989.

———. *Sabbath's Theater.* London: Jonathan Cape, 1995.

———. *American Pastoral.* London: Jonathan Cape, 1997.

——. *I Married a Communist.* London: Jonathan Cape, 1998.

——. *The Human Stain.* London: Jonathan Cape, 2000.

Rowe, John Carlos. *At Emerson's Tomb: The Politics of Classic American Literature.* New York: Columbia University Press, 1997.

Ruttenburg, Nancy. "Melville's Handsome Sailor: The Anxiety of Innocence." *American Literature* 66, no. 1 (March 1994): 83–103.

Sandel, Michael. *Liberalism and the Limits of Justice.* 1982. Cambridge: Cambridge University Press, 1998.

——. *Democracy's Discontent: America in Search of a Public Philosophy.* Cambridge, Mass.: Harvard University Press, 1996.

Schier, Steven E. "American Politics After Clinton." In *The Postmodern Presidency: Bill Clinton's Legacy in U.S. Politics,* edited by Steven E. Schier, 255–265. Pittsburgh, Pa.: University of Pittsburgh Press, 2000.

Schlesinger Jr., Arthur. *The Vital Center: The Politics of Freedom.* 1949. New York: Transaction Publications, 1997.

——. *The Disuniting of America: Reflections on a Multicultural Society.* 1991. New York: W. W. Norton, 1992.

Schudson, Michael. *The Good Citizen: A History of American Civic Life.* Cambridge, Mass.: Harvard University Press, 1998.

Shalhope, Robert E. "Toward a Republican Synthesis: The Emergence of an Understanding of Republicanism in American Historiography." *William and Mary Quarterly* 29, no. 1 (January 1972): 49–80.

Skinner, Quentin. *Liberty Before Liberalism.* Cambridge: Cambridge University Press, 1998.

Smith, Henry Nash. *Virgin Land: The American West as Symbol and Myth.* Cambridge, Mass.: Harvard University Press, 1950.

Sollors, Werner. *Beyond Ethnicity.* New York: Oxford University Press, 1986.

Spanos, William V. "American Studies in the 'Age of the World Picture': Thinking the Question of Language." In *The Futures of American Studies,* edited by Donald E. Pease and Robyn Wiegman, 387–415. Durham, N.C.: Duke University Press, 2002.

Spitzer, Alan, B. "John Dewey, the 'Trial' of Leon Trotsky, and the Search for Historical Truth." *History and Theory* 29, no. 1 (February 1990): 16–37.

Steinfels, Peter. *The Neo-Conservatives: The Men Who Are Changing America's Politics.* New York: Simon and Schuster, 1979.

Stephanopoulos, George. *All Too Human: A Political Education.* New York: Little, Brown, 1999.

Strozier, Charles B. *Lincoln's Quest for Union: Public and Private Meanings.* New York: Basic Books, 1982.

Styron, William. *The Confessions of Nat Turner.* 1967. New York: Vintage, 1993.

Summers, Anthony. *The Arrogance of Power: The Secret World of Richard Nixon.* New York: Viking Penguin, 2000.

Tallack, Douglas. *Twentieth-Century America: The Intellectual and Cultural Context.* Harlow: Longman, 1991.

Teichgraeber, Richard F. *Sublime Thoughts and Penny Wisdom: Situating Emerson and Thoreau in the American Market.* Baltimore, Md.: Johns Hopkins University Press, 1995.

Teres, Harvey M. *Renewing the Left: Politics, Imagination, and the New York Intellectuals.* New York: Oxford University Press, 1996.

Thoreau, Henry David. *Walden and "On the Duty of Civil Disobedience."* New York: Signet Classics, 1960.

Tocqueville, Alexis de. *Democracy in America.* 2 vols. 1835–1840. Translated by George Lawrence. London: Fontana Press, 1994.

Tomes, Robert R. *Apocalypse Then: American Intellectuals and the Vietnam War, 1954–1975.* New York: New York University Press, 1998.

Trenchard, John, and Thomas Gordon. *Cato's Letters: Essays on Liberty, Civil and Religious, and Other Important Subjects.* 3 vols. New York: Da Capo Press, 1971.

Trilling, Lionel. *E. M. Forster.* Norfolk: New Directions, 1943.

——. *The Middle of the Journey.* 1947. Harmondsworth: Penguin, 1977.

——. *The Liberal Imagination: Essays on Literature and Society.* London: Secker and Warburg, 1951.

——. *Prefaces to the Experience of Literature.* New York: Harcourt Brace Jovanovich, 1967.

——. *The Moral Obligation to Be Intelligent: Selected Essays.* Edited by Leon Wieseltier. New York: Farrar, Straus & Giroux, 2000.

Trotsky, Leon. *The Revolution Betrayed.* 1937. Atlanta: Pathfinder Press, 1989.

Venkataraman, M. S. "Leon Trotsky's Adventure in American Radical Politics." *International Review of Social History* 9 (1964): 1–46.

Vidal, Gore. *Burr.* 1973. London: William Heinemann, 1974.

——. *Lincoln.* London: William Heinemann, 1984.

——. *Empire.* London: Grafton, 1987.

——. *Hollywood: A Novel of the Twenties.* 1989. London: Grafton, 1991.

——. *United States: Essays, 1952–1992.* New York: Random House, 1993.

——. *Palimpsest: A Memoir.* London: Andre Deustch, 1995.

——. *The Smithsonian Institution.* New York: Random House, 1998.

——. *The Golden Age: A Novel.* New York: Random House, 2000.

——. *Inventing a Nation: Washington, Adams, Jefferson.* New Haven, Conn.: Yale University Press, 2003.

——. *Imperial America: Reflections on the United States of Amnesia.* New York: Nation Books, 2004.

Villa, Dana. *Arendt and Heidegger: The Fate of the Political.* Princeton, N.J.: Princeton University Press, 1996.

Wald, Alan. *The New York Intellectuals: The Rise and Decline of the Anti-Stalinist Left from the 1930s to the 1980s.* Chapel Hill: University of North Carolina Press, 1987.

Walker, Brian. "John Rawls, Mikhail Bakhtin, and the Praxis of Toleration." *Political Theory* 23, no. 1 (February 1995): 101–127.

Warren, Robert Penn. *John Brown: The Making of a Martyr.* 1929. Chicago: Ivan R. Dee, 1993.

——. *All the King's Men.* 1946. New York: Harcourt, 2001.

Warren, Frank A. *Liberals and Communists: The "Red Decade" Revisited.* Bloomington: Indiana University Press, 1966.

West, Cornel. "Lionel Trilling: Godfather of Neo-Conservatism." In *Lionel Trilling and the Critics: Opposing Selves,* edited by John Rodden, 395–403. Lincoln: University of Nebraska Press, 1999.

Whalen-Bridge, John. *Political Fiction and the American Self.* Urbana: University of Illinois Press, 1998.

White, Hayden. *Metahistory: The Historical Imagination in Nineteenth-Century Europe.* Baltimore, Md.: Johns Hopkins University Press, 1975.

——. *The Content of the Form: Narrative Discourse and Historical Representation.* Baltimore, Md.: Johns Hopkins University Press, 1990.

——. "Introduction: Historical Fiction, Fictional History, and Historical Reality." *Rethinking History* 9, no. 2/3 (June/September 2005): 147–157.

White, Ronald C. "Lincoln's Sermon on the Mount: *The Second Inaugural.*" In *Religion and the American Civil War,* edited by Randall M. Miller, Harry S. Stout, and Charles Reagan Wilson, 208–225. New York: Oxford University Press, 1998.

——. *Lincoln's Greatest Speech: The Second Inaugural.* New York: Simon & Schuster, 2002.

Whitebrook, Maureen. *Real Toads in Imaginary Gardens: Narrative Accounts of Liberalism.* London: Rowman & Littlefield, 1995.

Wills, Garry. *Nixon Agonistes: The Crisis of the Self-Made Man.* 1970. New York: Mariner Books, 2002.

——. *Inventing America: Jefferson's Declaration of Independence.* New York: Doubleday, 1978.

Wilson, Douglas L. "Thomas Jefferson and the Character Issue." *Atlantic Monthly* 270, no. 2 (November 1992): 41–49.

——. *Honor's Voice: The Transformation of Abraham Lincoln.* New York: Alfred A. Knopf, 1998.

Wilson, Edmund. *Patriotic Gore: Studies in the Literature of the American Civil War.* New York: Oxford University Press, 1962.

Wood, Gordon. *The Creation of the American Republic, 1776–1787.* 1969. Chapel Hill: University of North Carolina Press, 1998.

——. "Hellfire Politics." Review of *The Lost Soul of American Politics: Virtue, Self-Interest, and the Foundations of Liberalism,* by John Patrick Diggins. *New York Review of Books* 32, no. 3 (February 28, 1985): 29–32.

——. *The Radicalism of the American Revolution.* New York: Alfred A. Knopf, 1992.

Zarefsky, David. *Lincoln, Douglas, and Slavery: In the Crucible of Public Debate.* Chicago: University of Chicago Press, 1990.

Zuckert, Catherine H. *Natural Right and the American Imagination: Political Philosophy in Novel Form.* Savage, Md.: Rowman & Littlefield, 1990.

Zuckert, Michael P. *Natural Rights and the New Republicanism.* Princeton, N.J.: Princeton University Press, 1994.

——. *Launching Liberalism: On Lockean Political Philosophy.* Lawrence: University Press of Kansas, 2002.

INDEX